TOOLS OF THE TRADE

ABOUT THE AUTHOR

Stephanie L. Brooke is a private practitioner and organizational consultant in Rochester, New York. She received training as an art therapist at Hillside Children's Center in Geneseo, New York and her certification in art therapy from Nazareth College in Rochester, New York. Additionally, she is an online instructor for the University of Phoenix, Cayuga Community College, and Jamestown Community College. She teaches face-to-face classes as an adjunct in sociology and psychology for Nazareth College.

Second Edition

TOOLS OF THE TRADE

A Therapist's Guide to Art Therapy Assessments

By

STEPHANIE L. BROOKE, PH.D., NCC

With a Foreword by

Barry M. Cohen, M.A., A.T.R.

CHARLES C THOMAS • PUBLISHER, LTD.
Springfield • Illinois • U.S.A.

Published and Distributed Throughout the World by

CHARLES C THOMAS • PUBLISHER, LTD.
2600 South First Street
Springfield, Illinois 62704

© 2004 by CHARLES C THOMAS • PUBLISHER, LTD.

ISBN 0-398-07521-2 (hard)
ISBN 0-398-07522-0 (paper)

Library of Congress Catalog Card Number: 2004048020

With THOMAS BOOKS *careful attention is given to all details of manufacturing
and design. It is the Publisher's desire to present books that are satisfactory as to their
physical qualities and artistic possibilities and appropriate for their particular use.*
THOMAS BOOKS *will be true to those laws of quality that assure a good name
and good will.*

Printed in the United States of America
MM-R-3

Library of Congress Cataloging-in-Publication Data

Brooke, Stephanie
    Tools of the trade : a therapist's guide to art therapy assessments / by
Stephanie L. Brooke with a foreword by Barry M. Cohen.–2nd ed.
      p. cm.
    Rev. ed. of: A therapist's guide to art therapy assessments. c1996.
    Includes bibliographical references and index.
    ISBN 0-398-07521-2 – ISBN 0-398-07522-0 (pbk.)
    1. Art therapy. 2. Psychodiagnostics. I. Brooke, Stephanie L. Therapist's
guide to art therapy assessments. II. Title.

RC489.A7B75 2004
616.89'1656–dc22
                                         2004048020

FOREWORD

Stephanie Brooke has graciously invited me to write an introductory note to the new edition of her book, reflecting on my experience of creating and shepherding an art therapy assessment over the period of two decades. When I accepted her invitation, I had no idea of the complexity of the issues and feelings that would surface.

In 1981, a couple of years out of graduate school, I moved to metropolitan Washington, D.C. Once settled in our nation's capitol, I set out to create a national slide library of artwork representing the various psychiatric diagnoses. As an ambitious art therapist surrounded by national collections of "this and that," it seemed like a natural project to initiate. But I quickly found that I could not get adequate slide donations from senior practitioners and educators. For the most part, they did not trust the accuracy of diagnoses in samples submitted by others, and were understandably protective of their clients' work. It became clear that I would have to create the collection on my own, from scratch.

Spontaneous works and those made in art therapy sessions cannot be compared for diagnostic research purposes. Differences in materials, formats, and directives make it impossible to compare "apples to apples." So I decided to develop a standardized format for creating a series of pictures that would ultimately allow clinicians around the country to compare artwork by clients along with a standardized research format for studying these pictures. And that is how the Diagnostic Drawing Series (DDS) was born around 1982.

My supervisor, art therapist Barbara Lesowitz and I created a three drawing tool using twelve square chalk pastels and three sheets of large format white paper that could reflect a rich profile of behavioral and psychological information about the artist/patient by using rating criteria that were primarily based on pictorial structure instead of the traditional narrative content. We were encouraged by psychiatrist Thomas Wise to improve the project's potential for publication by obtaining concurring diagnoses from a pair of psychiatrists for each client in the DDS research sample. We began to collect

v

DDSs within our hospital corporation's several facilities for our first pilot study. Soon after, Lesowitz left town (and subsequently the profession), but fellow art therapists Anna Reyner and Shira Singer joined me in completing that pilot study, which eventually won us the Research Award of the American Art Therapy Association (AATA) in 1983.

From the beginning of this adventure, I have enjoyed receiving inquiries from clinicians in this country and overseas. Mail crossed my desk from the former Soviet Union, Australia, Israel, Italy, Belgium, Great Britain, Norway, and other far-flung places around the globe. In addition to the letters and lovely postage stamps, the idea that people all over the world had heard about the DDS and were interested in using it with their clients was very gratifying. In fact, I met my future colleague/collaborator/wife, Anne Mills, when I was invited to speak at my first international art therapy conference in Canada in 1984.

Training workshops around the country have always been a wonderful way to spread the word, see hundreds of new examples, and to learn more about the DDS from our participants. In particular, a number of trips to the Pacific Northwest were wonderful experiences. A couple of these were organized by our west coast DDS Training Associate, art therapist Kathryn Johnson, who is currently completing a DDS study on bipolar disorder for her doctoral research in psychology.

In recent years, the founding of multiple DDS study groups in the Netherlands has been among my greatest rewards for the often grueling and relatively thankless time spent writing criteria, rating drawings, working with statisticians, shooting slides, responding to inquiries, spraying pictures, preparing presentations, publishing articles, and mailing out packets during those early years.

A few short weeks after 9/11, Anne and I traveled to Utrecht to teach a two-day introductory DDS training session, along with our European DDS Training Associate, Jon Fowler, who is now based in England. It was followed by a special master class with Dutch study group members. This was our second invited training trip to Holland, but the first to be held inside a windmill! The warmth of our hosts and their avid interest in our work stood in sharp contrast to those horrific recent events, and resulted in the most memorable experience of my career as an art therapist.

Looking back at my reaction to the welcome given us–really, to the DDS– in Holland, I am certain my response was somewhat exaggerated by many of the challenges and disappointments that I have faced in raising the DDS to adulthood here in the United States.

Although the last twenty years has been a interesting and pivotal time for the field of art therapy assessment in this country, it is highly unlikely that there will ever be a broad level of interest in art therapy diagnosis and research here in the United States. Our Dutch colleagues have told us that their interest in the DDS stems from the lack of such information in their training, which is primarily oriented to process issues. But what about American art therapists and their training?

Could it be that American art therapists are so well instructed in this area that they have no need for continuing education? To my knowledge, many of the faculty that teach the DDS to graduate students, or supervise their use of it, have never themselves taken the requisite training (now two days in length, because of the time necessary to convey and integrate the material through practice), yet they feel competent to teach it, write about it, or critique it.

Naturally, the vast majority of American art therapists are less interested in, or comfortable with, assessment or evaluation than clinical work; it stands to reason that art therapists would much rather engage in the activities they are trained to do, such as making art with their clients and otherwise helping them to heal. Moreover, as a general rule, artists tend to shy away from anything that smacks of scientific studies, especially those that involve numbers or statistics.

Now, after twenty years of publications and presentations, there is not a single active DDS study group in North America that I am aware of, but in a small country such as the Netherlands, there are several. In my opinion, this reflects the impact of role modeling by our graduate faculty, coupled with an unproductive form of rebelliousness among American art therapists which manifests in different ways. Here is one that that I find particularly destructive:

Rather than turning to established and even validated art therapy assessment tools like the DDS, art therapists seem to prefer creating their own highly idiosyncratic assessments to use with their clients. Stephanie Brooke's *Tools of the Trade II,* is mercifully lacking these creations. However, their annual proliferation points to the naiveté among practitioners who believe that pairing a metaphor with drawing materials is all it takes to make a useful art therapy assessment. And their acceptance annually by the conference program committee may appear to some, I believe, to be a tacit form of approval or endorsement.

So, when art therapists create an ongoing flow of novelty assessments without investing the necessary years of work to render their tools meaningful, who suffers? In my opinion, when they persist in assessing their clients with them and proudly encourage others to use them at our annual conferences, we all do.

I believe that many art therapists simply do not understand or accept the importance of evidence-based work, or explicitly reject standards that the DDS project is based upon, such as objectivity, replicability, and the scientific method. This split in the field is reflected in the American Art Therapy Association's current ethics standards on assessments.

The introduction of the DDS was an important step away from simplistic, psychoanalytically-based symbol analysis in art therapy. In devising rating criteria for the research component of the project that were primarily based on pictorial structure, not narrative content, I was rebelling against what I felt were the "touchy-feely" roots of art therapy which came of age in the late 1960s.

At the time, I noted that I was trying to help art therapists in psychiatric facilities identify and develop essential skills to deal with the arrival of diagnosis-driven short-term treatment. But back in the 1980s, many influential art therapists did not want to "label" their patients nor did they want to deal with numbers or statistics.

They saw the research-associated DDS which was designed to be equally useful to clinicians from all schools of psychotherapy as somehow contrary to the values of humanism, psychodynamic psychotherapy, feminism, spirituality, and intuition.

Once the "hardball" managed care era of the 1990s hit, art therapy positions were seen as luxuries and staffing was cut around the country. Art therapists had little to point to that would show their budget makers why their skills were necessities, especially at higher salaries than recreational therapists, and not reimbursable, either, like occupational therapists. Had the art therapy profession taken a bit of preventive medicine with some outcome studies and the like, perhaps some jobs would have been saved and the field would have moved forward by now.

Just recently, for instance, a young sniper's portfolio of jailhouse drawings was entered into evidence by the defense in a highly notorious murder case, which was tried nearby an art therapy graduate training program. Was a single art therapist called in to look at the pictures and offer a professional opinion? Did the attorneys on either side call for an art evaluation in a case being tried on an insanity plea? Please prove me wrong; this was our profession's best chance to enter the national dialogue on anything, and we clearly missed out because we had not prepared the way. The media and legal professions do not yet realize the unique assessment and diagnostic skills that art therapists have to offer because our profession is still ambivalent about them, and has not promoted itself effectively, if at all, in this regard.

Little did I realize back in the early eighties that the creation of a valid art-based assessment, especially if it is correlated with psychiatric diagnostic nomenclature, is ultimately a lifetime's work. And it is not just one person's lifetime work. Like other things of importance in this world, it definitely takes a communal effort.

But, as Anne Mills has pointed out in one of her conference presentations, everyone thinks that research, like dirty dishes or other forms of housework, is up to somebody else to do. And once someone comes forward and actually does it, they are roundly criticized, and usually by people who have not read, studied, or even understood their work. In fact, the DDS has taken more than its share of misinformed critiques over the years on this side of the Atlantic and abroad, largely because it is a highly visible target.

The DDS, as I originally conceived it, was a multifaceted project with a number of ambitious but viable goals, most that I believed could be achieved within a matter of years through the support of my fellow art therapists. And I was correct in my assumptions to a certain extent. The resource library of DDSs has grown to over 1000 sets over the years. But the amount of samples submitted over the past decade or more has been minimal, especially when considering the number of students who graduate from training programs annually, and the thousands of registered practitioners in the United States alone.

Still, after twenty years, our achievements as a worldwide network of collaborating clinician-researchers are significant and many. The DDS offers a quick and easy-to-administer art interview, which, through associated research has a large centralized library of carefully collected standardized samples, along with an unparalleled body of multicenter studies by multiple investigators from around the world; add to this its status as the first major scientific study correlating art productions with psychiatric diagnoses. Also, through its handbook of defined structural criteria, the DDS Project provides an objective, common language to describe pictorial communications. It was the first art therapy assessment to norm the art of "healthy" adults, and arguably the first projective drawing tool ever to do so. And, after two decades of use and study, published DDS research has achieved a level of validity unprecedented in the study of art expression and psychiatric diagnosis. As early as 1993, the number of published validity and reliability studies on the DDS effectively doubled the total number of such studies in the entire art therapy literature. Additionally, the DDS has become the best known and most commonly taught art therapy assessment in the United States, and possibly the world.

The DDS, first presented publicly at an AATA conference in 1983, first entered the published literature in 1985, when the handbook was made widely available. Also that year, the test itself was profiled in the American Psychological Association's *Monitor,* prompting a good deal of interest from psychologists. An overview in a Dutch psychological journal appeared in 1986, and the first DDS research results were presented in the expressive therapies literature in 1988. The DDS was featured on National Public Radio's "All Things Considered" in 1984, and illustrated in two college psychology textbooks in 1987.

Approximately 35 DDS studies have been completed to date; some are replication studies, but most norm different DSM diagnostic groups. They include: Nonhospitalized controls, children and adolescents (Leavitt, 1988; Neale, 1994; Shlagman, 1996); adults (Cohen, Hammer, & Singer, 1988; Morris, 1995); and seniors (Couch, 1992). Schizophrenia (Cohen, Hammer, & Singer, 1988; Mills & Yamashita, 1996; Morris, 1995; Ricca, 1992). Mood disorders, major depressive disorder, children and adolescents (Leavitt, 1988); adults (Cohen, Hammer, & Singer, 1988; Morris, 1995); Dysthymic Disorder (Cohen, Hammer & Singer,1988); Bipolar disorder (McHugh, 1997). Dissociative Disorders, Dissociative Identity Disorder (Fowler & Ardon, 2000; Heitmajer & Cohen, 1993; Kress, 1992; Mills & Cohen, 1993; Morris, 1995; Ricca, 1992), Dissociative Disorder Not Otherwise Specified (Fowler & Ardon, 2000). Eating Disorders (Kessler, 1994). Borderline Personality Disorder (Mills, 1988). Posttraumatic Stress Disorder (Des Marais & Barnes, 1993). Dementia (Couch, 1994). Adjustment Disorder, children (Neale, 1994). Conduct Disorder (Neale, 1994).

There are many directions in which the DDS Project and its myriad off-shoot studies could be developed in the future. Perhaps some of the present generation of art therapists who have been educated in the importance of reliable and valid art assessment tools, as well as other professionals, will explore ways to expedite the completion of this valuable and still ongoing work. In an aspect of the field almost devoid of scholarly research until relatively recently, we've made a great deal of progress, even if the definitive DDS book is not on your local merchant's shelf . . . yet.

I think the most important goal of Stephanie Brooke's book is its attempt to digest and accurately report on a lot of detailed material for people who would otherwise not take the time to do it for themselves, but who are conscientious, and know that choosing an art assessment must be a well-informed decision, not one simply dictated by training program bias. Keep that in mind as you read on.

BARRY M. COHEN, M.A., A.T.R.

PREFACE

Tools of the Trade is a volume that provides critical reviews of art therapy tests with some new reviews of assessments and updated research in the field. It is comprehensive in its approach to considering reliability and validity evidence provided by test authors. Additionally, it reviews research on art therapy assessments with a variety of patient populations. The book contains helpful suggestions regarding the application of art therapy assessments.

Specific areas covered include individual, group, family, and multicultural assessment techniques. The desirable and undesirable features of a variety of art therapy assessments are deliberated. This is a valuable resource for practitioners who use art therapy as an adjunct or primary therapy. The book will serve to enhance clinical skills, making therapy more effective for each patient who participates in the assessment process.

This volume critiques a series of art therapy assessments from traditional art therapy approaches to current releases. The goal of this work is to assist mental health professionals in selecting assessments that yield reliable and valid clinical information regarding their clients. Of special interest is the author's approach to writing the results of a series of art therapy assessments in an effort to provide a more complete indication of client dynamics and issues.

ACKNOWLEDGMENTS

I would like to express my sincere appreciation to Dr. Barry M. Cohen for writing the foreword to this book. I was deeply honored when he accepted this undertaking and shared his experience with developing and refining the DDS. I would also like to thank the following art therapy assessment authors for their communication with me on the writing of the reviews of their chapters: Donna Betts, Linda Gantt, Ellen Horovitz, Myra Levick, and Rawley Silver. I commend them for their endeavors to contribute to the creation of an art therapy assessment and commitment to establishing further reliability and validity to the field of art therapy. To Bodan Petriev, a dear friend, I would like thank him for the photography of the artwork in this book. I would like to thank my friend, Dr. Michael Hand, who started out with me in my Ph.D. program at Walden University, for his undying support during this work! My deepest appreciation goes to my long-time mentor and friend, Dr. Jack Dilendik, who watched me grow from a novice researcher and writer to a published author.

CONTENTS

TOOLS OF THE TRADE

Chapter 1

INTRODUCTION

Due to the increasing isolation, dehumanization, and overintellectualization of our culture, there is an increasing focus on affect and getting in touch with the inner self (Prinzhorn, 1972; Moreno, 1975; McNiff, 1992; Anthony, 2003). Jung (1958), a novice artist himself, was using art as a method to get in touch with his psyche. Although known as a landscape painter, Jung was focused, the images that emerged from the inner psyche Edwards (2001). Accordingly, therapists are inclined to use creative modalities such as art, music, dance, and drama for psychological healing and growth. Although these methods may be unorthodox to some, people can encounter important self-data by approaching themselves from a new perspective or through a new medium.

> Aside from the therapeutic benefit of nonverbal communication of thoughts and feelings, one of the most impressive aspects of the art process is its potential to achieve or restore psychological equilibrium. This use of the art process as intervention is not mysterious or particularly novel; it may have been one of the reasons humankind developed art in the first place–to alleviate or contain feelings of trauma, fear, anxiety, and psychological threats to the self and the community. (Malchiodi, 1990, p. 5)

Art has been used as a means of self-expression for centuries, the evidence of which remains today with pottery, cave drawings, hieroglyphics, masks, and much more. People have used art materials to "make images and connect them to feelings and bodily states [that] bring into the open thoughts that have been only vaguely sensed" (Keyes, 1983, p. 104). Edwards (1986) asserted that drawing exists as a parallel to verbal language and was the simplest of nonverbal languages. Art does not have the restriction of linguistic development in order to convey thoughts or feelings.

JUNG AND ART

> I had to abandon the idea of the superordinate position of the ego. . . . I saw that everything, all paths I had been following, all steps I had taken, were leading back to a single point–namely, to the mid-point. It became increasingly plain to me that the mandala is the centre. It is the exponent of all paths. It is the path to the centre, to individuation. . . . I knew that in finding the mandala as an expression of the self I had attained what was for me the ultimate. (Jung–Mandala Gallery, 2003)

Initially a follower of Freud, Carl Jung, a Swiss psychiatrist, was one of the founding fathers of depth psychology. Jung (2003) inspired the New Age Movement with its interest in spirituality, occultism, Eastern religions, I Ching, and mythology. From *Psychology and Literature* (1930), Jung noted the power of art as a tool to work with the unconscious (cited in Jung, 2003) (http://www.kirjasto.sci.fi/cjung.htm).

> The artist is not a person endowed with free will who seeks his own ends, but one who allows art to realize its purposes through him. As a human being he may have moods and a will and personal aims, but as an artist he is "man" in a higher sense–he is "collective man," a vehicle and moulder of the unconscious psychic life of mankind.

Given that art was a natural mode for getting in touch with his own emotions and inner images, Jung used art as a tool to help his patients get in touch with their inner self. According to Stone (2002), Jung's work prompted Irene Champernawne to set up a center for "Psychotherapy through the Arts." Irene (a psychotherapist) and her husband, an art teacher, ran the center. Art therapy has also been used in psychiatric institutions. In addition, Freudian psychoanalysists used the drawings as tools for gathering information on the patient's current mental state (Stone, 2002).

Recently, I attended a presentation by Harriet Wadeson, who wrote the forward to the first edition of this book. She was presenting at Nazareth College (September 26, 2003). Her workshop focused on the use of Jungian principles in relation to art therapy. Specifically, she used art exercises to get in touch with the shadow. Other art therapists have used the concept of the shadow in conjunction with art therapy. For instance, Bouchard (1998) implemented experiential art exercises as a method of transforming the negative elements of the shadow into positive creations. These projective methods designed to explore motivation are not new to the field of psychotherapy.

ART THERAPY ASSESSMENTS

Machover (1949) observed the power of projective methods in discovering unconscious determinants of self-expression that were not apparent in direct, verbal communication. Langer (1953) stressed that "there is an important part of reality that is quite inaccessible to the formative influence of language: that is the realm of the so called 'inner experience,' the life of feeling and emotion . . . the primary function of art is to objectify feeling so that we can contemplate and understand it" (pp. 4–5). Art expression offers the opportunity to explore personal problems without dependence on a verbal mode of communication. Naumburg (1966), a renowned art therapist, contended that "by projecting interior images into exteriorized designs art therapy crystallizes and fixes in lasting form the recollections of dreams of phantasies which would otherwise remain evanescent and might quickly be forgotten" (p. 2). According to Knoff and Prout (1985), projective drawings were used for the following purposes:

1. as an icebreaker technique to facilitate child-examiner rapport and the child's comfort, trust, and motivation.

2. as a sample of behavior that involves a child's reactions to one-on-one child-examiner interaction with a semi-structured task.

3. as a technique that investigates the interaction between a child's or adolescent's personality and his/her perceptions of relationships among peers, family, school, and significant others.

4. as a technique linked to a clinical, diagnostic interview that moves discussion beyond a drawing's actions and dynamics to more pervasive psychological issues and concerns.

Therapists have found that drawings serve as an indication of the client's current level of functioning (Wadeson, 1980; Cohen, 1986; Gantt, 2001 a & b). Often, drawings are part of an initial interview with a client. Over the years, these techniques have formed the foundation of art therapy assessment.

What are the nature and objectives of art therapy assessments? "The purpose of the assessment process is to study an individual's behavior through observation of his/her performance and through a systematic examination of his/her finished product" (Oster & Gould, 1987, p. 13). Further, art therapy assessments may be viewed as tests of personality. Anastasi (1988) defined personality tests as "measures of such characteristics as emotional states, interpersonal relations, motivations, interests, and attitudes" (p. 17). Generally, there are three types of personality assessments: self-report inventories, performance tests, and projective techniques. Most art therapy assessments may be considered the latter type. Anastasi (1988) defined projective techniques as tests in which "the client is given a relatively unstructured task that permits wide latitude in its solution. The assumption underlying such methods is that the individual will project her or his characteristic modes of response into such a task" (p. 19). These tests are disguised in their purpose, somewhat similar to the performance tests. This reduces the likelihood that the client will "fake" or generate a desired response. The purpose of this book is to discuss the advantages and disadvantages of the various art therapy assessments. As Anastasi (1988) noted:

> Research on the measurement of personality has attained impressive proportions since 1950, and many igneous devices and technical improvements are under investigation. It is rather the special difficulties encountered in the measurement of personality that account for the slow advances in this area. (p. 19)

SCOPE OF ART THERAPY ASSESSMENTS

An area of controversy concerning projective assessments centers on validity and reliability. This is often a concern when trying to use art therapy assessments in court proceedings (Brooke, 1997). "The psychologist trained in research design and statistics, sought to demonstrate the validity and reliability of projective drawings, while chief interest of the therapists (who had no training in research) was in how art could contribute to understanding individual patients and therefore, might assist in developing therapeutic technique" (Wadeson, 1992, p. 136). Some psychologists stated that projective drawing techniques were not valid indications of personality traits (Swenson, 1957; Chapman & Chapman, 1967; Swenson, 1968; Chapman & Chapman,1969; Wanderer, 1969, Klopfer & Taulbee, 1976). Despite these findings, researchers still use projective drawings for diagnosis and treatment. Groth-Marant (1990) provided evidence of validity and reliability with respect to projective drawings. The question of validity is still being debated today.

Controversy also focused on structured drawing tasks and spontaneous drawings. Often there is overlap, as Naumburg (1953, p. 124) observed:

> The line of demarcation between studies . . . that employ spontaneous art as a

primary means of psychotherapy and those that deal mainly with structured art in diagnosis is not always easy to define. In some cases the therapeutic approach that uses spontaneous art may also include more formal diagnostic art elements; similarly structured art tests may include elements free of art expression as employed in art therapy. An example of this overlapping of areas of therapy and diagnosis is evident in those diagnostic papers which discuss figure and family drawings; in such cases, it can be observed that while the theme for a specific type of figure drawing is set by the therapist, spontaneity is nevertheless encouraged in the execution of this task by the patient.

Neale and Rosal (1993) reviewed some common projective drawing techniques. These authors noted the value of these techniques as instruments of insight and information that can be utilized across professions. Although the projective techniques have great potential in revealing personality characteristics, there were several questions that the authors had (p. 37):

- how accurate is the diagnostic information taken from drawings and paintings?
- should strengths as well as weaknesses be sought in drawings?
- can drawings be used to assess pathology?
- how sensitive are drawings to clinical and therapeutic changes?
- should drawings and paintings be used to assess pathology and to diagnose?

These are questions typically asked by psychologists who use projective techniques. Art therapy assessments are sometimes designed differently from the projective techniques created by psychologists. Neale and Rosal (1993) outlined some concerns that art therapists have regarding assessments (p. 38):

- can objective drawing characteristics be identified without losing the holistic view of the drawing?
- can diagnostic indicators be identified?
- can diagnosis be reached through one drawing?
- how is a scoring manual developed?
- can free drawings as well as set drawing tasks be used in diagnosis and how does one score a free drawing?

These are just a few of the questions that will be considered in this book. Where applicable, I will analyze reliability and validity information. Some of the assessments considered in this book are newly created, thus reliability and validity information is not yet available. If that data is not present for a particular assessment, information that the test purports to yield will be considered.

Another factor that will be deliberated is the cookbook approach to art therapy assessment:

> In the "cookbook" method you look up the meaning of each sign and come up with a ready made diagnosis without regard for the total figure drawn and irrespective of the child's age, sex, intelligence, and social-cultural background. The circumstance under which the drawing was produced are also ignored. (Koppitz, 1968, p. 55)

There are obvious disadvantages to looking up the meaning of images in a dictionary fashion. Images have various meanings to different individuals. Additionally, observation of the client while completing the assessment provides valuable information about affect and personality. Despite the limitations discussed, art therapy assessments are a valuable source for understanding client issues and dynamics. Although many assessments in this book do not yield quantitative information, they provide a rich source of client information:

> Even without this quantification, clinicians are holding firm to the belief that drawings can be considered a unique, personal expression of inner experiences which, when used appropriately, can offer clues that are of value both diagnostically and therapeutically. Even though the value of drawings cannot be measured independently from the accumulated knowledge of the clinician, this does not diminish their intrinsic value as aids in working with both impaired and growth-oriented populations. (Oster & Gould, 1987, p. 8)

In order to gain credibility in the field, to establish validity and reliability, and to use art therapy assessments in court proceedings and continued research, art therapy assessments must be standardized.

> So, when art therapists create an ongoing flow of novelty assessments without investing the necessary years of work to render their tools meaningful, who suffers? In my opinion, when they persist in assessing their clients with them and proudly encourage others to use them at our annual conferences, we all do. (Cohen, 2004)

Many creative art therapists are highly resistant to standardizing assessments (Phillips, 1994, Gantt, 2000, Cohen, 2004). Cohen (2004) hits the nail on the head with respect to this problem:

> Naturally, the vast majority of American art therapists are less interested in, or comfortable with, assessment or evaluation than clinical work; it stands to reason that art therapists would much rather engage in the activities they are

trained to do, such as making art with their clients and otherwise helping them to heal. Moreover, as a general rule, artists tend to shy away from anything that smacks of scientific studies, especially those that involve numbers or statistics.

Standardization is the key to developing a sound foundation in this field , without which, we would not be able to reliably compare the response of one person to another. In her special feature article, Gantt (2000, p. 18) notes the key questions that must be addressed regarding art therapy assessments:

- What are we assessing that other related fields are not or cannot?
- What can we devise that would be a credible addition to the battery of existing psychological and psychiatric tests?
- Are there generic assessments that could be applied to any population or setting?
- Are we able to demonstrate that we have reliable and valid instruments?
- Do our assessments mean anything to others besides those of us in the particular discipline?

Since each art therapy assessment has its own value and limitations, this book will include structured as well as unstructured approaches. I commend the authors of these assessments for their effort to provide objective and meaningful assessments, which contribute immensely to the creative art therapy disciplines. The challenges of developing an assessment can often take years of work, as Cohen (2004) notes with his Diagnostic Drawing Series (DDS). Although we have made a great deal of progress in the effort to establish art-based assessments, there is still room for growth. The novel ideas that are generated must be transformed into psychometrically sound assessments. Further, there is need to conduct reliability and validity studies. This means that creative art therapists must overcome any resistance to conducting this research. One way to do this is to have more of a focus on assessment and research in graduate creative therapy programs.

Although this new Second Edition does not include all art therapy assessments available, it is my hope that this book will provide counselors and therapists with a rich selection of assessments that can be used in conjunction with their treatment goals and objectives. The book will begin with some traditional art therapy assessments and then proceed to more recent measures. It should be noted that the assessments reviewed in this book represent those more commonly used in graduate programs, private practices, and clinical settings. This book introduces new chapters on assessments such as Draw a Story (DAS; Silver 2002), the Art Therapy Dream Assessment (ATDA; Horovitz, 2004), the Face Stimulus Assessment (FSA; Betts, 2001), Formal Elements Art Therapy Scale and Person Picking an Apple from a Tree

(FEATS & PPAT; Gantt & Talbone, 1998), and the Levick Emotional Cognitive Art Therapy Assessment (LECATA; Levick, 2001 a & b). The most current research information on the assessments is provided.

REFERENCES

Anastasi, A. (1988). *Psychological testing* 6th ed. New York: Macmillan Publishing Company.

Anthony, E. (2003). The revealing image: Analytic art psychotherapy and practice. *Transcultural Psychiatry, 40*(2), 290–291.

Betts, D.J. (2001). *Projective drawing research: Assessing the abilities of children and adolescents with multiple disabilities.* 32nd Annual Conference of the American Art Therapy Association, Albuquerque, NM.

Bouchard, R.R. (1998). Art therapy and its shadow. A Jungian perspective on professional identify and community. *Art Therapy: American Journal of the American Art Therapy Association, 15*(3), 158–164.

Chapman, L., & Chapman, J. (1967). Genesis of popular but erroneous psychodiagnostic observations. *Journal of Abnormal Psychology, 72,* 193–204.

Chapman, L., & Chapman, J. (1969). Illusory correlation as an obstacle to the use of valid psychodiagnostic signs. *Journal of Abnormal Psychology, 74,* 271–280.

Cohen, B.M. (2004, January 5, 2004). *Personal communication.*

Cohen, B.M. (Ed.). (1986). *The Diagnostic Drawing Series Rating Guide.* Alexandria, VA: Barry Cohen.

Edwards, B. (1986). *Drawing on the artist within.* New York: Simon and Schuster.

Edwards, M. (2001). Jungian analytic art therapy. In Judith Aron, (Ed), *Approaches to art therapy: Theory and technique.* NY: Brunner-Routledge.

Gantt, L. (2001). The Formal Elements Art Therapy Scale: A measurement system for global variables in art. *Art Therapy: Journal of the American Art Therapy Association, 18* (1): 51–56.

Gantt, L. (2000). Assessments in the creative art therapies: Learning from each other. *Music Therapy Perspectives, 18,* 41–46.

Gantt, L., & Tabone, C. (1998). *Formal elements art therapy scale: The rating manual.* Morgantown, WV: Gargoyle Press.

Groth-Marant, G. (1990). *Handbook of psychological assessment.* (2nd ed.) New York, NY: John Wiley & Sons.

Horovitz, E. (2004, January 21). *Personal communication.*

Jung, C.G. (2003). Carl Gustav Jung (1875-1961). [Online] http://www.kirjasto.sci.fi/cjung.htm

Jung, C.G. (1958). *Psyche and symbol.* Violet de Laszlo (Ed.), New York, Doubleday.

Keyes, M.F. (1983). *Inward journey: Art as therapy.* Lasalle, IL: Open Court.

Klopfer, W., & Taulbee, E. (1976). Projective tests. In: M. Rosenzweig & L. Porter, Eds. *Annual Review of Psychology, 27.* Palo Alto, CA: Annual Reviews Inc.

Knoff, H.M., & Prout, H.T. (1985). The kinetic drawing system: A review and integration of the Kinetic Family and School Drawing techniques. *Psychology in the Schools, 22* (January), 50–59.

Koppitz, E.M. (1968). *Psychological evaluation of children's human figure drawings.* New York: Grune & Stratton.

Langer, S. (1953). *Feeling and form.* New York: Charles Schribner's Sons.

Levick, M.F. (2001-a). *The Levick Emotional and Cognitive Art Therapy Assessment (LECATA): Procedures.* Florida: Myra F. Levick.

Levick, M.F. (2001-b). *The Levick Emotional and Cognitive Art Therapy Assessment (LECATA): Test administration and scoring manual.* Florida: Myra F. Levick.

Machover, K. (1949). *Personality projection in drawing of the human figure.* Springfield, IL: Charles C Thomas, Publisher.

Malchiodi, C.A. (1990). *Breaking the silence: Art therapy with children from violent homes.* New York: Brunner/Mazel.

Mandala Gallery. (2003). Carl Jung and the mandala. [Online] http://www.netreach.net/~nhojem/jung.htm

McNiff, S. (1992). *Art as medicine: Creating a therapy of imagination.* Boston, MA: Shambala.

Moreno, Z.T. (1975). *Group psychotherapy and psychodrama.* New York: Beacon House Inc.

Naumburg, M. (1953). *Psychoneurotic art: Its function in psychotherapy.* New York, NY: Grune & Stratton.

Naumburg, M. (1966). *Dynamically oriented art therapy.* New York: Grune and Stratton.

Neale, E.L., & Rosal, M.L. (1993). What can art therapists learn from the research on projective drawing techniques for children? A review of the literature. *The Arts in Psychotherapy, 20,* 37–49.

Oster, G.D., & Gould, P. (1987). *Using drawings in assessment and therapy: A guide for mental health professionals.* New York, NY: Brunner/Mazel.

Phillips, J. (1994). Commentary on the assessment portion of the art therapy practice analysis survey. *Art Therapy: Journal of the American Art Therapy Association, 11,* 151–152.

Prinzhorn, H. (1972). *The artistry of the mentally ill.* New York, NY: Springer-Verlag.

Silver, R. (2002). *Three Art Assessments: The Silver Drawing Test of Cognition And Emotion; Draw a Story: Screening for Depression; and Stimulus Drawing and Techniques.* New York: Brunner-Routledge.

Stone, A. (2002). Art therapy. [Online article]. http://www.naturalhealth.org/articles/arttherapy.htm

Swenson, C. (1957). Empirical evaluations of human figure drawings. *Psychological Bulletin, 54,* 431–466.

Swenson, C. (1968). Empirical evaluations of human figure drawings: 1957–1966. *Psychological Bulletin, 70,* 20–44.

Wadeson, H. ed. (1992). *A guide to conducting art therapy research.* Mundelein, IL: The American Art Therapy Association.

Wadeson, H. (2003). Presentation on the Shadow and Art Therapy, at Nazareth

College, Rochester, New on September 26, 2003.

Wadeson, H. (1980). *Art psychotherapy*. New York: John Wiley & Sons.

Wanderer, Z. (1969). Validity of clinical judgments based on human figure drawings. *Journal of Consulting and Clinical Psychology, 33,* 143–150.

Chapter 2

HUMAN FIGURE DRAWING TEST

TITLE: Human Figure Drawing Test (HFD)
AGE: Ages five to twelve
YEAR: 1968 (See also Koppitz, 1984)
PURPOSE: designed to determine developmental level as well as provide information on personality characteristics
SCORES: two scores: (1) developmental items Present (total of 30 points) and (2) emotional indicators Present (total of 30 points)
MANUAL: manual (341 pages); illustrations (111 pages); profile (4 pages); reliability data (1 page); validity data (44 pages)
TIME LIMIT: no time limit for administration
COST: $12–$65 for testing manual
http://dogbert.abebooks.com/servlet/BookSearchPL
AUTHOR: Koppitz, Elizabeth M.
PUBLISHER: Grune & Stratton Inc., 111 Fifth Avenue, New York, NY, 10003.

INTRODUCTION

Some Human Figure Drawing (HFD) tests focused on emotional indicators while ignoring or minimizing the developmental aspects of a drawing. In addition, other HFD tests considered only developmental signs and neglected emotional indicators. Some test developers viewed items as a measure of both development and personality characteristics. Due to the confusion of previous human figure drawing tests, Koppitz (1968) designed the HFD to include separate indices of development and personality characteristics. For example, the omission of the neck or feet on HFDs was not uncommon for normal five-year-old boys, developmentally speaking. Yet, by the age of ten, boys should be including these features in their drawing, the omission of which may indicate immaturity or emotional problems. "It appears, therefore, that a meaningful interpretation of HFDs of children presupposes a thorough knowledge of both developmental and emotional indicators on drawings at each age level and a clear differentiation between the two" (Koppitz, 1968, p. 3). Koppitz (1968) systematically investigated the HFDs of children ranging in age from five to twelve. Her intention was to redesign the assessment so that it served as a development test and as a projective test.

PURPOSE AND RECOMMENDED USE

The HFD was the product of an interpersonal situation in which the clinician asked the child to draw a whole person. The structure of the drawing was said to indicate the child's maturational level whereas the style indicated the child's attitudes. The HFD may serve as a self-portrait, a picture of the client's inner self and his/her attitudes. Only one drawing was required to yield clinical information about a child. The HFD was designed for psychologists who work in clinics, schools, hospitals, or in private practice.

DIMENSIONS THAT THE TEST PURPORTS TO MEASURE

The HFD measured a child's developmental level and attitude. The first measure, developmental items, included 30 features of human figures. Specifically, a developmental item was defined "as an item that occurs only on relatively few HFDs of children of a younger age level and then increases in frequency of occurrence as the age of the children increases, until it gets to be a regular feature of many or most HFDs at a given age level" (Koppitz, 1968, p. 9). The presence of these items was related to the child's maturational level not to his/her artistic ability, education level, or medium used.

The second dimension that the HFD purported to measure was emotional indicators. An emotional indicator was defined "as a sign on HFDs which meets the following three criteria:

1. It must have clinical validity, i.e., it must be able to differentiate between HFDs of children with and without emotional problems.

2. It must be unusual and occur infrequently on the HFDs of normal children who are not psychiatric patients, i.e., the sign must be present on less

than 16% of the HFDs of children at a given age level.

3. It must not be related to age and maturation, i.e., its frequency of occurrence on HFDs must not increase solely on the basis of the children's increase in age" (Koppitz, 1968, p. 35).

Thirty-eight items were selected. The indicators measured the quality of the drawing, unusual features, and characteristic omissions of children at a given age level. Out of 38 original items, 30 met the criteria as outlined by Koppitz (1968).

ADMINISTRATION

The HFD can be administered individually or in group settings. Koppitz (1968) recommended individual testing since the administrator was able to observe the child and ask questions if needed. Also, "most children produce richer and more revealing drawings in a one-to-one relationship with an accepting psychologist than in a group setting" (Koppitz, 1968, p. 6).

The HFD utilized a blank sheet of white paper size 8 1/2″ x 11″ with a Number 2 pencil and eraser. The following directions were given:

> On this piece of paper, I would like you to draw a WHOLE person. It can be any kind of a person you want to draw, just make sure that it is a whole person and not a stick figure or a cartoon figure. (Koppitz, 1968, p. 6)

There was no time limit for the administration of the HFD. Generally, children took 10 to 30 minutes to complete the assessment. The child was permitted to erase as needed. Koppitz (1968) instructed that the examiner should carefully observe the child to determine the sequence in which the figure was completed, noting affect, spontaneous comments, as well as behavioral changes.

In order to avoid copying, children should be seated as far apart as possible when administering the HFD to a group. When tested individually, the child should be seated in a manner that he/she does not see a picture of a person on a wall or on a magazine cover. Using the examiner as a model for the assessment should be discouraged. If a child was inclined to copy figures, the examiner should repeat the HFD with the added instruction to draw "a picture of a whole person out of your own head" (Koppitz, 1968, p. 7).

NORM GROUPS

The normative sample included 1,856 public school children from kinder-garten through sixth grade. The sample contained students from ten differ-ent schools. One-third of the students came from low-income communities (including black and white students), one-third came from a white middle-income community, and the last one-third lived in high-income areas. Other demographic characteristics of the sample were not discussed. Additionally, it did not appear to be a random sample. Koppitz (1968) provided a break-down of the sample by age and gender. In her opinion, the sample did not include children who were mentally retarded or physically handicapped. The students were given the HFD in a group format by their teacher. Koppitz (1968) checked the HFDs for the presence of the 30 developmental items and the 30 emotional indicators.

INTERPRETATION OF SCORES

For the developmental items, charts were provided to aid in the interpre-tation of scores. For example, if a child had an HFD score of seven or eight, his/her level of mental ability was rated as high average to superior (IQ 110 upward). If a child had an HFD score of one or zero, he/she was rated as mentally retarded (IQ less than 70). Charts were not provided for the emo-tional indicators; therefore, quantitative interpretation of this section of the test was not possible. Qualitative interpretation focused on how the child drew the figure, who the figure represented, and the child's verbalizations. Koppitz (1968) interpreted HFDs based on the following: (1) the child's approach toward life's problems; (2) attitudes toward significant events; and (3) attitude toward self. Her interpretations were supported by case studies. For instance, three of her cases approached life problems with ambitious atti-tudes. These children drew themselves climbing mountains.

SOURCE OF ITEMS

The developmental items were taken from the Goodenough-Harris (Harris, 1963) scoring system and Koppitz's own experience. Only items that pertained to elementary age school children were included. The develop-mental items were broken down into the following categories: (1) Expected items (occur on 86–100% of drawings); (2) Common items (occur in 51–85% of HFDs); (3) Not unusual items (occur in 16–50% of drawings); and (4) Exceptional items (occur in 15% or less of drawings). Koppitz (1968) then broke down the scores by gender and age. She indicated which features were expected, common, not unusual, and exceptional. For instance, a five-year-old boy can be expected to include six basic items on their HFDs: head, eyes, nose, mouth, body, and legs. It was exceptional for a five-year-old boy to draw pupils, two-dimensional feet, correct number of digits, arms at shoulder, nostrils, lips, and knees. Five-year-old girls were expected to include seven items on their HFDs: head, eyes, nose, mouth, body, legs, and arms. It was exceptional for five-year-old girls to draw nostrils, elbows, lips, arms at shoulders, and knees.

Emotional indicators were broken down by age and gender. Two criteria were used: (1) that the item was not related to child's developmental level; and (2) that the item was unusual and occurred in less that 15% of the sample. Eight items of the original sample of 38 did not meet the criteria; therefore, they were omitted from the assessment. For instance, 15% of the six year old children (N = 131) showed poor integration of their figure. For six-year-old girls (N = 133), 8% showed poor integration of their figure.

VALIDITY AS DETERMINED BY THE AUTHOR

To determine the validity of the developmental items on the HFD, Koppitz (1966) examined 45 boys and 49 girls who were attending kindergarten classes. She wanted to see if the drawing medium had an effect on the HFD. The children were administered the test individually. Koppitz (1966) observed behavioral differences between boys and girls. Boys were awkward, shy, and seemed inept at using the No. 2 pencil. On the other hand, girls appeared comfortable and at ease using a No. 2 pencil. A few weeks later, the classroom teachers administered the HFD in a group fashion, modifying the instructions. Children were instructed to use crayons and were given the following directions:

> Now that you are going into the first grade, I would like to have a picture of you to keep. So, make me a picture of what you look like. Do not look at anyone else's paper because no two boys and girls look alike. (Koppitz, 1968, p. 21)

It should be noted that these instructions differ from the original HFD directive. No time limit was set. All pencil drawings and crayon drawings were checked for the presence of developmental items. Some items were omitted since the children were so young (i.e., two lips, elbow, knee, profile, good proportion, two or more clothing items). Using the percentage of children who revealed the developmental items, Koppitz (1966) found "thirteen basic items on HFDs were truly developmental indicators for young children and were not much influenced by the drawing medium or by the instructions given to the children" (p. 22). Overall, girls used pencils better than boys did whereas boys were more proficient using crayons. She did find that children were more likely to draw hair and clothing more often when using crayons as compared to pencil. It was unclear if these were significant differences.

The effect of learning and maturation on HFDs was examined using 179 children (89 boys and 90 girls) attending kindergarten classes. Koppitz (1968) compared the HFDs of children, matched by age, who either did or did not have a year of kindergarten training. The test was administered at the beginning of the school year in a group fashion and then again, nine months later. The drawings were scored for the presence of the 23 developmental items. By the end of the school year, 20 of the 23 developmental items were found more often than in the beginning of the year. Since it was difficult to discern if the improvement on the HFDs was due to maturation or kindergarten training, Koppitz (1968) matched the HFDs of 35 children (16 pairs of boys and 19 pairs of girls). One set of HFDs came from 35 children who were the oldest students at the beginning of the school year. The other set came from a group of children who were the youngest students before beginning school. When comparing these groups, there was very little difference in the frequency of the developmental items. Learning appeared to be related to the presence of the following developmental items: two dimensions on arms and legs, two or more pieces of clothing, and the correct number of fingers. "None of the other 19 developmental items showed a marked increase in frequency of occurrence as the result of school learning, thus supporting the hypothesis that the basic developmental items are primarily related to maturation and are not greatly influenced by school learning" (Koppitz, 1968, p. 26).

To determine the influence of high and low performance ability on HFDs, Koppitz (1968) matched 24 pairs of children by age, gender, and WISC Full Scale IQ (Wechsler, 1949) scores. All the children participating in the study had been referred to the school psychologist for possible learning problems. They ranged in age from 6 to 12 years with a mean age of 10.5 years. One set of the 24 students had a WISC Performance IQ score ten points above their Verbal IQ score. The other set of children had Verbal IQ score that was ten points above their Performance IQ score. Being blind to which group the children belonged to, Koppitz (1968) scored the drawings for the presence of the 30 developmental items. Thereafter, students with high Performance IQ scores were compared to children with low Performance IQ scores. Since the results were not significant, Koppitz (1968) concluded that developmental items on HFDs were not influenced by performance ability; rather, they were related to age and maturation.

In order to learn the relationship between IQ scores and the presence of expected and exceptional items on HFDs, Koppitz (1968) developed a scoring method. Each Expected or Exceptional Item was given a score of (+1) and the omission of an item was given a score of (-1). To avoid negative scores, (+5) points was added to each item whether positively or negatively scored. For example, the omission of one Expected item was given a score of 4 [-1+5]. On the other hand, the presence of one Exceptional item was scored as 6 [+1+5]. This scoring system was applied to the HFDs of 347 children, ranging in age from 5 to 12 years. The children were evaluated by Koppitz (1968) for psychological difficulties, at which time the HFD was administered. Within one year of the HFD test, the WISC (Wechsler, 1949) or the Standford-Binet Intelligence Scale (Terman & Merrill, 1960) was administered to the participants. Although the children showed a wide range of learning difficulties, none was brain injured or suffered from gross physical disabilities. The drawings were scored for the presence of the Expected and Exceptional items and then correlated with the child's IQ score. At the .01 level of significance, Koppitz (1968) found that the child's HFD score correlated with his/her IQ score. She concluded that the HFD can be used as a rough screening device to assess a child's mental maturity.

Koppitz (1968) examined the validity of the emotional indicators using a sample that included 76 pairs of public school children matched for age and gender. These children were matched with 76 patients in a child guidance clinic, who demonstrated at least normal intelligence. The students were administered the HFD individually. Koppitz (1968) reported that twelve emotional indicators were found significantly more often in the clinical group than on the drawings of the well-adjusted students. The most significant items (.01 level) included poor integration, shading of body and/or limbs, slanting figure, and tiny figure. The indicators such as the sun and figure cut off by the page were deleted since they did not demonstrate clinical validity.

Next, Koppitz (1968) selected 114 psychiatric patients (82 boys and 32 girls) who displayed any one of the following behaviors: overt aggressiveness, extreme shyness (depression or withdrawal), neurotic stealing, or a history of psychosomatic complaints. They ranged in age from 5 to 12 years. None of the children had an IQ score below 70. Shy children were matched with aggressive children. The HFDs were administered individually and checked for the presence of the 30 emotional indicators. Koppitz (1968) found that shy children significantly drew tiny figures, omitted the mouth, nose and eyes more frequently, and showed more hands cut off than did aggressive children. Genitals and transparencies occurred more often in the HFDs of aggressive children. Koppitz (1968) warned that no one emotional indicator could distinguish between a shy or aggressive child. Rather, the indicators must be viewed holistically.

Koppitz (1968) then compared the HFDs of children who steal with those who had a history of psychosomatic complaints. Few significant differences were found. Koppitz (1968) did report that the children with psychosomatic complaints revealed more short arms, legs pressed together, omission of nose and mouth, and clouds. Children who had a history of stealing revealed more shading of hands and/or neck, tiny head, big hands, omission of body, arms, or neck. The omission of the neck was significant at the .01 level.

Koppitz (1968) examined the relationship between emotional indicators on HFDs and school achievement. Ranging in age from 5 to 10 years, 313 children (180 rated as good students and 133 as poor students) participated in the study. Using group administration, the HFD was given at the beginning of the school year. The Metropolitan Achievement Test (Hildreth, 1946) was given at the end of the year and was used to determine the achievement level of the students in the first and second grades. Thereafter, teacher ratings were used. For kindergarten students, the omission of the body and of the mouth distinguished good from poor students. Additionally, 12 of the 13 poor students showed two or more emotional indicators on their HFD compared to three of 13 good pupils. For first and second grade students, five emotional indicators (poor integration, slanting figure, omission of the body and arms, and three or more figures spontaneously drawn) distinguished between good and poor students. For the third and fourth grades, none of the 30 emotional indicators was able to differentiate between the HFDs of good and poor students.

RELIABILITY AS DETERMINED BY THE AUTHOR

Reliability of the developmental items and for emotional indicators was determined with the aid of another psychologist. Independently, Koppitz (1968) and the psychologist scored HFDs of ten randomly selected second graders. Also, they rated 15 HFDs completed by students referred because of learning and emotional problems. The drawings were checked for the presence of the 30 developmental items and 30 emotional indicators. The examiners reached 95% agreement on scoring.

RESEARCH USING THE HFD

Lingren (1971) attempted to replicate Koppitz' (1968) work with shy and aggressive children. Participants included 97 pairs of children (56 pairs of boys and 41 pairs of girls) matched by age, gender, and IQ. Children ranged in age from 5 to 12 years. Parents and teachers completed a behavioral checklist that was used to classify the children as shy or aggressive. Children completed the HFD individually. Drawings were scored by Lingren (1971) and a school psychologist for the 30 emotional indicators. They reached 91% agreement. Lingren's (1971) results conflicted with Koppitz's findings in that shy children were more likely to draw cut-off hands than aggressive children. Lingren (1971) concluded the 30 emotional indicators could not significantly distinguish shy children from aggressive children. Lingren's (1971) work was supported by Hammer and Kaplan (1966) who found that the HFD was not a reliable test. Hammer and Kaplan (1966) had a large sample, 1,305 students who were given the HFD and then retested one week later.

Black (1976) randomly selected 100 children ranging in age from 6 to 12 years who were identified as having learning disabilities. Other demographic characteristics of the sample were not discussed such as economic, educational, and religious background. How the children were diagnosed and the nature of the learning disabilities were not discussed. He looked at self-perceived height, actual height, and HFD height discrepancies. Black (1976) concluded that the HFD was an indicator of learning disabilities since he found a significant difference in the mean actual height and the mean estimated height. Younger children were highly inaccurate when estimating height. Also, females were significantly more accurate in estimating their height as compared to males. Since there was not a significant number of drawings where height was scored as either large or small, Black (1976) asserted that the HFD may not be a direct representation of body image. Neal and Rosal (1993) supported Black (1976) in that the height of the HFD may not be a reliable indicator particularly for learning disabilities.

Koppitz and Casullo (1983) examined cultural influences on HFDs. Using two matched groups of 147 Argentine and 147 American adolescents, the researchers found that the drawings reflected different cultural values. Argentine children were better controlled, less aggressive, more vague, and more concerned with appearance and behavior. On the other hand, American participants portrayed more outgoing, impulsive, insecure, and aggressive behaviors.

Glutting and Nester (1986) examined the HFDs of 161 kindergarten children (82 males, 79 females). Using two learning related behavior tests, the researchers wanted to examine the predictability of the HFD. Children were placed into one of three groups depending on the number of emotional indicators present: (1) well-adjusted (no EIs); (2) adequately adjusted (one EI); or (3) possibly maladjusted (two or more EIs). Glutting and Nester (1986) found support for the concurrent validity of the HFD in that it significantly distinguished between the three groups of children.

Johnson (1989) examined 32 hearing impaired boys ranging in age from

7 to 12 years attending residential facilities for the deaf. The IQ scores ranged from 70 to 131 with a mean of 106.8. Students were administered the HFD (Koppitz, 1968) and the Stress Response Scales (SRS: Chandler, 1986). Johnson (1989) found that the HFD showed a positive correlation with emotional status as indicated by the SRS. The HFD was highly sensitive to the impulsive and passive-aggressive modes of the SRS. Although he did not use a random sample nor a large sample, Johnson's (1989) work did provide moderate concurrent validity evidence for the HFD (Koppitz, 1968).

Norford and Barakat (1990) also used the HFD to examine possible differences between aggressive and nonaggressive children. The sample ranged in age from four to five years and included 16 aggressive children and 16 nonaggressive children. Aggression was determined by using information from teacher ratings. Ten clinical raters classified the drawings into two groups: aggressive and nonaggressive. The researchers concluded that the HFD was not a valid instrument for distinguishing between aggressive and nonaggressive students. The authors attributed their findings to the fact that preschool age children lack cognitive maturity and visual-motor coordination.

Cates (1991) compared HFDs of hearing impaired children with normally hearing children. Participants included 26 residential students at a public school for hearing impaired children. These children were matched by age and gender with 26 students in a community school corporation, ranging in age from 9 to 18 years. A diagnosis of profound hearing impairment, placement at the school for at least one year, and a minimum IQ of 80 were the requirements for the hearing impaired sample. For the normally hearing children, the following criteria were used: placement in a regular classroom setting, no history of special education, hearing within a normal range, and no disabling condition. Cates (1991) used the Goodenough-Harris Drawing Test (Harris, 1963) and Koppitz's (1968) emotional indicators. Children were instructed as follows: "I want you to draw a person–the very best person you can. Cartoon characters and stick figures don't count" (Cates, 1991, p. 33). Hearing impaired children were given instructions using American Sign Language (ASL). After completing the drawing, students were instructed to identify the sex of the person by writing it at the top of the page. Subjects who drew opposite sex figures were excluded. Drawings were evaluated using Koppitz's emotional indicators (EI) and the Goodenough-Harris (GH) scoring system for drawings of a male or female. Ten drawings were randomly selected, five from the hearing group and five from the hearing impaired group. Although Cates (1991) did not discuss the rater qualifications or the number of raters used, he reported reliability coefficients of .87 for the GH scoring system and .94 for the EI's. He did not find that hearing impaired children drew larger ears than normally hearing individuals, a point supported by Davis and Hoppes (1975). Cates (1991) found a significant correlation of omissions with age and GH scores that suggests that these items may be testing development rather than emotional indices. "Although the results support the comparability of projective drawings between people with a hearing impairment and those with normal hearing, the emotional indicators did not perform as predicted in determining emotional disturbance" (Cates, 1991, p. 33). He went on to question the validity of the emotional indicators. Cates (1991) admitted that the results of his study may not generalize to other samples due to the small sample size and the inability to control for emotional disturbance.

Hibbard and Hartman (1990) examined the discriminant validity of the HFD. Drawings from 65 alleged sexual abuse victims were compared to 64 drawings made by participants who were presumed not to be victims of sexual abuse. No significant differences were found between the two groups on emotional indicators. As a group, the alleged victims tended to draw some indicators more often: legs pressed together, big hands, and genitals. Additionally, the victim group significantly showed more anxiety than the comparison group. The researchers stressed that the emotional indicators be reevaluated since they were found in the comparison group. It may be that some subjects in the comparison group were survivors of sexual abuse who may not have disclosed the information to the researchers or may not remember the abuse.

Numminen (1996) and colleagues used the HFD with 3, 4, and 5-year-old children and found gender differences. Using a sample of randomly selected children from childcare centers, 150 participants completed the HFD, with an equal number of girls and boys for each age level. Saastamoinen's (1993) test battery was used to score the HFDs. Numminen (1996) and colleagues found significant developmental changes and marked gender differences with this population. Developmentally, children's drawings began as mandalas and tadpole figures at three years of age and developed into more sophisticated forms in the older groups. Girls added more hair and clothing to their figures than did boys. Further, the tadpole perception of the body appaered early in girls' drawings.

In 1998, Wang and colleagues used the HFD as a tool for detecting dementia in the elderly. The HFD was used in conjunction with the Mini Mental State Examination (MMSE) to assess for dementia with a population of 461 people recruited from a community-based study of the elderly. Of this sample, 95 were affected with dementia and 366 were nondemented. Wang et al. (1998) noted that there was a high dropout rate in completing the HFDs., possibility due to the inability of this population to draw. Therefore, they stated that the use of the HFD has limited applicability in detecting mild dementia cases. The researchers also noted that their population was highly educated so further investigation of using the HFD with illiterate or low educated individuals was recommended.

Webster (2000) used the HFD as a tool for identifying sexually abused children. The HFD was one in a battery of assessments used to make determinations of sexual abuse. Sixty-two sexually abused children were compared to a sample of 40 children who were not abused. Webster (2000) outlined emotional indicators of abuse and sexually abused children significantly showed more of these indicators, poor figure integration, face shaded, slanting figure, crossed eyes, short arms, etc., as compared to the control group. In my second book, I go into more detail about possible graphic indicators of sexual abuse (Brooke, 1997).

Teichman (2001) used the HFD to examine the development of images, "Jew" and "Arab," in a group of Jewish children, aged 4–15 years. The HFDs were scored on thematic and structural variables. The youngest of the group of children and the adolescents showed more favoritism toward the ingroup and stronger outgroup negativity, whereas children in the middle showed reductions of ingroup favoritism and outgroup negativity. The HFD was a useful tool for the examination of social images. Since children can express themselves in drawings differently at different ages, Teichman (2001) felt that this tool is applicable to multiple age groups. As a language-free instrument, it can also be used with children from different sociocultural and ethnic backgrounds. Although she noted the usefulness of the HFD for assessing social images, Teichman (2001) did mention some drawbacks. She felt that drawing ability is indeed a factor with HFDs which warrants attention in future studies, a factor that was also an issue in the study of people with dementia (Wang et al., 1998).

In a later study, Teichman and Zafrir (2003) examined cultural differences in HFDs drawn by Jewish and Arab children. Specifically, they were interested in the children's perception of ingroup and outgroup differences. The large sample included 166 Jewish children and 199 Arab children from two different age groups, 7–8 (children), and 11–13 (adolescents). Teichman and Zafrir (2003) examined the images of "Jew" and "Arab" using the HFD and a questionnaire that were scored on structure and content. Results showed that younger children favored the majority group while adolescents favored their ingroup. Cultural and cognitive factors were explored: the Israeli-Arab conflict for Jewish children and minority status for Arab children, which were revealed in their HFD drawings.

Rae and Hyland (2001) used the Koppitz' (1968) scoring system to measure interrater and intrarater reliability in children's HFDs. A group of 85 school children, 8–9 years of age, completed the HFD on two separate occasions. The HFDs were rated by the same four individuals, one psychology graduate student and three undergraduate psychology students. Although results revealed little measurement error among the raters, especially in light of the fact that the raters received very little training on the scoring system, the variance component for the interactions of persons was high, .47. Rae and Hyland (2001) concluded that in order to have satisfactory reliability and generalize the results with the Koppitz system, children have to be tested on several occasions.

Swan-Foster et al. (2003) used an adapted version of the FEATS Rating Scale (Gantt & Tabone, 1998) to examine HFDs of pregnant women. She was specifically interested in the structural elements of the HFD. Three groups of women participated in the study: 20 high-risk outpatient (HRO), 20 high-risk inpatient (HRI), and 20 low-risk outpatient (LR) prenatal women. Ten drawings were randomly selected from each group for a total of 30 drawings. The adapted scales on FEATS included the following: color, space, detail, person, and implied energy. Swan-Foster et al. (2003) found significantly low scores for the high-risk group, suggesting the possibility of depression. The low-risk prenatal group had high scores using the adapted scale, indicating that depression was less of a risk for this group. Swan-Foster et al. (2003) asserted that the HFD is a useful tool for exploring prenatal women's emotions. Further, it may be a useful index for discovering prenatal women at risk for developing depression.

DESIRABLE FEATURES

Koppitz (1968) clearly described each item in the developmental and emotional indicator lists. In addition, she used examples in the case studies to illustrate the items. One chapter included case studies that relate the HFD to mental development, school achievement, organic conditions, and personality characteristics.

UNDESIRABLE FEATURES

The quantitative scoring procedure for the emotional indicators seems pointless since Koppitz (1968) did not provide guidelines for interpretation. In addition, interpretation may be difficult without previous clinical experience. Koppitz (1968) discussed possible interpretations of HFDs but they were based on case studies. Quantitative scoring procedures were not demonstrated in the case studies used in the book.

OVERALL EVALUATION

Koppitz's (1968) HFD scoring system did show some discriminant validity, particularly with high achievers compared to low achievers. Although she demonstrated that the HFD can discriminate between shy and aggressive children, other researchers were unable to reach the same conclusion. Discriminant validity for the HFD was lacking. Additional research is needed on the developmental items on the HFD.

Motta et al. (1993) argued that the HFD was not a reliable or valid instrument for assessing intelligence. Also, information on the reliability of the HFD needs to be examined. Since the standardization sample was selected over 30 years ago, future research should focus on reestablishing norms for the HFD. The use of the HFD in court proceeding has been questioned although the use of ratings scales, such as Koppitz's system, comes closer to meeting the minimal standards for admissibility as court evidence (Lally, 2001).

REFERENCES

Black, F.W. (1976). The size of human figure drawings of learning disabled children. *Journal of Clinical Psychology, 32*(3), 736–741.

Brooke, S.L. (1997). *Art therapy with sexual abuse survivors.* Springfield, IL: Charles C Thomas Publishers.

Cates, J.A. (1991). Comparison of Human Figure Drawings by hearing and hearing impaired children. *The Volta Review,* January, 31–39.

Chandler, L. (1985). *The Stress Response Scale: A Manual.* Pittsburgh, PA: University of Pittsburgh Psychoeducational Clinic.

Davis, C.J., & Hoppes, J.L. (1975). Comparison of House-Tree-Person drawings of young deaf and hearing children. *Journal of Personality Assessment, 39,* 28–33.

Gantt, L., & Tabone, C. (1998). *Formal elements art therapy scale: The rating manual.* Morgantown, WV: Gargoyle Press.

Glutting, J.J., & Nester, A. (1986). Koppitz emotional indicators as predictors of kindergarten children's learning-related behavior. *Contemporary Educational Psychology, 11,* 117–126.

Hammer, M., & Kaplan, A.M. (1966). The reliability of children's human figure drawings. *Journal of Clinical Psychology, 22,* 316–319.

Harris, D.B. (1963). *Children's drawings as measures of intellectual maturity.* New York: Harcourt, Brace, and World, Inc.

Hibbard, R.A., & Hartman, G.L. (1990). Emotional indicators in human figure drawings of sexually victimized and nonabused children. *Journal of Clinical Psychology, 46*(2), 211–219.

Hildreth, G. (1946). *Metropolitan Achievement Test, Primary I Battery: Form R.*

Yonkerson-Hudson: World Book Co.

Johnson, G.S. (1989). Emotional Indicators in the Human Figure Drawings of impaired children: A small sample validation study. *AAD,* July, 205–208.

Koppitz, E.M. (1966). Emotional indicators on Human Figure Drawings of shy and aggressive children. *Journal of Clinical Psychology, 22,* 466–469.

Koppitz, E.M. (1966). Emotional indicators on Human Figure Drawings of children: A validation study. *Journal of Clinical Psychology, 22,* 313–315.

Koppitz, E.M. (1966). Emotional indicators on Human Figure Drawings and school achievement of first and second graders. *Journal of Clinical Psychology, 22,* 481–483.

Koppitz, E.M. (1968). *Psychological Evaluation of Children's Human Figure Drawings.* New York: Grune & Stratton.

Koppitz, E.M. (1984). *Psychological Evaluation of Human Figure Drawings by middle school pupils.* Orlando, FL: Gune & Stratton.

Koppitz, E.M., & Casullo, M.M. (1983). Exploring cultural influences on human figure drawings of young adolescents. *Perceptual and Motor Skills, 57,* 479–483.

Lally, S.J. (2001). Should human figure drawings be admitted into court? *Journal of Personality Assessment, 76*(1), 135–149.

Lingren, R.H. (1971). An attempted replication of emotional indicators in human figure drawings by shy and aggressive children. *Psychological Reports, 29,* 35–38.

Motta, R.W., Little, S.G., & Tobin, M.I. (1993). The use and abuse of human figure drawings. *School Psychology Quarterly, 8*(3), 162–169.

Neale, E.L., & Rosal, M.L. (1993). What can art therapists learn from the research on projective drawing techniques for children? A review of the literature. *The Arts in Psychotherapy, 20,* 37–49.

Norford, B.C., & Barakat, L.P. (1990). The relationship of human figure drawings to aggressive behavior in preschool children. *Psychology in the Schools, 27,* 318–325.

Numminen, P., Nevala, N., Pennanen, M., & Saakslahti, A. (1996). *Human Figure Drawing as a representative medium of perceptual motor development among 3 to 5 year old children.* Paper presented at the Biennial Meeting of the International Society for the Study of Behavioural Development. Quebec, Canada, August 12-16th.

Rae, G., & Hyland, P. (2001). Generalisability and classical test theory analyses of Koppitz's Scoring System for Human Figure Drawings. *British Journal of Educational Psychology, 71,* 369–282.

Saastamoinen, N. (1993). *5-vutiaiden ihmispiirrosten representaatio jo ekspressiivisyys.* [Representation and expression of 5-year old children's human figure drawings]. Jyvaskyla, Finland: University of Jyvaskyla, Department of Psychology.

Swan-Foster, N., Foster, S., & Dorsey, A. (2003). The use of human figure drawings with pregnant women. *Journal of Reproductive and Infant Psychology, 21*(4). 293–308.

Teichman, Y. (2001). The development of Israeli children's images of Jews and Arabs and their expression in *Human Figure Drawings. Developmental Psychology, 37*(6), 749–761.

Teichman, Y., & Zafrir, H. (2003). Images Held by Jewish and Arab Children in Israel of people representing their own and the other group. *Journal of Cross-Cultural Psychology, 34*(6), 658–676.

Terman, L.M., & Merrill, M.A. (1960). *Standford-Binet Intelligence Scale.* Boston, MA:

Houghton Mifflin.

Wang, H., Kjerstin, E., Winblad, B., & Fratiglioni, L. (1998). The Human Figure Drawing test as a screen for dementia in the elderly: A community-based study. *Archives of Gerontology and Geriatrics, 27*(1), 25–34.

Webster, R.E. (2000). *Identifying sexually abused children using Human Figure Drawings.* Paper presented at the 32nd Annual Meeting of the National Association of School Psychologist, New Orleans, LA, March 28–April 1.

Wechsler, D. (1949). *Wechsler Intelligence Scale for Children.* New York, NY: The Psychological Corporation.

Chapter 3

KINETIC FAMILY DRAWINGS

TITLE:	Kinetic Family Drawings (KFD)
AGE:	Age limit not stated
YEAR:	1972
PURPOSE:	designed to understand child development: self-concept and interpersonal relationships
SCORES:	interpretation is based on actions, styles, and symbols used in the drawing; scoring is based on using a grid to measure distance of the self from other figures and size of the figures; an analysis sheet is included that summarizes information from the grid and drawing characteristics
MANUAL:	manual (304 pages); illustrations (137 pages); profile (2 pages); reliability data (none reported); validity data (none reported)
TIME LIMIT:	no time limit for administration
COST:	$23.95–$36.95 for testing manual http://www.tandf.co.uk/homepages/bmhome.html
AUTHOR:	Burns, Robert C., and Kaufman, S.H.
PUBLISHER:	Brunner/Mazel, Inc., 19 Union Square, New York, NY, 10003.

INTRODUCTION

The Kinetic Family Drawing (KFD) was designed to address the limitations of static family drawings by adding a kinetic component. Burns and Kaufman (1972) asserted that the KFD reflected emotional disturbances faster than interviews or other techniques. The manual was set up in a dictionary fashion so that the reader can look up common actions, styles, and figures in KFDs. Additionally, the manual was filled with example drawings along with case histories. Information on the theoretical background and development of the KFD was not discussed.

PURPOSE AND RECOMMENDED USE

The KFD was developed as a children's assessment to gather information on self-concept and interpersonal relationships. Through the use of the KFD, the therapist can gather information about family dynamics as well as the child's adaptive and defensive functioning. Burns and Kaufman (1970) responded to the feedback given on their previous work, Kinetic Family Drawings, by providing interpretive information about the KFD. A recommended use was not presented.

DIMENSIONS THAT THE TEST PURPORTS TO MEASURE

Actions drawn by the client was one dimension that the KFD measured. Action was construed as movement or energy reflected in the various figures (Burns & Kaufman, 1972). For girls, the most frequent actions of the father included reading, cooking, working, burning, mowing, and helping. For boys, the most frequent actions of the father comprised mowing, cutting, reading, repairing, painting, watching television, or working. The percentage of the samples showing these actions were low. Similar procedures were used for the actions of the mother and self. Again, the percentages were low. According to the authors, girls most frequently drew their mothers cooking, washing dishes, making beds, playing, or vacuuming. Boys, on the other hand, drew their mothers cooking, helping, ironing, planting, vacuuming, sweeping, washing dishes, or sewing. Girls most often drew themselves playing, eating, walking, riding, or washing dishes whereas boys most often drew themselves playing, eating, throwing, riding, or watching television. Movement between figures was also considered. The authors denoted this as a field of force:

> These forces may be conceptualized in a number of ways. Kurt Lewin (1937) might have discussed the drawings in terms of positive and negative valences and various barriers. Freud's (1938) concept of libido, a form of energy, at times invested in a particular person or part of the environment might also be a way to describe the forces depicted in the K-F-D's. Behaviorists, such as B.F. Skinner (1938), might call the emphasized parts of the drawings "discriminative stimuli." (Burns & Kaufman, 1972, p. 46)

The actions were delineated in dictionary fashion including case examples. For instance, the authors began by stating that the most frequent form of an action involved a ball. "Often competition or jealousy is depicted by the path of the ball" (Burns & Kaufman, 1972, p. 54). A great majority of the cases included in this section were devoted to the movement and interpretation of balls. A few other examples of actions were electricity, lights, barriers, fire, and dangerous objects.

Another dimension that the KFD purported to measure was the style of the drawing. Although the authors did not define it, style refers to the way figures were organized on the page and indicated emotional disturbance (Handler & Habenicht, 1994). These styles comprised the following: Compartmentalization, encapsulation, lining at the bottom, underlining figures, edging, lining on the top, and folding compartmentalization. Using a combined sample of 193 children, 20.8% had a compartmentalized style of drawing. From the same sample, the lowest figure was 2.1% for the use of the folding compartmentalization style. The style categories were vaguely defined. According to the authors, compartmentalization referred to the closing off of one's self or others (Burns & Kaufman, 1972). The examples included figures in boxes. How this differs from encapsulation was not clear. Encapsulated figures were also closed off and in boxes. With respect to encapsulation, the authors stated that "Sometimes we are able to love some people openly, but others bother us, so we encapsulate them" (Burns & Kaufman, 1972, p. 122). Unless the reader was previously familiar with encapsulation and compartmentalization, the distinction between these two styles may be ambiguous. The remainder of the chapter discussed case examples depicting each of the styles outlined by the authors.

The symbols section contained the authors' interpretations of items commonly depicted on KFDs. Burns and Kaufman (1972) selected a series of recurring symbols to include in this section. For example, the symbol "A" was linked to high academic achievement. The authors reported that it was frequently used in a number of KFD drawings. There was some overlap between symbols and actions in that electricity was listed as a symbol as well as an action; yet, the meaning of electricity in both sections was the same.

The last dimension that the KFD purported to measure was size of figures and the distance between them. The authors created a grid that can be placed over the child's drawing to measure the height of figures as well as the distance of self from other family members. This was a wonderful way to quantify information in the assessment; yet, the authors did not discuss grid analysis in any of the cases presented in the book.

ADMINISTRATION

The KFD was designed to be an individual assessment. The drawing was completed on plain white paper (8 1/2″ x 11″) using a No. 2 lead pencil. The child was instructed as follows:

> Draw a picture of everyone in your family, including you, DOING something. Try to draw whole people, not cartoons or stick people. Remember, make everyone DOING something–some kind of action. (Burns & Kaufman, 1972, p. 5)

The authors stressed that the examiner should leave the room and check back periodically. No time limit was given. Examiner qualifications were not discussed.

NORM GROUPS

The actions of individual KFD figures were standardized on a population of 128 males and 65 females ranging in age from 5 to 20 years, with a mean age of 10 years. Although the number of boys outweighed the number of girls, the authors argued that "this ratio is representative of that found by many clinics treating disturbed children" (Burns & Kaufman, 1972, p. 44). With the exception of children completing "normal" KFDs, this sample included cases from their previous book, Kinetic Family Drawings (Burns & Kaufman, 1970). Other demographic characteristics of the sample were not discussed. One was left to believe that the tables in the book were based on a normative sample of emotionally disturbed children. No information was given on how the cases were selected. Moreover, the diagnostic criteria was not described. The population sample was not randomly selected; therefore, the results can not be expected to generalize to other populations.

INTERPRETATION OF SCORES

A large majority of the book discussed the various symbols, actions, and styles included on the KFD. Some examples were given in the previous section of this chapter, "Dimensions that the Test Purports to Measure." The authors interpreted the case drawings solely based on drawing style, actions, and symbols. They neglected to use the grid that would have provided information about figure sizes and distances between figures. Although the authors created a list of interpretations of common actions, styles, and symbols, they warned that:

> any attempt at hypothesizing the unconscious expression of any single symbol
> of a dream or projective instrument such as a drawing, one must weigh the
> alternate and sometimes seemingly incompatible interpretations. What is more
> essential is that the observer be capable, in the frame of reference of his own
> background, training and skills, to consider the totality of the individual. (Burns
> & Kaufman, 1972, p. 144)

The authors did not outline qualifications for administrators nor provide a set
of clear guidelines for interpretation. Since the KFD used a dictionary
approach and did not observe the drawing process, this method can be classified as a cookbook method (Koppitz, 1968). Although the authors also created a grid to measure size of figures and distances between them, they did
not present guidelines for the interpretation of the measurements. A few
questions that came to mind were: How small does a figure have to be to suggest low self-esteem? How far should figures be apart to indicate psychological distance?

SOURCE OF ITEMS

The source of the symbols, actions, and styles was based on the authors'
interpretation of drawings from a sample of children in a clinical setting.
Information on theoretical background and historical development of the
KFD were not discussed. No other information on the source of items was
presented.

VALIDITY AND RELIABILITY AS DETERMINED BY THE AUTHOR

The manual did not discuss validity and reliability data. With the creation
of the grid, the authors can feasibly present information on reliability and
validity of figure size and distances; yet, this was not done. In addition, it
should be noted that the information that did appear was based on a biased
sample that was not randomly selected and it was a clinical population.

RELIABILITY RESEARCH

McPhee and Wegner (1976) investigated interrater reliability of the KFD.
Using a group of emotionally disturbed children, KFD styles were interpret-

ed. Five judges were trained to score KFDs. Reliability scores ranged from .65 to 1.00 with a median reliability of .87. These scores were in response to compartmentalization, lining at the bottom, and lining at the top drawing styles. The least reliable drawing style was underlining individual figures. Since they occurred very little in their population sample, the authors rejected edging and folding compartmentalization. McPhee and Wegner (1976) also investigated validity of the KFD, which will be discussed in the next section of this chapter.

Another study that investigated interrater reliability was completed by Cummings (1980). Two male and two female examiners were trained to score KFDs using three objective scoring methods, one of which was developed by McPhee and Wegner (1976). Behavior disordered, learning disabled, and public school children were examined. High interscorer reliabilities resulted. Five weeks later, they retested the children but found that test-retest reliability of the KFDs were inconsistent. Essentially, the KFD could not distinguish between emotionally disturbed children and well-adjusted children. Cummings (1980) suggested that the KFD may be sensitive to transition in children's personality states; thus, it may not be an accurate measure of personality traits or characteristics.

Realizing the lack of an objecting scoring system in the KFD manual, Mostkoff and Lazarus (1983) developed their own system. Fifty elementary school children (25 boys and 25 girls), selected to receive services in reading and math, participated in the study. The group consisted of 14 second grade students, 14 third graders, 9 fourth graders, and 13 fifth graders. Using a two-week interval, each child was administered the KFD. The researchers selected 20 variables to interpret the KFDs. Using two raters, interrater reliabilities ranged from .86 to 1.00, with an average reliability of .97. Out of the 20 variables listed by the author, the following revealed significant test-retest reliability: self in picture, omission of body parts (self and others), arm extensions, rotated figures, elevated figures, evasions, barriers, and drawings on the back of the page. "This study shows that it is possible for an objective scoring system to be developed with high interjudge reliability" (Mostkoff & Lazarus, 1983, p. 20). In agreement with Cummings (1980), the authors asserted that the KFD was sensitive to a child's mood changes.

Elin and Nucho (1979) also developed a scoring system for the KFD. Three judges rated 48 KFDs taken from the Burns and Kaufman (1972) manual. They reported high interrater reliability. Additionally, they established concurrent validity using the Personal Adjustment Inventory. The authors argued that the KFD significantly distinguished between low self-esteem and high self-esteem.

Mangold (1982) established that interpretation of the KFD was sensitive to preceding testing conditions. The researcher found that if the KFD was preceded by the Wechsler Intelligence Scale for Children-Revised (WISC-R), it had a suppressing effect on the drawing. If the KFD was preceded by the Rorschach, it had an expanding effect on the drawing. The research was helpful in filtering out extraneous variables that may have affected the interpretation of the KFD.

VALIDITY RESEARCH

A majority of the studies reviewed in this section did not use Burns and Kaufman's (1972) interpretation method. This fact makes the comparison of the studies difficult. Some researchers have included variables not previously considered in the original KFD manual. When possible, I will attempt to distinguish between scoring systems and variables considered.

McGregor (1978) completed one of the most thorough validity studies of the KFD. Using three treatment groups, 157 children, ranging in age from 5 to 13 years, were administered the KFD. Group I was rated as "normal" children by their teacher. Group II consisted of a group of children experiencing conduct problems such as acting out, aggression, and unmanageable behavior. Group III included children who experienced problems with shyness, phobias, and overly controlling behaviors. Figure omissions were unrelated to a child's age, sex, and behavioral problems. McGregor (1978) did not find a relationship between figure size and age, sex, or problems experienced. On the other hand, older children separated their figures significantly more than younger children did. Also, "normal" children drew their parents farther apart than either problem group. As compared to Group III, conduct disordered children were more likely to place a barrier between self and father. McGregor (1978) concluded that the KFD was not a valid instrument when discriminating between "normal" and clinically labeled children. Instead of using the KFD for diagnosis, McGregor (1978) recommended that it be used to address behavioral issues that may be significant for the child. Knoff and Prout (1985) noted that McGregor's study had several limitations: (1) validation of the clinical groups' label; (2) neglecting to look at intelligence level and socioeconomic status; and (3) using only two age groupings, even though they have a range of eight years.

McPhee and Wegner (1976) found that the KFD was not a valid instrument when trying to distinguish between well-adjusted children and poorly adjusted children. Monahan (1986) supported their findings in that more psychopathology was found in drawings of high achieving children as compared to low achieving children. Additionally, Monahan (1986) noted that the children participating in the success condition (high achieving) spent 40% more time completing the KFD. This supported McPhee and Wegner's (1976) finding that well-adjusted children spend more time drawing; therefore, they provided more details that fell into Burns and Kaufman's (1972) categories. When comparing a group of children, ranging in age from 6 to 12 years, with behavioral, learning, and emotional problems with a matched group of well-adjusted children, Layton (1983) found no significant differences in the KFDs. As with the previous researchers, signs of pathology were found more frequently in the well-adjusted group.

On the other hand, Sobel and Sobel (1976) discovered that delinquent male adolescents omitted family members more often than well adjusted adolescent males. They found that most of the Burns and Kaufman (1972) scoring criteria did not distinguish between the two groups. Rhine (1977) observed that poorly adjusted children showed twice as much compartmentalization and encapsulation as well-adjusted children. Again, their results failed to support Burns and Kaufman's (1972) hypotheses of using the KFD to determine adjustment.

Brewer (1980) found significant differences between shy, average, and active children. For instance, shy children drew themselves as isolated whereas active children drew themselves with others (although not interacting). Developmentally delayed children also demonstrated significantly more isolation and rejection when compared to well adjusted children (Raskin & Pitcher-Baker, 1975, 1977; Raskin & Bloom, 1979).

RESEARCH USING THE KFD

The KFD and Studies of Abuse and Neglect

Much of the research on KFD considered its application to the study of child abuse. Schornstein and Derr (1978) viewed the KFD as a rapid and objective means for determining cases of child abuse and neglect. Their article delineated what they look for in KFDs. For instance, they noted transparencies, stick figures, omissions, and tensions as common depictions in KFDs.

> We have also seen the child drawn as a competitor. For example, fathers who draw their sons as being more masculine, aggressive, or larger than themselves, or as being with mother. Child abuse can develop in these instances when the parent regards the child as receiving more attention than the spouse—or an extension of the spouse. (Schornstein & Derr, 1978, p. 35)

Generally, the authors found the KFD was valuable in preventing further abuse and provided information for intervention.

Goodwin (1982) used the KFD when evaluating possible sexual abuse survivors. Although she implemented a series of drawings in the evaluation, only the KFD will be discussed. She examined 19 female children who were suspected sexual abuse survivors. Goodwin (1982) found evidence of isolation, compartmentalization, and role reversals in the drawings of sexual abuse survivors. Additionally, she observed that these children drew themselves larger than their mother did.

Hackbarth (1991) and others found that the KFD can significantly differentiate between abused and nonabused children. Thirty children, ranging in age from 6 to 13 years (mean age of 8.6), classified as sexually abused by the Department of Human Services were compared to 30 unidentified children in a public school district. They ranged in age from 6 to 11 years (mean age of 8.6). The participants were matched with those in the experimental group: 25 girls and 5 boys (26 were White and 4 were Black). Mothers also completed the KFD. Using a Like to Live in Family (LLIF) rating procedure (Burns, 1982), five counselors scored the KFDs on desirability of family life. Sexually abused children drew significantly less desirable family situations compared to their mothers. Mothers of sexually abused children drew significantly less desirable family settings than did mothers of unidentified children. Mothers and their unidentified children did not significantly differ in their KFDs. "The KFD shows enough promise as an evaluation tool in the area of sexual abuse that elementary counselors may want to consider this instrument for inclusion in their repertoire of assessment skills" (Hackbarth et al., 1991, p. 260).

The KFD has revealed common themes in the artwork of sexual abuse survivors (Brooke, 1997). For instance, red houses were typically drawn by survivors (Cohen & Phelps, 1985). Also, children who were sexually abused tend to omit bedrooms or if bedrooms were present, indicated bizarre sleeping arrangements or lack of privacy (Goodwin, 1982). Further, Goodwin (1982) found evidence of isolation, role reversals, and encapsulation in the KFDs of sexual abuse survivors. Cohen and Phelps (1985) discovered that the child will often omit self from the KFD. Burgess and Hartman (1993) observed family conflict in KFDs. Isolation, barriers, encapsulation, and sexual themes were also some indicators portrayed in the KFD (German, 1986). For more detailed information on possible graphic indicators of sexual abuse in individual, family, and group art therapy assessments, see Brooke (1997). Although these studies found positive results using the KFD, other studies were not as confident that the KFD could distinguish abused children from nonabused children.

Veltman and Browne (2000) wanted to see if teachers and mental health professionals could identify children who had been maltreated through the Favorite Kind of Day (Manning, 1987) and the KFD. The study used a sample of 33 mental health practitioners and 10 classroom teachers to examine sets of drawings to see if they could identify maltreated children's drawings. The KFD showed more promise than the FKD in identifying maltreated children's drawing, only if it was known in advance that maltreatment was definitively present. Without this knowledge, the KFD could not be used as a reliable indicator of maltreatment. Despite this, Veltman and Browne (2000) felt that the KFD was useful that it "can help illicit information from children about distressful events and, when used by mental health professionals in case conferences for example, may provide extra evidence that maltreatment has occurred" (p. 335). They called for future studies to utilize larger sample sizes.

In a later study, Veltman and Browne (2001) administered Favorite Kind of Day (FKD) and the KFD with maltreated children. Specifically, there were interested in determining if the FKD and KFD would be useful screening devices for child maltreatment. With the KFD, they were interested in indicators of emotional distress. Using a sample of 28 10-year-old children, they found that the KFD was three times better than the FKD for identifying maltreated children. It should be noted that the raters were blind to the abuse status of the children completing the drawings. Although this seemed promising, Veltman and Brown (2001) stated that the false alarm rate was too high to warrant either assessment to be used as a classroom screening device for maltreatment.

Holt and Kaiser (2001) used the KFD with a population of children from alcoholic families. They were interested in seeing if there were graphic indicators of parental alcoholism in the KFDs of children whose parents were being treated for substance abuse. Compared to the control group, Holt and Kaiser (2001) found that two indicators, isolation of self and isolation of family members, distinguished the children who had parents abusing substances.

Reddy et al. (2002) used the KFD to examine resistance and graphic indicators with neglected boys. Two hundred and fifty participants were from 8 to 12 years of age and resided in juvenile homes. The researchers found that when compared to a control sample, neglected boys drew more disoriented and irregular figures in their KFDs.

Veltman (2003) evaluated the KFDs of physically abused children. Specifically, Veltman (2003) was interested in how abused children draw themselves in relation to how they depict their family members. She asked, would physically abused children draw more indicators of emotional distress as compared to children who were not physically abused? Six physically abused children, aged 4–8 years, were compared to 12 matched, control children. Physically abused children significantly showed more omissions and incomplete figures. Qualitatively, abused children showed more distortions in the KFD and drew themselves out of proportion in comparison to their family members. Follow-up studies at six months, and then at 12 months, showed that these emotional indicators began to disappear. Veltman (2003) stated that more research is needed to determine if the KFD is an effective assessment with physically abused children.

The KFD and Cross Cultural Studies

Cabacungan (1985) examined cultural variables related to the KFD. Using a sample of 197 children, 113 Japanese, and 84 Filipinos, ranging in age from 9 to 12 years, participated in the study. After the KFDs were administered, names were erased and the drawings were randomly numbered. One Japanese and one Filipino rater used an objective scoring system (Burns, 1982; Thompson, 1975) to rate all 197 drawings. Japanese children significantly drew their actual family size more often than Filipino children did. Also, they omitted less characters and added nonmajor figures. Filipino children omitted father and mother figures significantly more often. Both groups drew the mother as the largest figure. Japanese children drew their figures engaging in recreational activities whereas Filipino children showed figures engaged in work and pleasure. Actions of figures did not reveal cultural or gender differences. Japanese parents were drawn as less communicative as compared to the Filipino children's drawings. Cabacungan (1985) concluded that culture had a significant effect on the drawing of actual family size, actions depicted by major figures, and communication levels of the figures.

Deornellas (1997) examined cultural differences and similarities in children's KFDs. The sample included 161 third grade students from Caucasian (43% of the sample) , African American (24%), and Hispanic (33%) families. Three trained scorers rated the KFDs independently. It was proposed that since African American children come primarily from matriarchal families, they would draw the mother figure larger but this was not supported by the results. Although Hispanic children included more nuclear family members in their drawings compared to the other two groups, this result did not reach significance. There were significant results in that African American children were more likely to omit a parent figure compared to the other two groups. Overall, Deornellas (1997) asserted that the KFD should be included in test batteries used for assessing social-emotional adjustment for children of these ethnicities.

Friedlander et al. (2000) used the KDF to examine bicultural identity in adopted children. The researchers interviewed the parents and asked the adopted children to complete KFDs. Twelve parents and 12 children participated in the study. Parents were selected from a local adoption support group and were all of European-American descent. The children ranged in age from 6–15 years and came from either Korean or Latin American heritages. Generally, the KFDs indicated positive self-esteem and did not seem to reflect racial differences.

Sanchez-Rosado (2002) used the KFD as a tool to provide more sociocultural information on Hispanic children and their families, particularly in viewing the impact of acculturation on psychological testing. The children participating came from rural, semirural, small city, and urban schools and represented a nonclinical population. Of the sample, 320 children were of Mexican descent and 114 were Caucasian, in grades 3 through 6. Acculturation level was assessed and compared to the children's' KFDs. Sanchez-Rosado (2002) stated that acculturation was clearly reflected in the children's' KFDs. He asserted that future studies should focus on acculturation factors as they relate to psychological testing.

Other Studies Utilizing the KFD as a Screening Device

Stawar and Stawar (1987) researched the possibility of using the KFD as a screening device. They compared the KFD of two groups of white boys who ranged in age from 7 to 11 years. Group I consisted of 18 boys referred to a mental health center for a myriad of issues: learning problems, anxiety, phobias, attention deficit disorder, hyperactivity, and conduct disorders. The children had a full scale IQ above 75. Group II consisted of nine boys enrolled in a public school system who did not suffer from learning, emotional, or behavioral problems. No statistical differences were found between the distance of self to father. Group I boys drew themselves significantly closer to their mothers than Group II boys. The authors also found significant differences in the styles and self-actions. For instance, Group I used more edging and encapsulation which is generally associated with isolation, avoidance, and withdrawal. Group II showed more figure underlining and compartmentalization, which may suggest feelings of instability and separateness. Group I depicted themselves riding bikes or horses whereas Group II showed more play. "Although the present results do not support a wholesale endorsement of the test authors' interpretations, they suggest that certain variables (closeness to mother, style, and self-actions) may have potential as components of a screening instrument" (Stawar & Stawar, 1987, p. 810).

Rabinowitz (1991) examined the relationship of acceptance-rejection and KFDs. Although he proposed that peer accepted children would draw themselves closer to other figures than rejected children, the differences were not significant. He did find sex differences in that peer accepted girls drew themselves closer to other figures as compared to boys. The following year, Rabinowitz (1992) examined the height of parental figures in relation to peer acceptance or rejection. The researcher examined 55 boys and 61 girls in the fifth grade. They were given "a sociometric measure consisting of two questions requesting the names of four children with whom the child wished or did not wish to be paired on an outing, and rating of acceptance and rejection were obtained" (Rabinowitz, 1992, p. 329). Rejected children had higher rejection scores than acceptance scores whereas accepted children had higher acceptance scores. Unfortunately, this was the only information given regarding the test used. The nature of this instrument and the subsequent classification of the children was not clear. The researcher then administered the KFD. Sex differences were found only when dividing the children into peer accepted and peer rejected groups: Peer accepted girls drew taller mother and father figures than boys did. Rabinowitz (1992) suggested that the family has greater significance for accepted girls than it did for accepted boys. No significant differences were found between peer accepted and rejected boys with respect to the size of parental figures. Accepted girls drew significantly taller mothers than rejected girls. No differences were found with the father figure. Rabinowitz (1992) concluded that it was important to note peer acceptance-rejection when evaluating the size of parental figures in the KFD.

Michael and Dudek (1991) examined creativity and mother-child relationships. The researchers assessed the degree of differentiation in both creative and uncreative children using a series of tests. Only the KFD will be considered. Differentiation referred to the mother's ability to encourage the child to develop a separate identity. The initial sample included 133 eight-year-old public school children (60 girls and 73 boys). Using the Torrance Tests of Creative Thinking (TTCT; Torrance, 1966), 15 of highest scoring children and 15 of the lowest scoring children were selected. Comparing the mothers' interview with the children's KFDs, the researchers found that highly creative children were significantly more differentiated than less creative children.

Lyons (1993) discussed the use of the KFD in evaluating children in custody cases. When the custody of a child was disputed, Lyons (1993) served as a consultant to provide information on the determination. Her evaluation consisted of four tasks, the second of which will be considered. She used the KFD as a tool since it "appears to be quite directly related to the issues involved in much child forensic work" (Lyons, 1993, p. 156). She examined how the figures were drawn, interaction and space between figures, environmental characteristics, and omissions. When children included a parental figure, it suggested attachment and "may reveal the real and honest need for this family member to remain a part of their emotional life and remain 'in the picture'" (Lyons, 1993, p. 158).

Finger (1997) used a case approach to examine the sensitivity of the KFD to changes during the therapeutic process. Alan was a seven-year-old first grader whose parents were divorced. He had no siblings. In school, Alan was having difficulty with reading and arithmetic. In general, he demonstrated much anxiety and had poor academic progress. At home, he had difficulty sleeping, plagued by bad dreams. He completed the KFD before and during therapy. According to Finger (1997), Alan was resistant to drawing the pretherapy KFD. In the drawing, Alan is alone. He describes himself as going downstairs to have breakfast, watch television, and go to school. He had an anger outburst and stated that his father does not live there anymore. Finger (1997) equates the going downstairs with feelings of depression possibly associated with the estrangement with his father. During therapy, Alan's KFD showed a feeling of being part of a family. Finger (1997) noted possible sexual feelings arising in relation to his mother.

DESIRABLE FEATURES

The KFD was an interesting approach to understanding the client's perception of self and familial relationships. The grid was a wonderful method of quantifying information about the KFD; yet, the authors did not present guidelines for the interpretation of measurements. The case examples were helpful in understanding how the authors intended the KFD to be used. Overall, the KFD potentially yields valuable information about familial relationships as well as self-concept.

UNDESIRABLE FEATURES

There was overlap between some of the features of the test. For instance, "light" was used as both a symbol and an action. However, the terms were not clearly defined. Moreover, there was not enough information on how the test was developed, especially the theoretical background. No information was given on who was able to administer the KFD and their qualifications. Interpretation can be difficult given the ambiguity in the test terms and lack of examples for the grid information.

OVERALL EVALUATION

Although not presented in the manual, objective scoring systems have been developed for the KFD. With training, interrater reliability has been established. However, test-retest reliability evidence was weak suggesting that the KFD may be sensitive to mood changes and pretest conditions. Additionally, it may not be a reliable indicator of personality traits.

Validity evidence was also mixed. Research suggested that the KFD cannot distinguish between emotionally disturbed children and well-adjusted children. In addition, cultural differences as well as sex differences were found when using the KFD. It was difficult at times to compare validity studies since researchers used a variety of scoring methods. Studies that examined only one variable, such as underling at the bottom, were not considered in this review. Examining only one variable did not seem to provide evidence of an assessment's validity. The exact nature of what the KFD measured was not clear.

The completed summary sheet at the end of the manual can be a useful tool. It would have been more helpful to the reader to have a blank summary sheet to be used for therapeutic or research purposes. Additionally, the use of the grid to measure size of the figures and distances was helpful. More information was needed on the interpretation of these measurements. Overall, the authors were not clear when outlining the test dimensions. At times, the meanings were ambiguous, such as the distinction between encapsulation and compartmentalization.

The KFD shows promise as a tool that yields information about a child's personality state. It seemed to be a particularly useful tool when evaluating children who were suspected sexual abuse survivors (Brooke, 1997; West, 1998). Further evidence was needed to determine whether or not the KFD can adequately distinguish between other groups such as clinically labeled versus well-adjusted children. Overall, the KFD may be a useful approach to gather information about a child's view of self in relationship to family members.

REFERENCES

Brewer, F. (1980). *Children's interaction patterns in Kinetic Family Drawings.* Unpublished doctoral dissertation, United States International University. Cited in Handler & Habenicht (1994).

Brooke, S.L. (1997). *Healing through art: Art therapy with sexual abuse survivors.* Springfield, IL: Charles C Thomas, Publishers.

Burgess, A.W., & Hartman, C.R. (1993). Children's drawings. *Child Abuse & Neglect, 17,* 161–168.

Burns, R.C. (1982). *Self-growth in families.* New York: Brunner/Mazel.

Burns, R.C., & Kaufman, S.H. (1970). *Kinetic Family Drawings (K-F-D): An introduction to understanding children through kinetic drawings.* New York: Brunner/Mazel.

Burns, R.C., & Kaufman, S.H. (1972). *Actions, styles, and symbols in Kinetic Family Drawings (K-F-D): An interpretive manual.* New York: Brunner/Mazel.

Cabacungan, L.F. (1985). The child's representation of his family in Kinetic Family Drawings (KFD): A cross-cultural comparison. *Psychologia, 28,* 228–236.

Cohen, F.W. & Phelps, R.E. (1985). Incest markers in children's art work. *Arts in Psychotherapy, 12,* 265–284.

Cummings, J.A. (1980). An evaluation of an objective scoring system for the KFDs. *Dissertation Abstracts, 41*(6-A), 2313.

Deornellas, K.L. (1997). A comparison of the Kinetic Family Drawings of African American, Hispanic, and Caucasian third graders. *Dissertation Abstracts International: Section B: The Science and Engineering, 58*(5–B), 2716.

Elin, N., & Nucho, A.O. (1979). The use of kinetic family drawing as a diagnostic tool in assessing the child's self-concept. *Arts in Psychotherapy, 6,* 241-247.

Finger, D.R. (1997). Child case study Alan, before and during therapy. In *Advances in projective drawing interpretation.* E. F. Hammer (Ed). Springfield, IL: Charles C Thomas. pp. 263–267.

Friedlander, M.L., Larney, L.C., Skau, M., Hotaling, M., Cutting, M.L. & Schwam, M. (2000). Bicultural identification: Experiences of internationally adopted children and their parents. *Journal of Counseling Psychology, 47*(2), 187–198.

German, D. (1986). *The female adolescent incest victim: Personality, self-esteem, and family orientation.* Unpublished doctoral dissertation, Andrews University. Cited in Handler & Habenicht, 1994.

Goodwin, J. (1982). Use of drawings in evaluating children who may be incest victims. *Children and Youth Services Review, 4,* 269–278.

Hackbarth, S.G., Murphy, H.D., & McQuary, J.P. (1991). Identifying sexually abused children by using Kinetic Family Drawings. *Elementary School Guidance & Counseling, 25,* 225–260.

Handler, L., & Habenicht, D. (1994). The Kinetic Family Drawing technique: A review of the literature. *Journal of Personality Assessment, 62*(3), 440–464.

Holt, E.S., & Kaiser, D.H. (2001). Indicators of familial alcoholism in children's Kinetic Family Drawings. *Art Therapy: Journal of the American Art Therapy Association, 18*(2), 89–95.

Manning, T.M. (1987). Aggression depicted in abused children's drawings. *The Arts in Psychotherapy, 14,* 15–24.

Murphy, H.D., & McQuary, J.P. (1991). Identifying sexually abused children by using Kinetic Family Drawings. *Elementary School Guidance & Counseling, 25,* 225–260.

Knoff, H.M., & Prout, H.T. (1985). The Kinetic Drawing System: A review and integration of the Kinetic Family and School Drawing Techniques. *Psychology in the Schools, 22,* 50–59.

Koppitz, E.M. (1968). *Psychological evaluation of children's human figure drawings.* New York: Grune & Stratton.

Layton, M. (1983). *Special features in the Kinetic Family Drawings of children.* Unpublished doctoral dissertation, Temple University. Cited in Handler & Habenicht, 1994.

Lyons, S.J. (1993). Art psychotherapy evaluations of children in custody disputes. *The Arts in Psychotherapy, 20,* 153–159.

Mangold, J. (1982). *A study of expressions of the primary process in children's Kinetic Family Drawings as a function of pre-drawing activity.* Unpublished doctoral dissertation,

Indiana State University. Cited in Handler & Habenicht (1994).

Manning, T.M. (1987). Aggression depicted in abused children's drawings. *The Arts in Psychotherapy, 14,* 15–24.

McGregor, J. (1978). *Kinetic Family Drawing Test: A validity study.* Unpublished doctoral dissertation. Auburn University. Cited in Handler & Habenicht (1994).

McPhee, J., & Wegner, K. (1976). Kinetic-Family-Drawing styles and emotionally disturbed childhood behavior. *Journal of Personality Assessment, 40,* 487–491.

Michael, M., & Dudek, S.Z. (1991). Mother-child relationships and creativity. *Creativity Research Journal, 4*(3), 281–286.

Monahan, M. (1986). Situation influences on children's Kinetic Family Drawings. *Dissertation Abstracts International, 46,* 4444.

Mostkoff, D.L., & Lazarus, P.J. (1983). The Kinetic Family Drawing: The reliability of an objective scoring system. *Psychology in the Schools, 20,* 16–20.

Rabinowitz, A. (1991). The relation of acceptance-rejection to social schemata and Kinetic Family Drawings. *Social Behavior and Personality, 19*(4), 263–272.

Rabinowitz, A. (1992). Acceptance-rejection and height of parental figures on the Kinetic Family Drawings. *Perceptual and Motor Skills, 74,* 329–330.

Raskin, L., & Bloom, A. (1979). Kinetic Family Drawings by children with learning disabilities. *Journal of Pediatric Psychology, 4,* 247–251.

Raskin, L., & Pitcher-Baker, G. (1975). The use of Kinetic Family Drawings in the assessment of children with perceptual-motor delays and developmental disabilities. *Journal of Pediatric Psychology, 3,* 4–5.

Raskin, L., & Pitcher-Baker, G. (1977). Kinetic Family Drawings by children with perceptual-motor delays. *Journal of Learning Disabilities, 10,* 370–374.

Reddy, K.S., Bhadramani, G., & Samiullah, S. (2002). Placement of family members by normal and neglected boys: A study of family drawings. *Social Science International, 18*(1), 72–82.

Rhine, P. (1977). *Adjustment indicators in Kinetic Family Drawings by children: A validation study.* Unpublished doctoral dissertation, Purdue University. Cited in Handler & Habenicht, 1994.

Sanchez-Rosado, K.A. (2002). Levels of acculturation of children of Mexican decent as perceived in their Kinetic Family Drawings. *Dissertation Abstracts International Section A: Humanities & Social Science, 62*(7-A), 2596.

Schornstein, H.M. & Derr, J. (1978). The many applications of kinetic family drawings in child abuse. *British Journal of Projective Psychology and Personality Study, 23,* 33–35.

Sobel, H., & Sobel, W. (1976). Discriminating adolescent male delinquent through the use of Kinetic Family Drawings. *Journal of Personality Assessment, 40,* 91–94.

Stawar, T.L., & Stawar, D.E. (1987). Family Kinetic Drawings as a screening instrument. *Perceptual and Motor Skills, 65,* 810.

Thompson, L.V. (1975). Kinetic Family Drawings of adolescents. *Dissertation Abstract International, 36*(06B), 3077.

Torrance, E.P. (1966). *Torrance Tests of Creative Thinking: Norms and technical manual.* Princeton, NJ: Personnel Press.

Veltman, M.W., & Browne, K.D. (2001). Pictures in the classroom: Can teachers and

Mental health professional identify maltreated children's drawings. *Child Abuse Review, 9,* 328–336.

Veltman, M.W., & Browne, K.D. (2001). Identifying childhood abuse through favorite kind of day and Kinetic Family Drawings. *Arts in Psychotherapy, 28*(4), 251–259.

Veltman, M.W. (2003). Trained raters' evaluation of Kinetic Family Drawings of physically abused children. *Arts in Psychotherapy, 30*(1), 3–12.

West, M.M. (1998). Meta-analysis of studies accessing the efficacy of projective techniques in discriminating child sexual abuse. *Child Abuse & Neglect, 22*(11), 72.

Chapter 4

KINETIC SCHOOL DRAWING

TITLE:	Kinetic Drawing System
AGE:	Age limit for the Kinetic Family Drawing (KFD) is 5 to 20 years whereas the Kinetic School Drawing (KSD) was limited to school-aged children
YEAR:	1985
PURPOSE:	designed to understand a child's relationships within the family and school setting
SCORES:	scoring was based on qualitative interpretations (actions between figures, figure characteristics, distance between figures, drawing style, and symbols)
MANUAL:	manual (65 pages); illustrations (18 pages); profile (2 pages); reliability data (1 page); validity data (1 page)
TIME LIMIT:	no time limit for administration
COST:	$70 for testing manual; 25 scoring booklets https://www-secure.earthlink.net/www.wpspublish.com/Inetpub4/catalog/W-208.htm
AUTHOR:	Knoff, Howard M., and Prout, H. Thomas
PUBLISHER:	Western Psychological Services, 12031 Wilshire Boulevard, Los Angeles, CA, 90025-1 http://www.wpspublish.com/Inetpub4/index.htm

INTRODUCTION

The Kinetic Drawing System (1985) incorporated the Kinetic Family Drawing (KFD; Burns, 1970, 1972) and the Kinetic School Drawing (KSD). Since the KFD was previously reviewed within this text, only information relating to the Kinetic School Drawing (KSD) will be evaluated. The KSD was designed to investigate the child's psychological status and relationship dynamics within the school setting. In addition, the KSD was constructed to reveal a child's attitude toward school.

PURPOSE AND RECOMMENDED USE

The Kinetic Drawing System (1985), as a whole, was used to assess any difficulties that the child was experiencing at home or in school. The system was created to isolate particular relationships that may be contributing to the child's difficulties. Further, it was used to identify family issues that may be affecting school behaviors or vice versa. Overall, Knoff and Prout (1985) expressed that the Kinetic Drawing System can serve as a projective technique, which investigates the child's personality and perceptions of significant relationships. The authors also stipulated that the system can be used to monitor the child's progress in the counseling setting.

DIMENSIONS THAT THE TEST PURPORTS TO MEASURE

The dimensions that the KFD measured were discussed previously. The KSD purported to reveal the child's relationships with the instructor and peers. Generally, this section of the test measured the child's attitude toward school. In essence, the KSD manifested the child's concept of self and other self-perceptions as they related to the school milieu.

ADMINISTRATION

Depending on the individual client, the Kinetic Drawing System may take between 20 and 40 minutes to administer. The authors recommended giving the KFD first and then the KSD, since family issues may affect the child at home and in school. For instance, "a child's self-concept is often primarily determined by his or her interactions with parents (and siblings), their attitudes toward his or her achievement and potential, and the identification process, which occurs during the child's early years before school age" (Knoff & Prout, 1985, p. 3). Additionally, the authors felt that administering the KSD may taint the directions as well as the drawing styles of the KFD. Both the KFD and the KSD consist of a performance phase and an inquiry phase.

The performance phase of the KSD immediately followed the KFD inquiry phase. Here, the child was given the following directions:

I'd like you to draw a school picture. Put yourself, your teacher, and a friend or two in the picture. Make everyone doing something. Try to draw whole people and make the best drawing you can. Remember, draw yourself, your teacher, and a friend or two, and make everyone doing something. (Knoff & Prout, 1985, p. 4)

In a personal communication to the authors, Burns, one of the creators of the KFD, suggested that the directions read as follows:

I'd like you to draw a school picture. Put yourself, your teacher, and two or more students in the picture. Try to draw whole people, not stick or cartoon figures. Remember, draw yourself, your teacher, and two or more students doing something. (Knoff & Prout, 1985, p. 4)

Although some children may not feel that they have friends, Knoff and Prout (1985) emphasized that it was important to include the word in the directions since it may reveal clinical information about peer relationships. They also retained the phrase, "make the best drawing you can" because it required a performance demand, similar to the school setting.

The inquiry phase attempted to clarify the child's perception of the drawing. The authors required that the examiner ask the child to describe what was happening in the picture, what each figure was doing, and identify each human or animal figure with a name and age. Although no rigid procedures were required beyond this inquiry, the authors did provide a list of questions that may be helpful in yielding clinical information. The authors did not discuss the qualifications of the examiners. In addition, they did not state if group administration was appropriate.

NORM GROUPS

Prout and Celmer (1984) examined 100 fifth grade students (44 boys and 56 girls) in a regular education program. It did not appear to be a random sample. Other demographic characteristics of the students were not discussed. The researchers only reported the mean height and distance between figures. For instance, the average height of the teacher was 54.25 mm. The average distance between the self and teacher was 90.00 mm. Although these measurements were interesting, it only revealed information about average fifth grade students. Since the sample was not random, the information may not generalize to other fifth graders.

The authors did include normative information from Sarbaugh's (1982) technique for assessing the child's attitude toward school. Although it was not the exact same test, the authors implied that since this assessment was similar to their own, the normative information would be useful. Sarbaugh (1982) examined school-aged children, from kindergarten through high school. Knoff and Prout (1985) summarized her work in their manual. For example, Sarbaugh (1982) found that kindergarten students had difficulty with visual-motor coordination. This may be a confounding variable. They also had difficulty putting all of their class members into the picture. By first grade, children included desks and other features of the classroom. Second-grade students featured buildings, rooms, and objects whereas people were de-emphasized. In third grade, students made use of props and equipment. By fourth grade, children drew complete pictures and used a more linear perspective. Fifth graders displayed more detail, differentiation of figures, and activities. With junior, middle, and high school students, stick figures were common. Also, drawings were completed more rapidly. This was the extent of the normative information for the KSD.

INTERPRETATION OF SCORES

Interpretation of the KSD included five diagnostic areas: (1) Actions of and between figures; (2) figure characteristics; (3) position, distance, and barriers; (4) style, and (5) symbols. The qualitative interpretation of the KSD was based on the work of Sarbaugh (1982) and Prout and Celmer (1984). Although Knoff and Prout (1985) warned that the examiner should be sensitive when interpreting the work of special populations, they did not provide guidelines. They stated that drawings completed by learning disabled, gifted, and behaviorally disturbed children will differ from typical children. The nature of these differences and instructions for interpretation for special populations were not discussed.

As for actions of and between figures, the examiner was instructed to look for the self figure engaged in academic behavior. Greater incidence of academic activity was related to greater achievement (Prout & Celmer, 1984). When the self was engaged in disruptive behaviors such as yelling or running, it was associated with lower academic achievement. When a child drew the self in recess activities or nonacademic activities (lunch, music, gym), it may indicate avoidance or anxiety issues.

Figure characteristics were based on the interpretation of subjects drawn in the KFD. Globally, using more than two peers in a drawing was significantly related to lesser academic achievement (Prout & Celmer, 1984). Lack of people drawn or drawing people symbolically was related to avoidance of social interaction (Sarbaugh, 1982). Large self (greater than 49.25 mm) was significantly related to academic achievement (Prout & Celmer, 1985). If the teacher was larger than self, it may reveal feelings of inadequacy. Yet, the authors went on to say that if the teacher was large (greater than 55 mm), it was significantly related to positive academic achievement. This information was contradictory. Excessive detail of the teacher figure was related to possible conflicts, perceptions of a dominating teacher, or authority issues.

Position, distance, and barrier interpretations were based on the KFD (Burns, 1970, 1972). The drawing style of the KSD involved transparencies that may reflect compulsive preoccupations, impulsivity, or poor reality testing. Emphasis of the physical features of a room was said to indicate a need for structure and avoidance of social interaction. Bear in mind that the authors previously stated that second grade students characteristically emphasized the physical features of the room. Children who drew outdoor pictures were said to dislike school and resisted task demands.

The last section focused on a few symbols used in the KSD. For instance, apples may represent oral or dependency needs. Also, apples may symbolize school and teacher activities indicating issues of nurturance and authority. Drawing a school bus was said to indicate avoidance, dislike and conflict of school activities. Further, the authors stated that it served to isolate the child from others. "For a clear analysis, one needs to ask or determine whether the bus is coming to or leaving school and the child's affective relation to either possibility" (Knoff & Prout, 1985, p. 20). Drawing the chalkboard or bulletin board may indicate anxiety about self-adequacy in school. Drawing the principal may reveal conflict with authority or a need for male identification. It was not clear if the authors were assuming that all principals were males?

SOURCE OF ITEMS

The KSD appeared to be based on the KFD (Burns, 1970, 1972). Interpretation was similar to the KFD. Also, the KSD was related to the work of Sarbaugh (1982) who used a kinetic drawing of the school. It was not clear what similarities and differences existed between Sarbaugh's (1982) school drawing and the KSD.

VALIDITY AND RELIABILITY AS DETERMINED BY THE AUTHOR

Reliability of the KSD was not examined by the authors. Validity information was primarily based on the work of other researchers. One study compared Hispanic children with Anglo children who were referred for psychological evaluation. The number of participants and the manner of selection were not discussed. Using seven objectively scored KSD characteristics, no significant differences were found between these groups. The authors concluded from this one study that:

> The KSD may be a relatively culturally unbiased technique with Hispanics for whom emotional disturbance placement decisions are being considered. At worst, it appears that some KSD style and content characteristics have equal probabilities of occurring on Hispanic or Anglo children's drawings. (Knoff & Prout, 1985, p. 61)

A follow-up study was briefly discussed that examined special populations such as learning disabled and emotionally disturbed children. Since the categorization of the sample was unclear and the methodology limited, Knoff and Prout (1985) did not discuss the implications of the research.

Prout and Celmer (1984) used the KSD to predict academic achievement with 100 fifth grade students. This study was part of the normative information previously discussed. Out of ten KSD variables, six correlated significantly with academic achievement (SRA scores). A large number of peers, overall score, and drawing of self engaged in undesirable behaviors negatively correlated with the SRA scores. Positive correlations involved the child's height, teacher's height, and drawing self engaged in academic behaviors.

The authors included the work of Schneider (1978) who examined the validity of the KSD. Children referred to the school psychologist were assessed. The total sample size and demographic characteristics were not discussed. Schneider (1978) used ratings of the severity of the child's school problems and the severity of the family's problems as dependent measures. Since the KSD could not predict age and IQ, he concluded that his work offered little support of the validity of the KSD.

RESEARCH USING THE KSD

Andrews and Janzen (1988) developed a scoring sheet and reference guide for the KSD. The scoring sheet was a checklist of 17 items related to the KSD. The reference guide demarcated a list of characteristics that would indicate pathology such as disorganization, distorted body image, and drawing rain to mention a few. Activities were rated as positive, negative, neutral, or uncertain. Guidelines for scoring were discussed. Andrews and Janzen (1988) also constructed a rating scale to determine the degree of behavioral issues such as depression, aggression, isolation, etc. They examined an equal number of learning disabled (LD) and nonlearning disabled (NLD) children in fifth grade attending eight different schools. A total of 96 drawings were examined by two sets of three trained raters. Interrater reliability was reported to be above .70. Significantly more NLD children showed structure in their drawings. Further, significantly more LD drawings indicated negative interactions with peers and instructors. Also, they depicted themselves more often outside of school and involved in nonacademic activities or undesirable forms of behavior compared to NLD students. Significantly more LD children were rated as depressed, impulsive, and competitive. The scoring sheet, reference guide, and rating scale were able to differentiate between the two groups of students. The authors concluded that their instruments demonstrated reliability and some discriminant validity.

Neale and Rosal (1993) evaluated a series of projective assessments. In reviewing the literature, some of which was previously discussed, Neal and Rosal (1993) found that the KSD indicated strong concurrent validity when correlated with achievement measures. The authors evaluated the research on problem, design, procedure, and analysis. Based on the research on KSD validity, the authors gave the instrument 46 points out of 50 possible points.

Lifson (1996) used Andrews and Janzen's (1988) objective scoring method with the KSD in order to provide information on possible cultural differences expressed in the KSD. Participants included 171 third grade public school students with Hispanic (42% of the sample), Caucasian (31%), African American (28%), and Asian (1%)backgrounds. Three independent raters, graduate students, scored the KSDs and were blind to the participants completing the drawings. The average inter-rater reliability was reported to be .63, with a range of .14 to .92 across items on the scoring sheet. Race and ethnicity did not appear to impact scoring of the KSDs. Students who were classified as learning disabled showed significant differences in the KSDs in terms of negative self-concept, pathology, defensiveness, and teacher activities and relationships. No significant differences were found with students classified as gifted and the other groups. Lifson (1996) stated that this may have been due to the broad definition of "gifted" student. In an earlier study, Armstrong (1995) used the KSD with 60 educationally gifted elementary students and found the KSD a useful tool for identifying students' perceptions of their current school experience. Further, the KSD was useful for identifying changes that students wanted to see in their program.

DESIRABLE FEATURES

The KSD was easy to administer and did not require much time. The manual included several case examples, which were helpful when interpreting drawings. Overall, the manual was easy to read and clear.

UNDESIRABLE FEATURES

Interpretation of the KSD may be difficult. Only qualitative information was considered. A scoring guide that was objective in nature would have been more helpful and was later developed by other researchers. At times, the information appeared contradictory. For instance, the authors stated that drawing a large teacher was related to feelings of inadequacy in school. In the next paragraph, they stated that drawing a large teacher was related to positive school achievement. How can one adequately interpret school achievement based on the size of the instructor given this information? Normative information was lacking. Also, guidelines for interpreting the drawings completed by special populations was nonexistent.

OVERALL EVALUATION

The reliability of the KSD was not established in the manual. Andrews and Janzen (1988) did create a scoring guide, reference sheet, and rating scale that demonstrated some reliability. Additional information regarding the stability of the KSD is needed.

Overall, the KSD did demonstrate some concurrent validity. Discriminant validity information was needed. For example, it would be helpful to know how emotionally disturbed children's KSDs differ from children who were not diagnosed with emotional disorders. Guidelines for the interpretation of drawings from special populations should be established.

The normative information was weak at best. Although there was a normative study of fifth grade students, norms were not established for other age groups. Since the normative sample was unreliable, the interpretation of the KSD was difficult. Additionally, the authors used a norm sample from a test that was similar to their own. It cannot be assumed that these assessments were similar. Additionally, it cannot be assumed that the normative information from Sarbaugh's (1982) work will be useful when interpreting the KSD.

As opposed to Neale and Rosal's (1993) findings, I do not agree that the KSD was a valid instrument. Although the manual did report some concurrent validity, additional research was required. There was not enough information on the KSD to warrant its use within the school or counseling settings. At most, the KDS can be included in a battery of assessment and may be helpful in revealing the child's perception of the school environment.

REFERENCES

Andrews, J., & Janzen, H. (1988). A global approach for the interpretation of the Kinetic School Drawing (KSD): A quick scoring sheet, reference guide, and rating scale. *Psychology in the Schools, 25,* 217–237.

Armstrong, D.C. (1995). The use of Kinetic School Drawings to explore the educational preferences of gifted students. *Journal for the Education of the Gifted, 18*(4), 410–439.

Burns, R.C., & Kaufman, S.H. (1970). *Kinetic Family Drawings (K-F-D): An introduction to understanding children through kinetic drawings.* New York: Brunner/Mazel.

Burns, R.C., & Kaufman, S.H. (1972). *Actions, styles, and symbols in Kinetic Family Drawings (K-F-D): An interpretive manual.* New York: Brunner/Mazel.

Knoff, H.M., & Prout, H.T. (1985). *Kinetic Drawing System for Family and School: A Handbook.* Los Angeles, CA: Western Psychological Services.

Knoff, H.M., & Prout, H.T. (1985). The Kinetic Drawing System: A review and integration of the kinetic family and school drawing techniques. *Psychology in the Schools, 22,* 50–59.

Lifson, C.R. (1996). Racial/ethnic school differences in Kinetic School Drawings using an objective scoring method. *Dissertation Abstracts International: Section B: The Sciences and Engineering, 57*(1-B), 0726.

Neale, E.L., & Rosal, M.L. (1993). What can art therapists learn from the research on projective drawing techniques for children? A review of the literature. *The Arts in Psychotherapy, 20,* 37–49.

Prout, H.T., & Celmer, D.S. (1984). School drawings and academic achievement: A validity study of the Kinetic School Drawing technique. *Psychology in the Schools, 21,* 176–180.

Sarbaugh, M.E.A. (1982). Kinetic Drawing-School (KD-S) Technique. *Illinois School Psychologists' Association Monograph Series, 1,* 1–70.

Schneider, G.B. (1978). A preliminary validation study of the Kinetic School Drawing. *Dissertation Abstracts International, 38,* 6628A.

Chapter 5

DIAGNOSTIC DRAWING SERIES

TITLE:	Diagnostic Drawing Series (DDS)
AGE:	Adolescents and adults
YEAR:	1983
PURPOSE:	designed to link picture analysis to DSM-III, DSM-III-R, and DSM-VI diagnoses: Assesses an individual's response to structured and unstructured drawing tasks
SCORES:	interpretation was based on a rating guide (considers 23 categories for rating)
MANUAL:	rating guide(10 pages); reliability & validity data (none reported in manual—follow-up studies are included in this chapter)
TIME LIMIT:	up to 15 minute time limit for each drawing task for a maximum of 45 minutes
COST:	$20/Packet (handbook, DDS style guide, collection forms, drawing analysis form, resource list)
AUTHOR:	Cohen, Barry M.
PUBLISHER:	Cohen, Barry M., PO Box 9853, Alexandria, VA, 22304.

INTRODUCTION

The Diagnostic Drawing Series (DDS) was designed to gather clinical information about a client in a single session. By presenting structured and semi-structured drawing tasks, the DDS provides information toward the clarification of *DSM-III, DSM-III-R*, and *DSM-IV* diagnoses. "This instrument was created because of the clinical imprecision of existing art therapy assessment procedures and the absence of a research foundation on which to base clinical judgments" (Mills, Cohen, & Meneses, 1993, p. 83). Art therapists and mental health professionals alike can use the DDS. Additionally, it is compatible with psychiatric diagnostic research.

PURPOSE AND RECOMMENDED USE

The DDS was designed to be used in clinical settings. When assessing adolescent and adults, the DDS provides information on cognitive capacity as well as behavioral and affective states of the client. Also, the DDS furnishes information about the client's strengths, defenses, and issues. For research purposes, within three to five days of admission to a mental health facility, the DDS should be administered to the client. Cohen (1985) recommended that two psychiatrists or one psychiatrist and one psychologist fill out a psychiatric diagnosis form to be used in conjunction with the DDS. The information obtained from the three drawing tasks was correlated with the *DSM* diagnoses established by concurring psychiatrists. The DDS can be used in individual sessions, group therapy, educational planning, and as a guide in treatment planning (Cohen, Mills, Kijak, 1994). A 15-minute time limit for each drawing as well as strict adherence to administration requirements were recommended if results are to compare with research.

DIMENSIONS THAT THE TEST PURPORTS TO MEASURE

The initial, free drawing reveals the defensive functioning of the client. Additionally, the free drawing indicated the individual's response to a relatively unstructured task. The second directive, the tree drawing, "provides a rich portrait of the individual's vegetative/psychic state" (Cohen, 1985, p. 2). This structured task yielded information about the person's life energy or life force (Burns, 1987). According to Cohen (1985), the tree drawing can be used as a diagnostic aid when considering organic impairment. The last directive, make a picture of how you are feeling using lines, shapes, and colors, reflects the client's ability to access and represent an affective state.

> This semi-structured task allows for self-assertion and self-reflection by the patient. The feeling picture also promotes abstract thinking. (Cohen, 1985, p. 2)

As with the first drawing, this task may gage flexibility and defensive functioning of the client.

A graphic profile of pictorial characteristics, such as line, color, and shape, were rated and correlated with the client's psychiatric diagnosis. Twenty-three categories of variables were defined and used to rate each drawing. For instance, when viewing a DDS drawing, the number of colors used, blending, and the use of idiosyncratic colors were noted. Representation versus abstraction, structural integration, and line quality were also recorded. Rather than "measuring" these variables, the scoring method requires noting their presence or absence.

ADMINISTRATION

The administration requirements for the DDS were clearly delineated. Within three days (no more than five days) of admission to a psychiatric setting, the patient should complete the DDS. A strict, 15-minute time limit was used for each drawing task. A box of 12 Alphacolor square pastels, three sheets of 18" x 24" (60 LB) white drawing paper, and Krylon Crystal Clear spray fixative were required. Although Krylon is not a requirement, it is suggested for those who wish to archive the series or submit them for research.

The administrator gives the following directive, " You have one sheet of paper for each picture. The page may be turned in any direction. The directions for the first picture is to make a picture using these materials." When the first drawing was complete, the administrator immediately proceeded with the second drawing: "Draw a picture of a tree." This was completed even if the patient drew a tree in the first picture. The last directive was "Make a picture of how you're feeling, using lines, shapes, and colors." If a patient cannot complete a drawing, a blank page was retained. The patient's verbal associations to a list of questions, a.k.a. drawing inquiry, were recorded following the last drawing task. Recommendations for writing up a DDS evaluation are provided in the packet, as well as a DDS style guide for writing up the assessment.

NORM GROUPS

The DDS Handbook and Rating Guide contained no information on the groups used to standardize the assessment. However, such information is contained in reports on research norming various groups in a number of publications. The DDS was standardized on a clinical population and control sample, submission from numerous clinicians around the United States. A later article was said to have established norms for the DDS; yet, the demographic characteristics of this sample were not discussed (Cohen, Hammer, and Singer, 1988).

INTERPRETATION OF SCORES

The DDS drawings were rated using a guide created by Cohen (1986) and colleagues. The Drawing Analysis Form (DAF) may be used to record the information for each drawing in the series. Interpretation of the DDS is not recommend without at least one day of training with an authorized teacher. Other than noting the presence or absence of the variables listed, no other interpretive guidelines were discussed in the rating manual or the handbook. In the absence of a two-day DDS training, clinicians must integrate 15 years of published research results. Cohen (1986) clearly delineated the categories for rating the DDS. Adequate guidelines for the interpretation of these variables would be helpful. In a personal communication, Cohen (2004) states that such a book is currently being written.

SOURCE OF ITEMS

Since Cohen (1985) did not discuss the historical and theoretical development of the DDS, the exact source of the items was not specifically delineated in the manual but a later publication discussed these issues (Cohen, Mills, & Kijak, (1994). The first exercise, a free drawing, was an activity used by some of the founders of art therapy (Kwiatkowska, 1978; Naumburg, 1987; & Wadeson, 1980). Free pictures were unstructured drawing tasks for which no subject was assigned. Kwiatkowska (1978) stressed that the free drawing contained the most important information about the client. The client's ego strength, defenses, and presenting issues often appeared in free drawings. Cohen (1985) related the first picture to the analysis of a first dream in that "the picture represents what the individual is willing to initially share of himself" (p. 2).

Cohen (1985) stated that the second directive was linked to the projective tree tests of the past:

> The tree is an ancient symbol and has been studied in the context of projective drawings. The tree symbol represents the deepest tapping of the psyche in the realm of projective drawing subject matter. (p. 2)

Assessments that describe personality based on tree drawings have been developed by a number of therapists (Buck, 1948; Bolander, 1977; Burns, 1987). A few of these tests have been reviewed within this text.

The last drawing task appeared to be originally created by the author. It was a semi-structured task designed to evoke the affective state of the client. The source of this task was inspired by Janie Rhyne's doctoral thesis on abstract drawings of mind states (Cohen, 2004).

VALIDITY AS DETERMINED BY THE AUTHOR

Reliability and validity information was not discussed in the handbook or the rating guide. In a separate article, 239 patients from multiple hospitals completed the DDS (Cohen, Hammer, & Singer, 1988). Demographic characteristics of the participants were not discussed. Although the sample was not random, 239 drawing series samples were collected. The cases were separated into the four groups based on the concurring psychiatrists' diagnoses: schizophrenia, depression, dysthymia, and nonpatients. Significant differences in the DDS were discussed for each group. For instance, dysthymia patients used light pressure, included animals in the free drawing, and drew disintegrated trees. Depressed patients showed unusual placement of images on the page, a characteristic not demonstrated by the other groups. In addition, depressed people lacked a landscape in the tree picture and included water images in the feeling picture. Schizophrenic patients drew monochrome feeling pictures. Also, they lacked integration in the free picture and depicted short tree trunks. The overall significance level for each group was below .05. This indicates that the DDS differentiated client populations.

Mills, Cohen, and Meneses (1993) examined the use of the DDS in identifying graphic characteristics associated with multiple personality disorder (MPD). They compared the DDS drawings of 24 hospitalized patients diagnosed, ranging in age from 19 to 46, with MPD and compared those drawings to a control group of nonhospitalized people and of inpatient populations from previous research studies. They were able to identify structural elements across the three drawings, which are characteristic of people with MPD. This article will be particularly helpful to those people not as familiar with recognizing graphic indicators of psychiatric conditions as Mills, Cohen, and Meneses (1993) delineate strategies to help recognize patients who are incorrectly diagnosed as MPD.

RELIABILITY AS DETERMINED BY THE AUTHOR

Interrater reliability was determined by examining 30 DDS series that were randomly selected from the DDS archive. After a two-month training period, Cohen, an experienced art therapist, and Meneses, a nonart therapist, rated each series. Interrater reliability was reported to be 95.7% (Mills, Cohen, & Meneses, 1993). The lowest agreement (.77) was with the category of representation. The remainder of the categories indicated agreement in the 90s. The study would have been more objective had Mills not included Cohen as a rater.

RESEARCH USING THE DDS

One of the claims of the DDS is that it correlates with psychiatric diagnoses. Gulbro-Leavitt (1989) examined the use of the DDS as a tool to measure depression in children and adolescents. Although the study found moderate validity for the use of the DDS in measuring depression, the correlation was based on self-report measures of children and parents. Gulbro-Leavitt (1989) states that the results have only equivocal validity.

In the handbook, Cohen (1985) stated that the DDS was helpful when diagnosing organic dysfunction. In 1994, Couch used the DDS when working with elderly people with organic mental syndromes and disorders. Using DSM-III-R criteria, 24 patients (16 females and 8 males) suffering from organic dysfunction were given the DDS. They ranged in age from 63 to 93 years. A control sample of ten subjects with no organic dysfunction completed the DDS. One-half of the subjects were given the DDS in a group setting whereas the other one-half were administered it individually. The participants were in the course of treatment at the time the research was conducted. Two art therapists trained to administer the DDS rated all three pictures. The researcher found that the treatment sample tended to use only one color, single images, and light line pressure. Trees were generally unrecognizable. Also, the pictures were impoverished with minimal inclusion of animals or people. Floating images, limited use of space, and unusual placement on the page characterized the organically impaired group. Pictures became more disorganized as the session progressed. Couch (1994) did note the limitations of the study: use of one racial group, raters were not blind to diagnoses, and the lack of a random sample. In conclusion, Couch (1994) stated that the DDS could be helpful when diagnosing possible cases of organic dysfunction.

Knapp (1994) used the DDS when working with Alzheimer patients. Participants were recruited from an ongoing treatment and research population. Fifty people matched by age participated in the study. The Alzheimer patients were early in the course of the illness and evidenced pathology (mean age of 69 with 9 males and 16 females). The control group did not suffer from psychiatric or medical disorders (mean age of 71 with 10 males and 15 females). Although Knapp (1994) used other assessments, only the results of the DDS will be considered. Knapp (1994) created a checklist of 39 variables which were rated by three independent art therapists. A total of 195 drawings were scored yielding a 90% agreement among raters. "Criterion-related validity was provided by establishing the 39 variables in the Graphic Indicator List from diagnostic criteria from the *DSM-III-R* for Primary Degenerative Dementia of the Alzheimer Type, since that constellation of symptoms distinguished the AD group of subjects from the control subjects" (Knapp, 1994, p. 134). The Alzheimer patients used fewer colors and less space compared to the control sample. Knapp (1994) did not make a final conclusion regarding the use of the DDS.

Kessler (1994) used the DDS with a group of individuals with eating disorders. People were selected from an inpatient eating disordered program for women. The group included 55 women with Bulimia Nervosa, 17 with Anorexia Nervosa, and nine with Eating Disorder NOS. They were diagnosed in accordance to *DSM-III-R* criteria. Other demographic characteristics of the sample were not discussed. Drawings were obtained in a group format within five days of admission to the center. Kessler (1994) used the DAF to note the occurrence and nonoccurrence of the DDS criteria. The combined sample showed significantly less use of a groundline. In addition, the group drew trees that were falling apart and had knotholes. Kessler (1994) concluded that the DDS might be helpful in establishing a tentative diagnosis for eating disorders.

Rankin (1994) used the DDS to examine possible graphic indicators of trauma in tree drawings. Specifically, Rankin (1994) was interested if knotholes, broken branches, damaged trunks, or leafless trees were indicative of trauma. Sixty drawings were selected from the DDS archive. Half of the drawings were from adults admitted to a psychiatric hospital for posttraumatic disassociative disorders. For the control group, 50 drawings were selected from staff at another psychiatric hospital. All tree drawings were observed for the following elements: knotholes, broken branches, damaged trunks, and the absence of leaves. Rankin (1994) used an independent rater and reported that there was 96% agreement between the primary observer and the rater. According to Rankin (1994), 60% of the drawings of people diagnosed with disassociative disorders contained at least one representation of a knothole, a broken branch, a damaged trunk, or a leafless tree. This was true in 27% of the drawings from the control group. Since knotholes were found in both groups, Rankin (1994) felt that knotholes were not a graphic indicator of trauma. Although no broken branches were observed in the control group, 30% of the diagnosed group depicted broken branches in their tree drawings. Again, 30% of the trees in the diagnosed group were leafless compared to 7% in the control group. Rankin (1994) asserted that there was a strong indicator of seasonal influence.

Neale (1994) used the Children's Diagnostic Drawing Series (CDDS) with a clinical population. A sample of 100 children from a private school served as the control group. A sample of 80 children from an outpatient mental health center comprised the treatment group. Neale (1994) clearly outlined the demographic characteristics of the sample. Additionally, she described the clinical diagnoses of the treatment group including the number of participants in each category. These participants were randomly selected from a larger pool. The CDDS differed from the DDS in that it used hard pastels and modified the instructions slightly. Instead of the original directive, "Make a picture using these materials" the administrator stated, "Make a picture using the pastels and paper." The drawings were collected in group and individual sessions. Using the 23 variables from the rating guide, the author and two trained DDS raters (blind to the study) evaluated the drawings. Twelve variables showed significant interrater reliability. Seven variables distinguished between the control and treatment groups: color type, line/shape, integration, groundline, inanimate objects, abstract symbols, and space usage. The clinical group drawings were impoverished, lacked a groundline, used only one color, and used less space. In addition, the author found that 20 variables significantly described children diagnosed with adjustment disorder. Neal (1994) noted the limitations of the study, and did an excellent job of describing the participants, outlining the method, and summarizing the results.

In 1995, Morris used the DDS and Creekmore's (1989) Tree Rating Scale with 80 people diagnosed with psychiatric conditions (20 with Multiple Personality Disorder, 20 with Major Depression and 20 with Schizophrenia). Further, 20 participants were in a control condition. As opposed to Gulbro-Leavitt's (1989) study, the pilot study results did provide evidence of differences between the groups. It was not clear who diagnosed the participants or how they came to be involved in the study. The largest weaknesses were the lack of information on the demographic characteristics of the sample as well as the rater qualifications.

The DDS is showing promise in working with other diagnostic groups such as individuals classified with substance related disorders. Billingsley (1999) completed the DDS with 27 outpatients (13 women and 14 men) classified with substance related disorder (SRD). DDS drawings from this group were compared to a control sample and other diagnostic categories including multiple personality, major depression, schizophrenia, and borderline personality disorder. Although the control and SRD group drawings were similar to one another as compared to the other diagnostic groups, Billingsley (1999) found some graphic indicators that distinguished the SRD group. In drawings 1 and 3, 50% of the pictures had water images or question marks.

Fowler and Ardon (2002) assessed the validity and reliability of the DDS with a sample of Disassociative Identity Disordered (DID) patients. Participants were given the DDS upon admittance to a clinic within the

Dutch State Mental Health Service. The DID group was compared to a control sample of people diagnosed with other psychiatric disorders. Interrater reliability was found unsatisfactory according to Fowler and Ardon (2002) as they felt that ratings were too heavily dependent on experience. Although they agreed that the handbook and training were clear and precise, their work suggests that clarifcation and precision are insufficient in practice (Fowler & Ardon, 2002). On the other hand, they did find significant differences providing support for structural elements characteristic of individuals with DID such as high scores on movement, controlled separation of drawing elements, and high levels of absorption.

DESIRABLE FEATURES

One advantage of using the DDS was that three drawings could be obtained in one session. The DDS employed one medium and allowed for the examination of color. The combination of structured and unstructured drawing tasks generated information about the client's cognitive capacities, defenses, and ability to respond to directives. This is one of the few assessments that employs pastels as the medium of choice. Another advantage is that the assessment entails three drawing tasks, which allow for the development of themes across pictures. This opens up great possibilities for gaining additional insight into the client's psyche. Additionally, the assessment also has validity when compared to psychiatric diagnostic criteria. The DDS uses artist grade materials and has an objective scoring system.

UNDESIRABLE FEATURES

The diagnostic interpretation of the DDS is difficult without the recommended training. Other than noting the presence or absence of pictorial characteristics, the handbook and rating guide did not provide information related to diagnostic categories. Clinicians in this regard must rely on their own skills of interpretation, as with any art production in therapy. Another possible limitation was the time factor. The pressure of completing a drawing in 15 minutes may cause stress and anxiety in some people. This has not been examined in the research on the DDS. However, the author states this quality expedites and clarifies the expression of psychopathology, which is the original purpose of the DDS (Cohen, 2004). Further Cohen (2004) notes that few people actually use the full 15 minutes, usually completing the series of three pictures in less than 20 minutes.

OVERALL EVALUATION

"Art therapy studies which utilize measurement tools, such as the DDS, meet the requirements of the scientific research process and work hard to achieve validity and reliability" (Burt, 1996, p.14). This assessment has a great deal of research interest in this country and abroad, which lends further support for its reliability and validity. Neale (1994) and Rankin's (1994) studies had promising and convincing results. As many research studies, there were limitations, which lends room for improvement with future research studies using the DDS.

The DDS is a tool that may be helpful in providing clinical information related to diagnosis. Research on the DDS, to date, has shown that it can distinguish between clinical populations and "normal" populations. This was true of the CDDS as well. People with dissociative disorders, posttraumatic stress, adjustment disorders, depression, dysthymia, schizophrenia, and organic syndromes have drawing styles characteristically different than well-adjusted individuals and from each other. The DDS also showed promise in providing as a screening device for people with eating disorders.

Cohen continues his research with the DDS. It would be helpful if a future revision of the handbook included a section on the historical development and the theoretical background of the assessment (AERAAP & NCME, 1985). Another researcher or the test author can complete this. Particularly important was information on the sample used to norm the DDS. Cohen may want to consider providing guidelines for the interpretation of the DDS, which will be helpful for those individuals who lack several years of clinical experience.

Overall, the DDS is a valuable tool to provide information on clinical diagnoses. A desirable feature was that the assessment could be completed in one session and allows for the development of themes across pictures. By changing the rating guide to a Likert scale or continuous scale, statistical analysis for the DDS would be enhanced. There is the risk that reliability would drop as this was not part of the initial design of the assessment (Cohen, 2004). These changes in the rating guide and the handbook would be helpful. The DDS has 20 years of research gathered and surpasses other art therapy assessments in terms of standardization, validity, and reliability.

REFERENCES

American Educational Research Association, American Psychological Association, & National Council on Measurement in Education. (1985). *Standards for educational and psychological testing*. Washington, DC: American Psychological Association

Billingsley, G. (1999). The efficacy of the Diagnostic Drawing Series with substance related disordered clients (outpatient, art therapy). *Dissertation Abstracts International: Section B: The Science & Engineering, 59*(10-B), 5569.

Bolander, K. (1977). *Assessing personality through tree drawings.* New York: Basic Books.

Buck, J.N. (1948). *The House-Tree-Person Technique.* Los Angeles, CA: Western Psychological Services.

Burns, R.C. (1987). *Kinetic-House-Tree-Person-Drawings: An interpretive manual.* New York, NY: Brunner/Mazel Publishers.

Burt, H. (1996). Beyond practice: A postmodern feminist perspective on art therapy research. *Art Therapy: Journal of the American Art Therapy Association, 12*(1), 12–19.

Cohen, B.M. (Ed.). (1985). *The Diagnostic Drawing Series Handbook.* Alexandria, VA: Barry Cohen.

Cohen, B.M. (Ed.). (1986). *The Diagnostic Drawing Series Rating Guide.* Alexandria, VA: Barry Cohen.

Cohen, B.M. (2004, January 5, 2004). Personal communication.

Cohen, B.M., Hammer, J.S., & Singer, S. (1988). The Diagnostic Drawing Series: A systematic approach to art therapy evaluation and research. *The Arts in Psychotherapy, 15,* 11–21.

Cohen, B.M., Mills, S., & Kijak, A.K. (1994). An introduction to the Diagnostic Drawing Series: A standardized tool for the diagnostic and clinical use. *Art Therapy, 11*(2), 105–110.

Couch, J.B. (1994). Diagnostic Drawing Series: Research with older people diagnosed with organic mental syndromes and disorders. *Art Therapy, 11*(2), 111–115.

Creekmore, J. (1989). *Diagnostic Drawing Series Tree Rating Scale Definitions.* (Available from Barry M. Cohen, PO Box 9853, Alexandria, VA: 22304.

Fowler, J.P., & Ardon, A.M. (2002). Diagnostic Drawing Series and disassociate disorders: A Dutch Study. *The Arts in Psychotherapy, 29*(4), 221–230.

Gulbro-Leavitt, C. (1989). A validity study of the Diagnostic Drawing Series as used for assessing depression in children and adolescents. *Dissertation Abstracts International, 49*(09, 4061B.

Kessler, K. (1994). A study of the Diagnostic Drawing Series with eating disordered patients. *Art Therapy, 11*(2), 116–118.

Knapp, N.M. (1994). Research with Diagnostic Drawings for normal and Alzheimer's subjects. *Art Therapy, 11*(2), 131–138.

Kwiatkowska, H.Y. (1978). *Family therapy and evaluation through art.* Springfield, IL: Charles C Thomas Publisher.

Mills, A., Cohen, B.M., & Meneses, J.Z. (1993). Reliability and validity tests of the Diagnostic Drawing Series. *The Arts in Psychotherapy, 20,* 83–88.

Morris, M.B. (1995). The Diagnostic Drawing Series and the Tree Rating Scale: An Isomorphic representation of Multiple Personality Disorder, Major Depression, and Schizophrenia populations. *Art Therapy: Journal of the American Art Therapy Association, 12*(2), 118–128.

Naumburg, M. (1987). *Dynamically oriented art therapy: Its principles and practices.* Chicago, IL: Magnolia Street Publishers.

Neale, E.L. (1994). The Children's Diagnostic Drawing Series. *Art Therapy, 11*(2), 119–126.

Rankin, A. (1994). Three drawings and trauma indicators: A comparison of past Research with current findings from the diagnostic drawing series. *Art Therapy: Journal of the American Art Therapy Association, 11*(2), 127–130.

Wadeson, H. (1980). *Art psychotherapy.* New York: John Wiley & Sons.

Chapter 6

HOUSE-TREE-PERSON TEST

TITLE:	House-Tree-Person Test (HTP)
AGE:	Age limit not presented
YEAR:	1987
PURPOSE:	designed to provide information on personality characteristics and interpersonal relationships
SCORES:	scoring was based on the presence or absence of features associated with detail, proportion, and perspective; two forms of test (chromatic and achromatic); quantitatively and qualitatively scored
MANUAL:	manual (350 pages); illustrations (58 pages); profile (6 pages); reliability data (none reported); validity data (none reported)
TIME LIMIT:	no time limit for individual administration; 90 minute time limit for group administration
COST:	$58.00–65.00 for testing manual
AUTHOR:	Buck, John N.
PUBLISHER:	Western Psychological Services., 12031 Wilshire Boulevard, Los Angeles, CA, 90025. http://www.wpspublish.com/Inetpub4/index.htm

INTRODUCTION

The House-Tree-Person Test (HTP) was designed to provide information on the client's personality. According to Buck (1987), the HTP yields details on the client's "sensitivity, maturity, flexibility, efficiency, degree of personality integration, and interactions with the environment" (p. 1). In addition, the HTP represents the client's level of intellectual functioning. In Phase One of the HTP, the client was instructed to use pencil to create a house, tree, and a person on separate sheets of paper. Phase Two was structured and verbal. The client used crayons to draw a house, tree, and person. This part of the assessment involved client associations to the objects drawn.

PURPOSE AND RECOMMENDED USE

Generally, the HTP was designed to furnish knowledge on the client's personality, behavior patterns, and interpersonal interactions. "The author feels strongly that the HTP may be employed usefully in individual examinations to provide the clinical psychologist, psychiatrist, or other qualified examiner with diagnostically and prognostically significant data concerning Ss [subjects] which otherwise might take much more time to acquire" (Buck, 1987, p. 2). In addition, Buck (1987) stated that the HTP may be used as a measure of change during the course of therapy. He felt that the HTP may be utilized as a screening device to measure maladjustment, appraise personality integration, and identify common personality characteristics of a specific population. In addition, he expressed that the HTP can serve as a pretest tool for entrance into a school, specialized training program, or an employment position.

DIMENSIONS THAT THE TEST PURPORTS TO MEASURE

The HTP measured an individual's response to an ambiguous task. Like other projective techniques, the HTP evoked projective material from the client. It accomplished this in a verbal as well as a nonverbal fashion. Additionally, the HTP calibrated intellectual functioning. Details, proportion, perspective, concept formation, and vocabulary comprised the appraisal of intellectual functioning. Each section of the test (house, tree, and person) was viewed as a psychological self-portrait. Buck (1987) asserted that the HTP stimulates conscious, subconscious, and unconscious associations. Since the house was the place of the client's most intimate interpersonal relationships, this part of the test suggested associations concerning the home and those living in the home. Teillard (1951) believed that the house represented the layers of the psyche: The outside symbolized the person's appearance, the upper floor exemplified conscious control, and the cellar depicted the unconscious. According to Buck (1987), the tree fostered associations concerning the person's life-role and satisfaction with the environment. Essentially, Buck (1949) viewed the tree as a symbol of the psychological development of the person with infancy at the bottom and present life age at the top.

The roots refer to the relationship to reality, the trunk to ego strength, and the branches and foliage refer to the ability to interact satisfactorily with the environment. A knothole indicates a traumatic event. (Ramirez, 1983, p. 44)

Essentially, the tree portrayed the person's psychological age. This section of the test aroused associations to past, present, and future interpersonal relationships.

Any emotion exhibited by the S [subject] while drawing or being questioned concerning his drawings is presumed to represent an emotional reaction to the relationships, situations, needs or pressures, or other dynamics which the S [subject] feels are directly or symbolically represented or suggested by one or more of his drawings or a part thereof. (Buck, 1987, p. 4)

Color use and affective reaction are related to the client's tolerance, control, and response to emotionally arousing stimuli. Comparison of the chromatic and achromatic forms of the test provided information on the constancy of intellectual functioning as well as attitudes, emotional reactions, and other behaviors.

ADMINISTRATION

Drawings were completed on white paper (6 sheets) 7″ x 8 1/2″. Several No. 2 lead pencils and a set of wax crayons (including red, green, blue, yellow, brown, black, purple, and orange) were required. A stopwatch and the four-page HTP Scoring Folder was also necessary.

The administrator began with the achromatic drawings. For the house drawing, the paper was placed horizontally with the word, HOUSE, written at the top of the page. For the tree and person drawings, the page was placed vertically. The following directive was given:

Take one of these pencils, please. I want you to draw me as good a picture of a house as you can. You may draw any kind of house you wish, it is entirely up to you. You may erase as much as you like, it will not be counted against you. In addition, you may take as long as you wish, just draw me as good a house as you can. (Buck, 1987, p. 18)

If the client objected due to his/her artistic abilities, the administrator explained that the HTP was not a test of artistic talent. Since the drawing must be freehand, the artist was not permitted to use a ruler. After giving the instructions, the administrator started the stopwatch. The initial latency period between the instructions and drawing, name and number of details, pauses, spontaneous comments, affect, and total time used to complete the drawing were recorded. The same procedure was followed for the tree and person drawings.

After the last drawing was complete, the therapist administered the Post-Drawing Interrogation (PDI). This gave the client an opportunity to describe, define, and interpret the objects drawn and give associations concerning them. The interrogation contained 60 questions and were labeled by object (H,T,P). Additional labels included "A" for Association, "P" for Pressure, and "R" for Reality testing. Pressure referred to any factors that may have a positive or negative influence on the client's behavior. For example, question T6 (tree question) read, "which does that Tree look more like to you: a man or a woman? (A & R)" (p. 22). This question apparently evoked associations and assessed reality testing. Buck (1987) stressed that the administrator should not adhere strictly to the PDI since other questions may arise during the assessment.

After the PDI, the chromatic drawings were completed. The administrator presented a set of crayons to the client and asked him/her to identify the colors. This was done to check for possible colorblindness. The administrator followed the procedure used for the achromatic version of the test. After the last drawing was complete, the therapist administered the chromatic PDI as long as the client was not too fatigued after drawing. This interview contained 22 questions broken down by test section: House, Tree, and Person.

For group administration, 90 minutes was allotted. The therapist recorded the time used by each person to complete the sections of the test, affect displayed, questions asked, and comments. With the PDI, the group was asked to write their responses down after the questions were asked. Next, the chromatic version of the test was administered. Artists identified colors by making check marks in the lower left corner of the page. The same procedure for the achromatic section of the test was followed. Administrator qualifications were not discussed.

NORM GROUPS

Participants were selected to represent the following intelligence categories: imbecile, moron, borderline, dull average, average, above average, and superior. Twenty participants were in each category. The people participating in the imbecile through average levels were white residents, patients, or employees of the Lynchburg State Colony. The average group consisted of college students in Nebraska and Virginia. They had completed at least two years of college. Superior participants were graduate students in a medical program. Buck (1987) presented a table listing the groups' intellectual level, gender, education achievement, and life age.

Using the individual administration guidelines that were previously discussed, 100 sets of drawings were obtained from the less than above average group. Group administration was used for the above average and superior groups. Group administration differed from individual administration in that participants were presented with a triple problem at once whereas the individual administration focused on only one section of the test at a time. In addition, the group administration involved writing comments about the drawings subsequent to the completion of the task.

One hundred and forty sets of drawing were analyzed to identify and list items that may distinguish intelligence level. Detail, proportion, and perspective appeared to differentiate the groups. Buck (1987) then provided definitions of detail, proportion, and perspective. Next, the drawings were rated as "good" or "flaw." A "good" item referred to as an item of detail, proportion, and perspective used by 50% of the sample and by less than 50% of the people below the borderline level. A "flaw" item was defined as an item presented by at least 50% of the group rated less than borderline intelligence and by less than 50% of the participants from the borderline group and up.

Factor symbols were then assigned to the drawings. The letter D was assigned to those items of detail, proportion, or perspective used by at least 50% of the participants of one of the "flaw" groups and by less than 50% of the people in the higher groups. The letter A was assigned to those items used by at least 50% of the people of one of the levels borderline through average and by less than 50% of the people in the upper levels. The letter S denoted those items used by 50% or more of the above average or superior groups and by less than 50% of the people in each lower level groups. For example, Buck (1987) found that 15% of the participants in the imbecile group, 30% of the moron group, 30% of the borderline group, 60% of the dull average group, 65% of the average group, and 95% of the above average and superior groups drew houses with more than one window.

The next sample involved a qualitative analysis of items that distinguished maladjustment as opposed to intelligence. A total sample of 150 people from two clinical settings completed the HTP. "The S [subject] population . . . indicated definitely that the HTP productions of Ss [subjects] with personality disorders differed in may respects from drawings produced by Ss who were not maladjusted" (Buck, 1987, p. 14). The well-adjusted group was not discussed. Detail, proportion, perspective, time, comments, associations, line quality, self-criticisms, attitude, drive, and concept served to differentiate between maladjusted individuals and well-adjusted people. How this determination was made was unclear. Additionally, the people involved in making the analysis of the drawings for this study and the previous study, along with their qualifications were not discussed. The breakdown of the participants into the intellectual levels and the diagnostic categories was not clear.

INTERPRETATION OF SCORES

The HTP may be scored quantitatively as well as qualitatively. The scoring for each method was clearly described and included illustrated case examples. The quantitative method viewed the detail, proportion, and perspective factors of each section of the test. For the house, tree, and person, the total scores were computed for the following categories: D3, D2, D1, A1, A2, A3, S1, S2. These categories were directly linked to the standardization sample and represented intellectual functioning. For instance, house drawing that lacked a roof was labeled D3 as representative of individuals with inferior intelligence. A house drawing that included roof material (shading, blocking, diagonal lines, etc) was labeled as S1 indicating superior intelligence. In addition to the verbal descriptions of the categories, Buck (1987) incorporated illustrations of the various possibilities. Raw scores were weighted to determine good scores and flaw scores. Overall, this method provided an indication of intellectual functioning. Buck (1987) furnished guidelines for interpreting the HTP IQ in relation to other standardized measures of intelligence.

Qualitative analysis considered details (relevant and irrelevant), proportion, and perspective. In addition, time consumption, line quality, criticality, attitude, drive, and color were examined. These sections were thoroughly outlined. For instance, the category of perspective involved placement on the page. When the tree drawing appeared in the upper portion of the paper, it indicated a person who was prone to fantasy, set unattainable goals, and felt frustrated. A tree placed in the lower portion of the page may reveal a person who felt insecure and may be mildly depressed. Guidelines for qualitative analysis were clearly outlined.

SOURCE OF ITEMS

Buck (1987) stated that the objects of the house, tree, and person were selected because they were familiar items for very young children as well as adults. Additionally, he felt that these objects were more accepted by clients of all ages compared to other suggested objects. Lastly, he found that the house, tree, and person seemed to foster more open and free associations than did other items. The nature of the "other suggested objects" was not discussed.

VALIDITY AND RELIABILITY AS DETERMINED BY THE AUTHOR

Buck (1987) did not present reliability and validity studies to support the use of the HTP. Several pilot studies have been conducted using the HTP. Unfortunately, these studies did not concentrate on establishing reliability and validity evidence. Nonetheless, they did provide information on the usefulness of this assessment.

RESEARCH USING THE HTP

Marzolf and Kirchner (1972) collected HTPs from 760 college students (454 women and 306 men) enrolled in psychology courses. On the same day or a few weeks later, the students were given the Sixteen Personality Factor Questionnaire Form C (Catell, 1962). The authors prepared a list of 108 characteristics of HTP drawings. All drawings were analyzed for the presence or absence of these characteristics. Using two assistants, the inter-rater reliability was better than 90%. Thirty-six percent of the 108 items showed sex differences. In relationship to the questionnaire, no reliable differences were found between those judged as disturbed and more well-adjusted individuals. Due to the sex differences found in the items, the authors underscored the importance of inquiry when interpreting the drawing.

Kline and Svaste-Xuto (1981) examined the cultural implications of the HTP. A total sample of 80 Thai children, ranging in age from 4 to 6 years, completed the HTP. A total of 40 British children of the same age completed the HTP. The samples were neither random nor matched and therefore, represented a restricted population. Further demographic characteristics of the participants were not discussed. The drawings were scored for the presence or absence of features. For instance, the following was an example of how the authors scored a drawing of a tree:

BRANCHES:	presence of branches	= 1 pt.,	absence = 0
BARK:	presence of bark	= 1 pt.,	absence = 0
ROOTS:	presence of roots	= 1 pt.,	absence = 0

The authors reported that the scoring system they developed was highly reliable, showing 90% agreement. The PDI questions were also objectively scored. Sex differences were found in the person drawings: Significantly more Thai girls indicated that their person was a young, healthy, woman.

The authors expressed that this supported the validity of Buck's statement that children were more likely to draw a person of the same sex. Significantly, more girls said that their house had one or two stories. No sex differences were found in tree drawings. Additionally, cultural differences were not found. The authors concluded that the HTP, when objectively scored, was a suitable personality assessment for cross-cultural use.

The HTP has been used to investigate physical abuse cases (Lewis & Goldstein, 1981). A sample 109 children completed the HTP. The physically abused-clinical group consisted of 32 children participating in therapy for child abuse (physical). A sample of 32 children, judged by their therapists not to have been physically abused, comprised the nonabused-clinical group. The well-adjusted group consisted of 45 children from a local elementary school, judged by their teachers to be highly well adjusted and to come from homes where physical abuse was unlikely. The authors found that the following items occurred significantly more often in the abused-clinical group than the other two: smoke coming from the chimney, absence of windows on the ground floor of the house, noticeable difference in the arms and legs of figures, and absence of feet, and disproportional size of the head. In conclusion, the authors stipulated that the items taken individually strongly distinguish between abused and normal children but not between abused and nonabused but disturbed children. This study may provide some valid evidence that the HTP distinguished between well-adjusted children and maladjusted children.

Ramirez (1983) examined the usefulness of the HTP in working through resistance ingroup settings. Resistance was defined as the conscious, preconscious, or unconscious opposition that envelops one's attitudes, ideas, impulses, thoughts, actions, and fantasies (Greenson, 1967). Ramirez (1983) presented case examples of groups where resistance impeded therapeutic progress. "The house, tree, and person drawing task is especially useful for group therapists unfamiliar with art therapy techniques because there is a large body of work available for help in interpreting the images and because patients have been found to be less resistant to drawing these particular subjects, which are familiar to everyone's experience" (Ramirez, 1983, p. 48). Although this study was qualitative in its approach, it illustrated how the HTP may be helpful in overcoming resistance patterns by reducing defensiveness and promoting group discussion.

Ouellette (1988) administered the HTP to 33 young deaf adults. Psychologists rated the drawings on scales measuring aggression, anxiety, insecurity, impulsiveness, immaturity, egocentricity, dependency, and feelings of inadequacy. Interrater reliability was established for aggression, impulsiveness, immaturity, and feelings of inadequacy. By comparing psychologists' ratings of the drawings with trained counselors' clinical observations, validity was established for five personality trait scales: Aggression, impulsiveness, immaturity, egocentricity, and dependency. In conclusion, Ouellette (1988) stressed that "while the validity and reliability of the House-Tree-Person technique remains to be fully demonstrated, this assessment instrument appears to hold promise for use with hearing-impaired adults to anticipate and intervene with potential personality difficulties" (p. 217).

The House-Tree-Person Test was used to work with middle-aged people facing a midlife crisis (Zahir, 1997). Zahir wanted to see if the chromatic and achromatic HTP would reveal issues typically associated with midlife. She presented the case of Leon, a 57-year-old male, who in his earlier years was studying to be a priest. Later, he left the ministry, married, and had two daughters. He was the youngest boy in an Irish family with three older brothers. According to Zahir (1997), he often felt unnoticed by his parents, particularly his father. Leon's marriage ended in divorce and he went through several relationships before and after his marriage.

Leon drew a house with stilts, on a hill, with large windows to see the ocean. The stilts appear unstable suggesting instability, uncertainty, and vulnerability with respect to his life events (Zahir, 1997). His drawing of self revealed defensiveness as he erased the legs and made them thicker and stronger. Zahir (1997) reported that Leon's chromatic drawings reveal his impulses as uncontrollable, unstable, and chaotic. The chromatic and achromatic drawings reveal a duality: " the priest in him and its inherent controls, on the one hand, and the other, the hedonist thrust breaking out, or as it were, the liberated Id escaping the control-invested alliance of Superego and Ego" (Zahir, 1997, p. 404). The duality is also suggested in the conflict between heterosexuality and homosexuality.

Finger (1997) used a case approach to examine the sensitivity of the HTP to changes during the therapeutic process. Alan was a seven-year-old first grader whose parents were divorced. He had no siblings. In school, Alan was having difficulty with reading and arithmetic. In general, he demonstrated much anxiety and had poor academic progress. His mother reported that he did not want to be alone or sleep by himself. Frequently, he had bad dreams. Alan feared abandonment by his mother. Also, Alan completed the chromatic and achromatic versions of the HTP before and during therapy.

Prior to therapy, Alan's achromatic house suggested a need for environmental access but fear of letting people close (Finger, 1997). His achromatic tree reflected his inner feelings of trauma, threat, and fear of being hurt. For the person, Alan drew a snow monster which "represents Alan's own feelings of rage and impotence. . . . Alan's sense of self is not of a solid and whole person, but one who is more amorphous and weird" (Finger, 1997, p. 266). Finger (1997) asserted that achromatic drawings tend to indicate what the artist wants to be whereas the chromatic drawing reveal what the artist wants to hide. In his chromatic drawing, Alan drew a house that was a cave of darkness. The constricted cave drawn in brown and black suggests depression (Finger, 1997). Although healthy, Alan's chromatic tree is starved for nourishment. The chromatic person is a man made of wood suggesting defense and fear of destruction (Finger, 1997). Further, it is drawn in brown suggesting depression.

During therapy, Alan's achromatic house becomes more imaginative showing more accessibility and acceptance of nurturance (Finger, 1997). His achromatic tree demonstrated grandiosity, fullness; yet, still contained feelings of trauma. Alan's achromatic person demonstrates an exaggerated sense of self in the tallness and weak sense of self in the thinness of the person. Finger (1997) noted that Alan has overcome the feelings of depersonalization. The chromatic house is drawn in blue suggesting emotional constriction yet moving away from depression noted in the pretherapy drawings. Additionally, his drawing of an orange tree suggested more security and environmental contact. The depersonalization has faded from his chromatic drawing of a person. Further, Finger (1997) notes that his drawing of a person indicates a health assertiveness.

The HTP was used with a sample of 589 Japanese college students to examine alexithymia characteristics in the drawing test (Fukunishi, Mikami, & Kikuchi, 1997). The authors defined an individual diagnosed with alexithymia as an individual "characterized by difficulty in identifying and describing emotions, paucity of fantasy life, and externally oriented thinking" (p. 939). This was measured using the Toronto Alexithymia Scale and compared to the students' HTPs. Poor relationship between figures was depicted on the HTPs of students having alexithymia.

Abell et al. (1998) examined the person component of the HTP in conjunction with the Goodenough-Harris Drawing Test and Wechsler Intelligence Scale for Children-Revised (WISC-R), comparing intellectual evaluations with human figure drawings with a sample of 200 adolescent boys from a residential treatment center. Abell and colleagues found that the person portion of the HTP showed promise for intellectually assessing young adolescent boys.

West (1998) used the HTP in a battery of projective assessments. The met-analysis found that the HTP and other projective assessments significantly discriminated between distressed, sexually abused children from nondistressed, nonabused children.

Louw and Ramkisson (2002) used the HTP in conjunction with the Draw A Person test, reviewed in Chapter 11 of this book, and the Roberts Apperception Test for Children (RATC) with sexually abused Indian girls. Participants included 23 sexually abused girls and 17 girls with no abuse history, 7 to 11 years of age, coming primarily from foster homes in Kswzulu-

Natal. The sexually abused girls differed significantly on the DAP and HTP. Although there were no significant differences on the RATC, Louw and Ramkisson (2002) noted that the sexually abused girls had more responses of a sexual nature. They asserted that the DAP and HTP assessments are useful in identifying sexually abused girls from India and should be included in a battery of tests for possible sexual abuse. This was not supported in an earlier study using the HTP with a population of sexually abused children. Palmer et al. (2000) collected HTPs from 47 sexually abused children and a control group of 82 children with no history of abuse. Although the two samples were matched for gender, age, and socioeconomic status, the quantitatively scored results did not yield significant differences between these groups.

Barrett et al. (2002) used the HTP to examine spatial bias using a sample of 30 Korean participants. Specifically, Barrett and colleagues (2002) were interested in biases that occur due to reading orientation. For instance, the Korean participants learned to read top to bottom, right to left (R-L group). Spatial-syntactic bias was tested by reading sentences to the participants and having them draw pictures of the sentence. They noted the placement of the subject on the page, left versus right. Placement of the HTP on the page was also measured. There were no spatial syntactical biases present in the R-L group compared to the L-R group; yet, they significantly placed their HTP on the left-hand side of the page. Barrett et al. (2002) concluded that left spatial bias may appear in people whose cultural background is Eastern and whose reading style is right to left.

Craig, Olson, and Saad (2002) used the HTP to determine if windows, doors, pathways, and size of house were graphic indicators of psychological and social accessibility by correlating the results with the MMPI-2, the Social Introversion scale. Participants included 153 adults from nonclinical settings and 146 people from a mental health center. There were strong correlations among the figure-drawing variables, which suggest common underlying dimensions. Yet, the scores did not correlate significantly with psychological accessibility as measured by the MMPI-2 Social Introversion scale.

Zannis (2003) examined the tree drawings from HTPs to determine if knotholes in trees significantly indicated trauma, and therefore had clinical validity as a screening device. Using an archived sample of 420 HTPs drawn by children, 6 to 16 years of age, from court-ordered evaluations of the Department of Children and Families and the Juvenile Justice Department, the tree drawings were examined for the presence of knotholes. Zannis (2003) found that children who were physically and/or sexually abused did not significantly draw more knotholes in their trees. On the other hand, children who witnessed domestic violence did tend to draw more knotholes in their trees.

DESIRABLE FEATURES

The HTP incorporated chromatic as well as achromatic features as part of the assessment. Guidelines for interpretation were clearly demarcated. In addition, Buck (1987) provided case examples that illustrated the quantitative and qualitative scoring methods. The manual was very detailed in its approach to design, administration, scoring, and interpretation.

UNDESIRABLE FEATURES

The quantitative method of the test was quite involved and may take the therapist some time in determining scores. The use of a stopwatch to time the client can be cumbersome and possibly intimidating to a client. Since the administrator was required to track a myriad of details during the assessment, important data may be missed. It seemed that the client may be prone to exhaustion after completing the drawings as well as the PDI. Interrupting the drawing tasks with a verbal component may interfere with the chromatic version of the test. The way the instructions were worded may develop performance anxiety in some clients. Additionally, the directions indicated that the drawing should be produced for the administrator. This may promote transference issues that may influence the manner in which the assessment was completed.

OVERALL EVALUATION

Reliability and validity evidence has yet to be established for the HTP. Some inter-rater reliability evidence was provided in the pilot studies; yet, they used their own scoring techniques as opposed to the one outlined by Buck (1987). From the studies presented, validity evidence appears mixed. With the quantitative method of scoring the HTP, validity evidence can be established by correlating the results of the HTP with well-known standardized measures of intelligence. Additionally, validity evidence can be produced by researching how the HTP distinguishes between clinical populations and well-adjusted individuals.

Buck (1987) recommended that the HTP be used as a screening device to measure maladjustment, appraise personality integration, and identify common personality characteristics of a specific population; yet, he did not provide evidence that the HTP was a valid device for screening in these areas. Additionally, he stated that the HTP can be used for employment and placement purposes. If the HTP was to be used to determine job classification decisions, evidence of differential prediction among job positions should be documented (AERA, APA, NCME, 1985). Validity and reliability evidence is required before the HTP can be used as a method of employment or academic placement. And research to date has not utilized the HTP as an employment screening assessment.

Several questions arise when viewing the standardization sample. First, the population was examined in the late forties. Can this information be used as a reliable guide for interpreting HTP IQs today? The exact nature of classification was not clear. How were these individuals rated? What assessment was used to measure their intelligence level? Was the same assessment used for all participants? The same questions hold true for the clinical sample. It is not clear how the participants were labeled and who was responsible for the diagnostic classification. Caution should be taken when using the HTP as a measure of intellectual functioning.

Buck (1987) was very thorough when outlining the administration and scoring sections of the manual. The case illustrations were helpful in providing insight on the use of the HTP. Another positive function of this assessment was that it incorporated color, a factor neglected by some art therapy tests.

Stone (2003) notes that the direct use of HTP questions may lead to widespread misuse of the assessment; therefore, specific guidelines for the interpretation of this assessment are essential. Future editions of the manual should include more information on the normative sample or develop new norms. Additional validity and reliability evidence would be welcome, particularly with respect to IQ and job placement and classification decisions.

REFERENCES

Abell, S.C., Horkheimer, R., & Nguyen, S.E. (1998). Intellectual evaluations of adolescents via human figure drawings: An empirical comparison of two methods. *Journal of Clinical Psychology, 54*(6), 811–815.

American Educational Research Association, American Psychological Association, & National Council on Measurement in Education. (1985). *Standards for educational and psychological testing.* Washington, DC: American Psychological Association

Barrett, A.M., Kim, M., Crucian, G.P., & Heilman, K.M. (2002). Spatial biases: Effects of early reading direction on Korean subjects. *Neuropsychologia, 40*(7), 1003–1013.

Buck, J.N. (1987). *The House-Tree-Person Technique: Revised Manual.* Los Angeles, CA: Western Psychological Services.

Buck, J.N. (1949). The H-T-P technique. *Journal of Clinical Psychology, 5,* 37–74.

Catell, R.B. (1962). *Handbook supplement for Form C of the Sixteen Personality Factor Questionnaire.* Champaign, IL: Institute for Personality and Ability Testing.

Craig, R.J., Olson, R.E., & Saad, S. (2002). Figure-drawing indices of psychological accessibility. *Psychological Reports, 91*(3), 1213–1222.

Finger, D.R. (1997). Child case study Alan, before and during therapy. In *Advances in projective drawing interpretation.* E. F. Hammer (Ed). Springfield, IL: Charles C Thomas, pp. 263–267.

Fukunishi, I., Mikami, N., & Kikuchi, M. (1997). Alexithymic characteristics in responses to the synthetic House Tree HTP Person Drawing Test. *Perceptual and Motor Skills, 85,* 939–942.

Greenson, R. (1967). *The technique and practice of psychoanalysis.* New York: International Universities Press.

Kline, P., & Svaste-Xuto, B. (1981). The House, Tree, Person Test (HTP) in Thailand with 4 and 5 year old children: A comparison of Thai and British results. *Projective Psychology, 26*(1), 1–11.

Lewis, M.L, & Goldstein, M.A. (1981). The use of objectively scorable House-Tree-Person indicators to establish child abuse. *Journal of Clinical Psychology, 37*(3), 667–673.

Louw, A.E., & Ramkisson, S. (2002). The suitability of the Roberts Apperception Test for Children (RATC), the *House-Tree-Person* (H-T-P) and *Draw-a-Person* (D-A-P) scales in the identification of child sexual abuse in the Indian community: An exploratory study. *South African Journal of Child and Adolescent Mental Health, 14*(2), 96–106.

Marzolf, S.S., & Kirchner, J.H. (1972). House-Tree-Person drawings and personality traits. *Journal of Personality Assessment, 36*(2), 148–165.

Ouellette, S.E. (1988). The use of projective drawing techniques in the personality assessment of prelingually deafened young adults: A pilot study. *A.A.D.,* July, 212–217.

Palmer, L., Farrar. A.R., Valle, M., Ghahary, N., Panella, M., & DeGraw, D. (2000). An investigation of the clinical case of the *House-Tree-Person* projective drawings in the psychological evaluation of child sexual abuse. *Child Maltreatment, 5*(2), 169–176.

Ramirez, C. (1983). Drawing out resistance: The use of the House-Tree-Person Test to facilitate communication in verbal therapy groups. *Group, 7*(3), 39–49.

Stone, E. (2003). A comment about the influence of http questions on our practice. *Art Therapy, 20*(3), 123–124.

Teillard, A. (1951). *II Symbolismo del Sogri.* Milan: Feltrineilli. Cited in Ramirez (1983).

West, M. (1998). Meta-analysis of studies assessing the efficacy of projective techniques in discriminating child sexual abuse. *Child Abuse & Neglect, 22*(11), 1151–1166.

Zahir, Y.L. (1997). An artists in mid-life crisis. In *Advances in projective drawing interpretation.* E. F. Hammer (Ed). Springfield, IL: Charles C Thomas, pp. 391–405.

Zannis, M.D. (2003). Child maltreatment and projective drawings: The role of holes in trees. Dissertation Abstracts International: Section B: *The Sciences and Engineering, 64*(1-B), 437.

Chapter 7

KINETIC HOUSE-TREE-PERSON TEST

TITLE: Kinetic House-Tree-Person Test (KHTP)
AGE: Age limit not discussed
YEAR: 1987
PURPOSE: designed to understand human development: Individual transformation process, reflections of scores included Attachments Present, Figures Other than Self Present, and Additional Figures Present
MANUAL: manual (213 pages); illustrations (47 pages); profile (5 pages); reliability data (none reported); validity data (none reported)
TIME LIMIT: no time limit for administration
COST: $31.95–$50.00 for testing manual
                      http://search.tandf.co.uk/bookscatalogue
AUTHOR: Burns, Robert C.
PUBLISHER: Brunner/Mazel, Inc., 19 Union Square, New York, NY, 10003.

INTRODUCTION

Because of the limitations of the House-Tree-Person Test (HTP) and the Draw a Person Test (DAP), researchers moved toward the development of kinetic assessments. "Projective, nonkinetic techniques are criticized because they restrict the depiction of important family dynamics that provide the greatest insight into a child's feelings and perceptions, and his family's roles, influences, and interactions" (Knoff & Prout, 1985, p. 51). One assessment that incorporated a kinetic component was the Kinetic House-Tree-Person Test (KHTP).

As opposed to the HTP, the KHTP combined all three images, house, tree, and person, on one page. In addition, the drawing introduced physical activity of family members. Despite the clinical value of the HTP, Burns (1987, p. 5) remarked on a few limitations:

1. The HTP was standardized on patients in a psychiatric setting. Literature on the HTP focused on diagnostic labeling such as "Organics, Schizophrenics, etc."

2. Placement of the images occurred on separate pieces of paper that did not allow for action or interaction.

3. Interpretation of the HTP was Freudian and reduced all images to fit within this matrix.

The KHTP was developed to surpass some of the limitations presented by the HTP, which resulted in more clinical information about the client.

PURPOSE AND RECOMMENDED USE

The purpose of the KHTP was to furnish information on the parameters of a client's perspective that may otherwise remain illusive using some traditional drawing techniques such as the HTP. "The K-H-T-P is useful in understanding the dynamics in many types of clinical situations, thus enhancing the healing process" (Burns, 1987, p. 7). The KHTP assessment was devised to tell a story; to create a visual metaphor about self.

DIMENSIONS THAT THE TEST PURPORTS TO MEASURE

Burns (1987) linked the KHTP to a developmental model, Maslow's (1954) Hierarchy of Needs, to qualitatively measure the results of this assessment. The first five levels of Maslow's (1954) Hierarchy were used to interpret the developmental stages of the person, tree, and house images. Essentially, the house represented the physical aspects of the client's life, the tree indicated life energy and direction, and the person symbolized the client. For instance, Level 1: Belonging to life, revealed desire for life, survival, safety and rootedness. In the drawing of the house, Level 1 was concerned with survival or the desire to die. Approachers viewed the house as a place of security and safety. Access was limited and the house was often depicted as a prison structure. Avoiders were people who considered death. The house may be crumbling, decaying, vacuous, or impermanent. In the tree drawings, Approachers drew trees that had talon-shaped roots. The tree may appear unfriendly and unclimbable. Avoiders drew trees that were dead or dying. Typically, the trunk was narrow and foliage was absent or sparse. In person drawings, Approachers tended to sketch people with an aggressive appearance or paranoid features. The figures were armed and/or suspicious. Avoiders, depicted vacuous faces or sad expressions. People seem dead or self-destructive.

ADMINISTRATION

Using a sheet of 8 1/2" x 11" white paper placed horizontally, the client was asked to "Draw a house, a tree, and a whole person on this piece of paper with some kind of action. Try to draw a whole person, not a cartoon or stick person" (Burns, 1987, p. 5). Group administration, administrater qualifications, and test requirements for special populations were not discussed.

NORM GROUPS

The manual contained several case examples but the assessment was not standardized on a population. Regardless of Burns' (1987) complaint that the HTP was standardized on a psychiatric population, the KHTP was not standardized on any population. The manner in which the cases were selected remains unclear. Most of the cases appeared to come from a psychiatric population so that the interpretation of drawings made by better-adjusted individuals may be difficult.

INTERPRETATION OF SCORES

The KHTP was scored for the presence or absence of attachments. For instance, the therapist may observe if the house attached to the tree (H-T) or if the house attached to the person (H-P). Other combinations included the person attached to the tree (P-T), all items attached (H-T-P), or no attachments (none). The KHTP can be scored for figures other than self. For instance, the counselor may record the presence of an antihero, deceased person, parent, friend, hero, relative, unknown person, or other person. Other than summarizing the presence or absence of these items, no other scoring information was discussed.

SOURCE OF ITEMS

The items appeared to originate from the HTP (Buck, 1948). Using other researchers as a guide, Burns (1987) interpreted the meaning of images drawn on the KHTP. For instance, emphasis of chimneys was said to suggest concern with psychological warmth at home (Buck, 1948; Jolles, 1964) and sexual concern about masculinity (Buck, 1948; Jolles, 1964; Hammer, 1969). Burns (1987) also expressed that emphasis of the chimney suggested concern about power and/or concern about activating creativity; yet, the source of these items remains unclear. Overall, Burns (1987) appeared to draw on the work of previous researchers when discussing interpretation of the objects drawn.

VALIDITY AND RELIABILITY AS DETERMINED BY THE AUTHOR

Burns (1987) did not incorporate reliability or validity information in his book. He mentioned that kinetic drawings have been reliably scored (Burns & Kaufman, 1972; Knoff & Prout, 1985); yet, he did not provide further information. To date, reliability, and validity for the KHTP has not been examined. Although the KHTP was based on the HTP, it cannot be expected to rely on the research used to support the HTP. Additional research was necessary in order to confirm that the KHTP was a reliable and valid art therapy assessment.

RESEARCH USING THE ASSESSMENT

Kukanich (2001) used the KHTP to examine the sign approach method of interpretation versus the holistic method of interpreting projective assessments. According to Kukanich (2001), the holistic method focuses on the overall affect and tone of the artist's drawing, taking into account the emotional reaction of the person interpreting the drawings. On the other hand, the sign approach uses traditional indicators to gain meaning from the drawing. Four graduate students were trained on the interpretation methods of the KHTP. Next, they interpreted four drawings using each method of interpretation. The Drawing Rating Form was used to record the graduate school students' impressions of the drawings. Although both methods were found to be effective, Kukanich (2001) reported that the holistic method yielded more clinical information compared to the sign approach method.

In a second portion of his doctoral dissertation study, Kukanich (2001) examined the personality characteristics of the participants that predicted accurate holistic projective drawing interpretation. The KHTP drawings were compared to the Millon Index of Personality Styles to determine their level of empathy-Feeling, intuition-Intuitive, and cognitive flexibility-Innovative. Kukanich (2001) found that clinical personality styles do predict holistic KHTP interpretation, particularly on the Feeling component. Kukanich (2001) concludes by presenting a model that integrates the drawer's social emotional issues, level of projection in the KHTP, clinician's interpretation strategy, clinician's personality characteristics, and the interpreter's clinical decision-making process.

DESIRABLE FEATURES

The test was easy to administer. Further, the manual included several case examples to assist the therapist with interpretation. Adding a kinetic component was a valuable idea. Moving figures will yield more information about personality as compared to static figures. Additionally, combining the house, tree, and person all on one page produces more information than when viewed separately. For instance, when the tree was leaning slightly away from the house, this may indicate growing independence and moving away from family attachments (Burns, 1987). Another possibility was having a person attached to the house. This may suggest a need for nurturing (Burns, 1987). By viewing the interaction of these objects, the therapist was able to glean more information than viewing the house, tree, and person separately.

Not only were attachments and proximity important, but also the order in which the items were drawn may reveal information about the client's personality. When the client draws the tree first, it may reveal that "life energy and growth are most important to the drawer. This was typical of people trying to grow or stay alive" (Burns, 1987, p. 102). If the client draws the house first, it may show a need to belong to the earth (a place to survive), need to belong to the body (body needs or obsessions), a need to belong to society, a home for nurturing, or a home for giving and receiving nurturing (Burns, 1987). If the client draws the person first, it may suggest concern with control of feelings, showing off or hiding the body, showing success, a nurturing person, or a joyful person.

Another desirable feature of the KHTP was the incorporation of Maslow's (1954) theory to create a developmental model for the assessment. Burns (1987) modified Maslow's approach to interpret the items on the KHTP. He came up with the following five levels (p. 54):

Level 1: Belong to Life: Desire for life, survival, safety, rootedness.

Level 2: Belong to body: Acceptance of body, seeking control of body addictions and potential.

Level 3: Belong to society: Search for status, success, respect, and power.

Level 4: Belong to self and not self: Self now defined to include not self as a pregnant woman accepts her child; compassion, nurturing, giving love; meta motivation.

Level 5: Belong to all living things: Giving and accepting love; self-actualization; sense of good fortune and luck; creativity; celebration of life.

Burns interpreted each item on the KHTP within this framework. Further, he divided each level into Approachers and Avoiders. Burns (1987) provided a similar breakdown for the developmental levels of the tree and person. In addition, he included several examples of drawings to indicate the various stages of development.

Burns (1987) also presented an appendix that summarized the general characteristics of the images drawn. These were hypotheses used when judging projective drawing techniques: They involved pressure factors, line or stroke characteristics, drawing size, and placement of the drawing. For instance, if a drawing was placed low on the page, it was said to suggest feelings of insecurity (Buck, 1948; Jolles, 1964; Burns & Kaufman, 1972), feelings of inadequacy (Buck, 1948; Jolles, 1964; Hammer, 1971; Burns & Kaufman, 1972), or depressive tendencies (Buck, 1948; Machover, 1949; Jolles, 1964; Hammer, 1971). Burns (1987) also furnished a summary of individual characteristics of the house, tree, and person.

UNDESIRABLE FEATURES

The KHTP may be difficult to interpret when a symbol occurs that were not included in the case examples or the summary tables. For instance, this I had one client who drew her person in the shape of a mandala, with two legs, and several eyes. It was not clear how to interpret this figure or where to place it within the developmental model presented by Burns (1987).

Although Burns (1987) provided a table for the scoring of attachments, he did not include scoring information when presenting the case examples. These tables were simplified in that they only note the presence of attachments and figures. Their significance was not discussed. For instance, I would have liked more information on clients who included deceased persons or political figures in their drawings. Obviously, these figures were important; yet, Burns (1987) did not present a framework for interpretation.

As Gould (1990) notes, the manual was not organized and is often unclear. The intended use of developmental levels is not made clear in the manual; therefore, interpretation from a Maslowian perspective is difficult.

OVERALL EVALUATION

Many have argued about the universal interpretation of symbols. Whether archetypes or cultural symbols, interpretation without the client's input is not valid. Burns (1987) warned against the overinterpretation of drawing symbols.

> Interpretation of all symbols depends on the level of consciousness of the producer of the symbol at the time the symbols was produced and the level of consciousness of the interpreter at the time of interpretation. There is obviously room for a great deal of error. (Burns, 1987, p. 143)

With this thought in mind, Burns (1987) suggested a procedure for interpreting symbols based on level of consciousness. For example, water can have various meanings depending on the consciousness level (p. 147):

Level 1:   Survival, embryonic stage
Level 2:   "Juices flowing," hedonistic
Level 3:   "Power of sea", water beats rock
Level 4:   Nurturing, refreshing, useful
Level 5:   Flexible, humble, serene, calm

This breakdown was provided for only a few of the symbols. It was not clear how the therapist would use this breakdown when other symbols were present. This point addressed the main weakness of the manual: The interpretation of symbols or drawing features that were not presented by Burns (1987). Granted, the client was the source for interpreting all symbols but what if the client was nonverbal or was unable to communicate the meaning of the item? Regardless of this weakness, the KHTP yielded some valuable information about the client's perception of self, the environment, and the family. The kinetic component was a valuable addition to the HTP. The interaction of the items as well as the developmental model was a strong improvement over the HTP.

Overall, the test was easy to administer and the case examples were interesting. Additional research information is needed on this assessment, especially the reliability and validity of symbol interpretation. In addition, it would be interesting to have information on the chromatic version of the test.

Color choice may reveal additional information about the client. The investigation of possible cultural differences that may be found in the KHTP would be worthwhile.

REFERENCES

Buck, J.N. (1948). *The House-Tree-Person Technique*. Los Angeles, CA: Western Psychological Services.

Burns, R.C. (1987). *Kinetic House-Tree-Person Drawings: An interpretive manual*. New York, NY: Brunner/Mazel Publishers.

Burns, R.C., & Kaufman, S.H. (1972). *Actions, styles and symbols in kinetic family drawings (K-F-D): An interpretative manual*. New York: Brunner/Mazel.

Gould, P. (1990). Book reviews. *American Journal of Art Therapy, 28*(4), 118–120.

Hammer, E.F. (1969). Hierarchical organization of personality and the H-T-P, achromatic and chromatic. In Buck, J.N., & Hammer, E.F. (Eds.) *Advances in the House-Tree-Person Techniques: Variations and   Applications*. Los Angeles, CA: Western Psychological Services.

Hammer, E.F. (1971). *The clinical application of projective drawings*. Springfield, IL: Charles C Thomas.

Jolles, I. (1964). *A catalog for the qualitative interpretation of the House-Tree-Person (H-T-P)*. Los Angeles, CA: Western Psychological Services.

Knoff, H.M., & Prout, H.T. (1985). The kinetic drawing system: A review and integration of the Kinetic Family and School Drawing techniques. *Psychology in the Schools, 22 (January)*, 50–59.

Kukanich, D.M. (2001). Clinician personality traits, the Kinetic House-Tree-Person Drawing, and holistic method assessment: Integrating the evaluator and the Technique. *Dissertation Abstracts International: Section B: The Sciences & Engineering, 61*(10-B), 5610.

Machover, K. (1949). *Personality projection in the drawing of the human figure*. Springfield, IL: Charles C Thomas.

Maslow, A.H. (1954). *Motivation and personality*. New York: Harper and Row.

Chapter 8

FAMILY-CENTERED CIRCLE DRAWINGS

TITLE: Family-Centered Circle Drawings (FCCD)
AGE: Age limit not discussed
YEAR: 1990
PURPOSE: designed to understand parent-self relationships
SCORES: drawings were not scored; guidelines for interpretation were presented; four types of FCCDs: (1) Mother-centered; (2) Father-centered: (3) Self-centered; and (4) Parent-self-centered
MANUAL: manual (198 pages); illustrations (49 pages); profile (12 pages); reliability data (none reported); validity data (none reported)
TIME LIMIT: no time limit for administration
COST: $29.95–$46.95 for testing manual
                 http://search.tandf.co.uk/bookscatalogue
AUTHOR: Burns, Robert C.
PUBLISHER: Brunner/Mazel, Inc., 19 Union Square, New York, NY, 10003.

INTRODUCTION

The Family-Centered Circle Drawings (FCCD; Burns, 1990) assessment was based on the concept of inner parents and the relationship to the self. Through the creation of symbol systems in drawings, therapists may determine how clients relate to their parents. Specifically, clients' emotions towards their parents and barriers between them were discussed in comparison to the clients' inner parents. Since symbol systems were created by the client, they were unique and served to bring the person closer to center (Burns, 1990).

FCCDs were based partly on Rorschach's findings relating to increased projective material with symmetry. Although standardized inkblot tests were previously used, Rorschach (1942) was the first to apply inkblots to assessment of personality as a whole (Anastasi, 1988). Rorschach (1942) discovered that symmetrical inkblots produced more responses and more unconscious material than asymmetrical inkblots. Burns (1990) incorporated this research by placing individual family members in a centered, symmetrical matrix. By drawing parents and self, the client may begin to see parent-self relationships more clearly and the impact on her own inner parents.

Jung's work with mandalas also contributed to the FCCD. According to Burns (1990), a mandala was a centered symbol in a symmetrical design.

> Psychologically speaking, a mandala image is one that emphasizes the totality of something, usually showing quite clearly a periphery and a center. In its historical sense, the term mandala refers to certain very structured meditation symbols used in Buddhism, often consisting of a four-gated square or circular city with a central image (to be meditated on) and lesser images surrounding it. (Hall, 1983, p. 76)

Jung extensively studied mandalas in his search for balance and health (Coward, 1985). Additionally, Jung was a novice artist who worked through his own conflicts by painting and sculpting: "In fact, Jung's theories can best be understood in the context of the value he attached to the subjective reality of spontaneously generated images" (Rubin, 1987, p. 93). The FCCD combined the use of the mandala with the concept of centering and artistic expression. Burns (1990) perceived that the key to these drawings was centering:

> By centering a symbol and focusing upon it in a symmetrical matrix, one may elicit deep emotional reactions. In the religious world focusing upon centered symbols such as a cross, star, lamb, divine figure, and so on may bring insights and healing. In the projective drawing world, centering upon the self-created images of the parents or of the parents and the self may also bring insights and healing. (Burns, 1990, p. 2)

By placing family figures in the center of the circle, Burns (1990) believed that it would increase projective material. Using this approach, the therapist fostered a dialogue with the client's inner parents in order to determine barriers and emotional conflicts.

PURPOSE AND RECOMMENDED USE

The purpose of the FCCD was to gain information about the client's family and relate it to the client's view of self and his/her inner parents. According to Burns (1990), this technique allowed the client to see self more clearly in relationship to each parent. Positive and negative associations were made around the symbols systems that the client created. The FCCD was recommended for those clients who need to get in touch with their inner parents. The objective of Burns' (1990) approach was to furnish counselors with an awareness of the client's visual communication potential. Also, therapists may be able to provide a broader interpretive context that was not heavily dependent on verbal skills.

DIMENSIONS THAT THE TEST PURPORTS TO MEASURE

The FCCD incorporated four types of drawings: (1) Mother-centered; (2) Father-centered: (3) Self-centered; and (4) Parent-self-centered. Each drawing generated information about the client's perception of family and self. The FCCD began by placing one parent in the center of a circle while the client free associated, doodled, or drew symbols around the perimeter of the circle. The FCCD was repeated with the parent of the opposite sex, and then with the self at the center of the circle. Parents-self-centered drawings (PSCD) involved placing both parents and self in the center circle. The client then free associated images around the circle. Symbol Centered Probes (SYMCP) focused on one particular symbol from the FCCD or PSCD. The client placed this symbol in the circle and then free associated images around this object. In turn, this generated additional information regarding client issues.

ADMINISTRATION

All drawings were to be completed on a standard sheet of typing paper 8 1/2″ x 11″ with the circle already drawn on the paper. The diameter of the circle ranged from 7 1/2″ to 9″. Three separate drawings were obtained for the FCCD. The instructions were as follows:

> Draw your mother in the center of a circle. Visually free associate with drawn symbols around the periphery of the circle. Try to draw a whole person, not a stick or cartoon figure. (Burns, 1990, p. 3)

This procedure was repeated substituting the father and then the self for the mother. The instructions were similar for the PSCD. For younger or educationally limited clients, Burns (1990) substituted the following instructions:

> Draw your parents and yourself in the middle of a circle. Try to draw whole people, not stick people or cartoons. Doodle whatever you want around the edge of the circle. (Burns, 1990, p. 109)

Other requirements for administration were not discussed, such as the administrator's qualifications, drawing media choices, group administration, or use with special populations.

NORM GROUPS

The FCCD was not standardized on a population. Burns (1990) used the case approach and presented example drawings with limited information on the client's background. The manner in which these clients were selected was unclear. Generally, the cases represented a clinical population. People dealing with eating disorders, addictive disorders, or family violence were just a few of the client issues. Although Burns (1990) posed a list of qualities seen in well-adjusted individuals, only one drawing was included. No background information was presented on the person who drew the "healthy" PSCD.

INTERPRETATION OF SCORES

Burns (1990) included a list of items to observe in an FCCD. For instance, the therapist should observe the size of the figure since it was often a reflection of the psychological size and the amount of energy invested in the figure. The omission or overemphasis of body parts and facial expressions should be considered. Also, the therapist should determine whether symbols surrounding the self were repeated in the parental drawings. Symbols directly above a figure should be noted since they were associated with primary feelings. For instance, a knife drawn above a figure may suggest anger (Burns, 1990). The positive and/or negative tone of the symbols should be observed. Although Burns (1990) admitted that these were just a few items to scrutinize, further guidelines for interpretation were not provided. Similar instructions were included for the PSCD. In the last chapter, Burns (1990) discussed a list of qualities observed in maladjusted individuals compared to a list of characteristics viewed in healthy people. The appendix contained recurring symbols in Kinetic Family Drawings (KFD) and FCCD that Burns (1990) considered important. The following represented a few examples from the appendix:

Butterflies: This symbol is associated with the search for illusive love and
                beauty.
Drums: A symbol found in the drawings for those who have difficulty in
                expressing anger openly and thus displace their anger onto the
                drum.

The instructions did not note the manner in which the drawing was completed, the client's affect during the drawing, or type of media used.

SOURCE OF ITEMS

The source of the circle drawings was previously discussed. Burns (1990)
based his approach on Freud's work with free association, Jung's work with
mandalas, and Rorschach's work with the standardized inkblot test. The
source of the interpretation of common symbols was ambiguous. For
instance, the list of items in the appendix incorporated interpretations for
various symbols. It was not clear if this list represented Burns (1990)'s interpretations or the interpretations based on the work of previous researchers.

VALIDITY AND RELIABILITY AS
DETERMINED BY THE AUTHOR

Burns (1990) did not present reliability or validity data on the FCCD.
Also, he did not use a population to standardize this assessment. The validity of the items in the appendix was questionable. The test manual did not
include many examples of children's or adolescents' work. Most of the
clients were in their thirties and forties. Other demographic characteristics of
the clients were not presented. Whether the FCCD was a valid and reliable
instrument for children or adults was unclear. It would be interesting to collect data on the interpretations of a variety of practitioners such as art therapists, counselors, and psychologists to see if there was reliable agreement
among professionals as to the interpretation of these drawings. To date, no
research was available that examined the reliability and validity of this
assessment, or research that used the FCCD as a therapeutic tool.

DESIRABLE FEATURES

The FCCD was an interesting assessment in that it provided information about the client with respect to their parents. It was different from the Kinetic Family Drawing (KFD; Burns & Kaufman, 1972) in that the therapist was able to see the client's relationship with one parent at a time and focus in on one particular symbol. When I implemented the FCCD in private practice, the client gained insight from the types of symbols that were drawn in relation to self and to their parents. This assessment seemed to be more helpful in uncovering the barriers in the client's past relationship with their parents as opposed to discovering or getting in touch with their inner parents.

UNDESIRABLE FEATURES

Burns (1990) did not outline what types of drawing media the administrator should make available to the client. It was difficult to tell from the drawings included in the book what type of medium was used and if it was consistently used. The addition of color may significantly influence the outcome of the assessment; yet, this was not addressed by Burns (1990).

Interpretation of the FCCD appeared limited. It focused only on the drawing and neglected other aspects of the domain. For instance, observing a client's affect while drawing does yield important information. In addition, the manner in which something was drawn or erased may be significant to the interpretation of the drawing. Some may consider the FCCD a "cookbook" approach (Koppitz, 1968). Burn's (1990) FCCD did not contain a list of symbols that the counselor looks up for interpretation. Much of the interpretation was left up to the client, which has a positive function. Yet, it did follow the cookbook approach to art therapy in that it neglected to observe the manner in which the drawings were completed. Valuable information regarding client affect may be missed if the therapist did not observe the drawing process.

OVERALL EVALUATION

Burns (1990) combined free association, family of origin work, object relations, and Jungian mandala symbolism to create an assessment that helped the client view self in relationship to parents and inner parents. Through a series of centered circle drawings, the client created a visual dialogue about his/her relationships with the family. The book contained many examples of each of these drawings.

Although Burns (1990) provided large collection of drawings and explained how to create them, they were in black and white. The colors and media used were not discussed. Thus, the reader lacks a complete visual sense of the drawings. Paint, pastels, inks, and watercolors were some of the materials that clients can manipulate when creating art. Texture of the material was often a reflection of the artist's inner experience or feelings:

> As one avenue to self-definition, we have usually had some choice of art materials, and have on occasion asked that people define themselves by choosing to be an art medium or process, and sharing their reasons. We have found that their choice is intimately related to how they see themselves, i.e., soft or hard, flexible or firm, fragile or strong, colorful or bland, etc. The choice of medium then evolves into a productive activity with that medium, in both cases self-defining and enhancing self-awareness. (Moreno, 1975, p. 113)

Art therapists use the characteristics of art materials for diagnostic purposes. For instance, watercolors involve complex layering. This medium was unpredictable and transparent in nature that allowed the artist spontaneous expression. Since watercolors were hard to control, Robbins (1987) stressed that people who employ this medium were spontaneous individuals who accepted change and relinquished omnipotence. Working with oils was a time-consuming process because it entailed layering. People who used this medium were patient, allowed change, and preferred a predetermined challenge (Robbins, 1987). The use of pencil indicated a need for control, structure, and firm boundaries (Robbins, 1987). Finger-paint was a direct form of expression. Betensky (1973) described finger-paint as an agent of regression that provided an important outlet for stress. These were just a few examples of media as they related to personality characteristics. Although painting may not be an appropriate medium for this assessment, the choice of color would be revealing. For instance, a client may use colored pencils, oil pastels, or crayons to create the FCCD.

Additional information was needed regarding the reliability and validity of the FCCD. It was an interesting approach that revealed information about the client's relationship with self and family; yet, the assessment lacked important data regarding administration requirements, interpretation, and a norm population. Riley (1991) felt that this assessment may be of more interest to mental health professionals as opposed to family therapists as family therapists may be reluctant to ascribe meaning to symbols.

Research on the relationship between the KFD and the FCCD would be beneficial. One advantage of the KFD was that it observed sibling systems. Sibling interactions greatly affect the dynamics of the family system. "There is a high level of interaction among siblings in the home and that the quality of this interaction is rich and varied" (Abramovitch et al. 1979, p. 1003). In my private practice, Burns' (1990) approach was modified to include siblings. This disclosed important information about the client's relationship issues.

Also, it would be helpful to have more information on the use of the FCCD with children and special populations such as learning disabled, hearing impaired, and culturally diverse individuals. Overall, the FCCD had great potential as an art therapy assessment. With additional research information, the FCCD may be a valuable tool when viewing the client's relationship to self and the family.

REFERENCES

Abramovitch, R., Corter, C., & Lando, B. (1979). Sibling interaction in the home. *Child Development, 50,* 997–1003.

Anastasi, A. (1988). *Psychological testing.* 6th ed. New York: Macmillian Publishing Company.

Betensky, M. (1973). *Self-discovery through self-expression: Use of art in psychotherapy.* Springfield, IL: Charles C Thomas Publisher.

Burns, R.C. (1990). *A guide to family-centered circle drawings.* Brunner/Mazel Publishers: New York.

Burns, R.C., & Kaufman, S.H. (1972). *Actions, styles, and symbols in Kinetic Family Drawings (K-F-D): An interpretive manual.* New York: Brunner/Mazel.

Coward, H. (1985). *Jung and eastern thought.* New York: State University of N e w York Press.

Hall, J.A. (1983). *Jungian dream interpretation: A Handbook of theory and practice.* Toronto, Canada: Inner City Books.

Koppitz, E.M. (1968). *Psychological evaluation of children's human figure drawings.* New York: Grune & Stratton.

Moreno, Z.T. (1975). *Group psychotherapy and psychodrama.* New York: Beacon House, Inc.

Riley, S. (1991). Book reviews. *American Journal of Art Therapy, 29*(4), 119–121.

Robbins, A. (1987). *The artist as therapist.* New York: Human Sciences Press.

Rorschach, H. (1942). *Psychodiagnostics.* Berne: Verlag Has Huber.

Rubin, J.A. (1987). *Approaches to art therapy.* New York: Brunner/Mazel.

Chapter 9

THE SILVER DRAWING TEST
OF COGNITION AND EMOTION

Silver Drawing Test

TITLE: Silver Drawing Test (SDT)

AGE: Ages five and over

YEAR: 2002

PURPOSE: designed to assess cognitive abilities in three areas: sequential concepts, spatial concepts, and association and formation of concepts

SCORES: scores included Predictive Drawing, Drawing from Observation, Drawing from Imagination, Total, Projection (Emotional Content) and Self-Image

MANUAL: manual (315 pages); profile (11 pages); reliability data and validity data (13 pages)

TIME LIMIT: 10-20 minutes for administration

COST: $34.95 for book containing all three of Silver's assessments (SDT; DAS; SDT); in *Three Art Assessments* (Silver, 2002)
Free download from
www.routledge-ny.com/testmaterials.cfm

AUTHOR: Silver, Rawley; Rawled@aol.com

PUBLISHER: Brunner-Routledge, 29 West 35th Street, New York, NY 10001

INTRODUCTION

Originally standardized in 1983, The Silver Drawing Test (SDT; 2002) was one of the few art therapy assessments that was written according to the Standards for Educational and Psychological Testing (AERA, APA, NCME, 1985). In 1996, the STD received the American Art Therapy's annual award for research. Since my first review of the assessment in *A Therapist's Guide to Art Therapy Assessments* (1996), the STD has gained wider recognition in the field. Additionally, more research has been conducted, adding to the assessment's reliability and validity support.

PURPOSE AND RECOMMENDED USE

The SDT measures a person's cognitive skills and adjustment. Additionally, it measures concepts critical to math and reading skills. According to Silver (2002), the SDT had the following goals: (1) to bypass language in assessing the ability to solve conceptual problems; (2) to provide precision in evaluating cognitive strengths or weaknesses that may not be detected by verbal measures; and (3) to provide a pre-post instrument for assessing the effectiveness of therapeutic or educational programs. By detecting low levels of cognitive development, the SDT aides in determining individuals in need of new educational programs and/or counseling. Silver (2002) designed the SDT based on the premise that drawings can be used to identify and evaluate problem-solving capabilities.

> Children's drawings are pictorial devices that can represent reality vicariously and economically, and thus reflect their thinking. Children with inadequate language ability are deprived of many opportunities to represent their experiences because they lack a major device for constructing models of reality. (Silver, 1990, p. 9)

The SDT was designed to assess cognitive abilities and emotional components for children and adults. The test manual reported that individual or group administration was appropriate. For children under seven or people who had difficulty understanding directions, individual administration was recommended (Silver, 2002). Individual administration was also recommended in clinical settings to allow for discussion and behavioral observation.

DIMENSIONS THAT THE TEST PURPORTS TO MEASURE

The SDT measures the individual's cognition in the following areas: (1) predictive drawing; (2) drawing from observation; and (3) drawing from imagination. The predictive drawing subtest evaluates sequencing abilities by asking respondents to predict changes in the appearance of objects by adding lines to outline drawings. In addition, this subtest assessed the ability to deal with hypothetical situations involving conservation. The drawing from observation subtest evaluates concepts of space particularly, horizontal, vertical, and depth reasoning. The ability to form concepts was assessed in the drawing from imagination subtest. Specifically, the skills of selecting, combining, and representing objects were tested. Also, the emotional content of the drawing and self-image are noted.

ADMINISTRATION

Generally, the SDT takes about 10 to 20 minutes to complete. The test can be administered individually or in groups with no limit on time. Silver (2002) recommended that group administration of the test was not appropriate for children below age seven and for those people who had difficulty understanding directions. For individuals who had difficulty reading, oral administration was recommended. Silver (2002) stated that the test can be used with hearing impaired children using pantomime or manual language (p. 26).

According to Silver (2002), the SDT can be administered and scored by teachers, therapists, or psychologists. From the reliability evidence in the manual, it seems that the assessment is most reliable when scored by art therapists, a finding common to other assessments reviewed within this book.

NORM GROUPS

1990 Manual Information

Originally, the SDT norms were developed from 547 students in grades 1 to 12 in rural, urban, and suburban schools (Silver, 1990). Grades 6, 7, 9, and 11 were not clearly represented. Although grade 6 does appear in the normative information, the students from this grade were grouped together with fourth and fifth graders with an N of 36. The students came from 13 different schools representing the low to middle socioeconomic backgrounds.

The SDT for adults was standardized on 77 participants. Silver (1990) stated that 250 workshop participants, including undergraduate students, graduate students, social workers, therapists, teachers, and parents of handicapped children completed the SDT from which 20 participants were randomly selected. No other information on the demographics of the standardization sample was presented.

2002 Manual Information

In her updated manual, Silver (2002) provides more information on the norms and case studies used to develop the STD. For instance, the norms for the 1996 edition of STD manual were based on the SDT drawings of 624 subjects, students from 6 to 18 years of age and 77 adults. Five schools participated and were located in New Jersey, Pennsylvania, California, and Canada. Three schools were suburban in high, middle, and lower socioeconomic communities and two were urban from low to middle socioeconomic communities. Although not included in the normative data, 700 students with disabilities completed the STD (Silver, 2002).

For the adult population, Silver (2002) stated that 250 adults completed the STD and consisted of art therapists, teachers, social workers, and students (graduate and undergraduate). The 77 selected represented a random sample for this population. In her recent update, Silver (2002) included some case data in her chapter on normative information. Additionally, she provided detailed charts and tables reflecting the expanded norms.

Using volunteers around the country, the STD was administered to additional youth, adults, and seniors in an effort to expand these norms and develop new ones (Silver, 2002). She reported that children came from diverse backgrounds and attended public and private schools. Although racial background was not recorded with the SDT, it did include information on grade level, age, gender, and any disabilities. Younger adults (20-50) were gathered from workshops or college audiences (students, teachers, and mental health professionals). Senior adults volunteered and were involved in recreational or other community programs. They lived independently or in retirement communities. Silver (2002) created norms based on this data, which included scores, in emotional projection and self-image.

INTERPRETATION OF SCORES

Scores were expressed as percentile ranks and T-scores conversions for emotional content and self-image scores on the drawing from imagination subtest. Similar tables are provided for predictive drawings and drawings from observation. Silver (2002) included the comment that these tables and scores were based on the age and gender of children living in the United

States. In a separate chapter, she provided information about the responses of children and adult in other countries.

Silver (2004) reported that 500 STDs of normal children and adolescents were administered by Ellen Horovitz, designer of the BATA (see Chapter 13 of this book) and the ATDA (see Chapter 14), at Nazareth College. Further, Silver (2002) informed me that Christine Turner of Marylhurst University will be administering the STD with a population of adult and exceptional children.

SOURCE OF ITEMS

The STD emerged from Silver's (2002) work with deaf children. Upon reading an article that hearing impaired children were unimaginative in their artwork compared to hearing children, she began to do more investigating as this seemed counter to her own experience working with this population. "It seemed to me that studio art had latent potential for developing the cognitive and creative skills of children with deafness" (Silver, 2002, p. 19). Silver's doctoral research was designed to ascertain if studio art could stimulate children's cognitive and emotional well-being with participants who were hearing impaired and language deficient.

The drawing tasks stemmed from Piagetian theory of cognitive development in children. According to Silver, the three subtests were created to assess one of three concepts critical to math and reading abilities. The first concept is of the group (classes and numbers), the second concept relates to sequential order and relationships, whereas the third, is the concept of space and is applicable to points of view and frames of reference. The drawing from imagination subtest has emotional and cognitive content components. For emotions, it considers wishes, fears, frustrations, conflicts in addition to inner strengths related to resiliency. The cognitive content of the drawing from imagination subtest relates to selecting, combining, and representing objects. The predictive drawing subtest focuses on sequential order, concept of horizontality, and concept of verticality. The drawing from observation subtest focuses on the development of spatial concepts.

VALIDITY AS DETERMINED BY THE AUTHOR

1990 Manual Information

Content validity evidence was lacking in the first edition of the STD (Silver, 1990). As to criterion-related validity, the manual reported correlations of .33, .16, .37, and .29 between the three SDT subtest scores and the total score with the WISC Performance Scale. WISC verbal correlations were near zero. Also, SDT subtest scores ranged from .59, .37, .50, and .60 with WAIS. Correlations with Draw a Man Test were .75, .31, .62, and .72. Correlations with the Bender were negative. Overall, concurrent validity was mixed. As for the achievement measures correlations, they were very low which may suggest discriminate validity. Yet, with aptitude measures, correlations were too low to indicate convergence.

When evaluating the correlations of the subtests, one category stood out (Silver, 1990): Drawing from observation, which consistently received very low correlations (ranging from -.15 to .47), most of which were not significant. In addition, predictive drawing received the second lowest correlations, ranging from .16 to .36, most of which were not significant. Inconsistencies in data collection were mentioned (Silver, 1990). For example, she used the Otis Lennon Test for most children; yet, used school records for test scores of deaf and learning disabled children. Since the Otis Lennon Test was not administered to this population, their scores should have been separated out. The only group Silver (1990) separated out was a group of deaf children and she used WISC Performance Scores to correlate with the SDT.

2002 Manual Information

Silver (2002) reports that in order to collect data for reliability and validity evidence, the STD was administered to 1,399 children, adolescents, and adults. Of this sample, 849 were relatively normal or typical in development whereas 550 had brain injuries, hearing impairments, emotional disturbance, or learning disabilities. Additionally, 21 art therapists, psychologists, and classroom teachers administered the SDT. This was done in different areas throughout the United States and Canada. In the updated manual, more detailed information is provided and the studies cited are clearly delineated. Silver (2002) discussed the correlational study by Hayes (1978). A classroom teacher in a parochial school, Hayes (1978) administered the SDT to 75 children in grades one through three. She compared the STD scored to the children's SRA scores. Hayes (1978) reported significant correlations between the reading achievement scores and the drawing from imagination subtest scores. Additionally, Hayes (1978) stated that the correlations between the drawing from observation and reading scores were stronger for girls than boys in the second and third grades. The correlation between reading scores and the drawing from imagination scores were significant for third graders only. Further, correlations between predictive drawing and reading achievement were weak for first graders and not significant for children in the second and third grades. Hayes (1978) also reported that the relationship between reading scores and artistic performance on the drawing from imagination subtest was stronger for boys in first grade and stronger for girls in the second and third grades.

Anderson (2001) examined the correlation between the SDT and the Gates–MacGinitie Reading Comprehension Test with a sample of 250 students. Of this sample, 24 students volunteered to have their scores correlated. The students ranged in age from 11 to 13. Anderson (2001) found a significant relationship between the scores on both measures. "Anderson's study seem to support the validity of the SDT to assess cognitive skills considered fundamental in comprehending written languages . . . and provides interesting observations for future investigation" (Silver, 2002, p. 72).

Another study examined the correlation between the STD and SRA survey of basic skills activity. The SDT was administered to 15 students, ages 13 and 14. Silver (2002) scored the assessments. There was a significant correlation reported between the SRA scores and the total SDT scores, and two out of three of the subtests (predictive drawing and drawing from imagination). No significant correlations were found for the drawing from observation and SRA scores.

Silver (2002) reported on a study, which compared SDT scores with scores from the Metropolitan Achievement Test (MAT), which measures math and reading abilities. Forty children, in grades one through three, completed the SDT. This was correlated with their MAT scores, which were previously administered. All three subtests correlated significantly with the MAT scores. In addition, the self-image scale also correlated significantly with the MAT scores.

Correlations between the SDT and six traditional languages oriented tests of intelligence and achievements were also examined. This sample included children participating in the National Institute of Education Project. Low but significant correlations were found between the SDT and these assessments (Canadian Cognitive Abilities Test, Metropolitan Achievement Test, Otis Lennon School Ability Test, SRA, Math Achievement Test, Iowa Test of Basic Skills, and the WISC Performance IQ). Moderate correlations were found with the drawing from imagination subtest whereas the drawings from observation correlations were significant only with the Iowa Composite Test.

RELIABILITY AS DETERMINED BY THE AUTHOR

1990 Manual Information

In a test-retest study, the SDT was administered to 10 third grade children one month later. Although all the third grade students were initially evaluated, the teacher selected ten "top students across the board." This was not a random sample. Other than coming from lower income families in an urban neighborhood, demographic characteristics were not discussed. Silver (1990) included herself along with four other individuals to score the SDTs. When viewing the subtests, predictive drawing was not significantly reliable for these third grade students. Silver (1990) provided a detailed explanation of what the children did differently. The use of only ten subjects did not lend itself to strong reliability evidence. It was possible that the test may be reliable for only third grade students, not adults, hearing impaired children, or other grade levels.

Moser (1980) administered the SDT to 12 learning disabled adolescents using a one month interval. Again, demographic information was limited. Moser (1980) found that all subtests were significant.

Excluding herself from the study, Silver (1990) used four judges from the previous study to examine the reliability of the emotional projection part of the SDT. The result was not significant. She attributed this to lack of practice and misunderstanding the scoring guidelines. Silver (1990) conversed with each judge to clear up any ambiguity and the resulting correlation was significant. Therefore, training was required to make the results significant.

Using one educator, an art therapist, and a psychotherapist, all with no special training, Silver (1990) provided evidence of reliability and included herself as a rater. Correlations of the subtests ranged from .45 to .99. The emotional projection part of the test was not examined.

2002 Manual Information

In the updated manual (Silver, 2002), rater reliability was examined by seven art therapists who scored the responses of STDs by children who were participating in the National Institute of Education Project. Of the raters, four were registered art therapists and three had a masters degree in art therapy or education. Silver (2002) stated that the raters attended several training sessions. The art therapists scored the responses of six children who were selected by the school administrator for performing at least one year below grade level in reading and math. Silver (2002) reported a high degree of inter scorer reliability with .93 for predictive drawing, .92 for drawing from observation, and .98 in drawing from imagination.

In another study, six raters scored the SDT responses of 11 children with visual motor disabilities. The qualification of the raters was not discussed. It is not known if the judges attended training sessions for scoring STD. Although the coefficients for predictive drawing were not reported, Silver (2002) stated that the reliability coefficient was .852 for drawing from imagination and .944 for drawing from observation.

To examine the reliability of the self-image and emotional content scales, five raters evaluated responses to the drawing from imagination task. Four of the judges were art therapists and one was a graduate student in an art therapy program. Five SDTs were randomly selected from 15 drawings by 4 children, 5 adolescents, and 6 adults. The raters met for an hour to discuss scoring procedures. Reliability coefficients were reported to be .94 for the emotional content scale and .74 for the self-image scale.

To see if training was an issue, Silver (2002) focused on raters who had not attended a specific training on scoring the STD. A registered art therapist with no training and Silver scored 16 tenth grade students and 20 fourth grade student responses to the STD. The drawing from observation subtest for fourth graders had the lowest coefficient .45. The coefficients ranged from .45 to .86, suggesting moderate reliability. "They suggest that the scoring guidelines alone are adequate when used by a registered art therapist, and that training sessions for such examiners are unnecessary" (Silver, 2002, p. 67).

A similar study used an art therapist and Silver to score the STDs of nine hospitalized adults with mental handicaps. The coefficients ranged from .89 (drawing from observation) to .99 (predictive drawing). There is strong reliability evidence suggesting that art therapists do not need training on STD scoring procedures.

Another study centered on evaluations completed by a classroom teacher, a psychotherapist, and three art therapists. This study specifically examined the impact of the change of wording in the scoring criteria for the updated manual. The STD of 10 third grade children were scored using the new guidelines. The overall coefficient was .66, which was significant at the .01 level.

In the updated manual, test-retest reliability was examined using the scores of 10 third grade children, described as top of the class, after a one month interval. The test was administered by the children's teacher and the responses were scored by five judges, blind to the participants. Silver (2002) reported moderate correlations for the drawing from imagination subtest and for the total test. Low correlations were found in the drawing from observation. No significant correlations were found for the predictive drawing. Silver (2002) stated that this test-retest reliability underestimates the overall reliability of the STD: "the variations in retest scores suggest that the visuospatial abilities measured by the Predicted Drawing task may be unstable in this age group" (p. 70).

RESEARCH USING THE SDT

Silver (2003) compiled a cross-cultural analysis of people's cognitive abilities, emotions, and self-images in response to STD drawing tasks. She wanted to determine if cultural differences existed in scores on the STD with children, adolescents, and adults. Together, the studies do show similarities as well as differences from the American norms that Silver (2002) developed.

Hunter (1991) used the SDT in a battery of assessments to examine individual and gender differences in a population of Australian students. The population included 65 males and 128 females, aged 15–53. The study, which implemented the SDT, focused on structure of spacial thinking and problem solving. Specifically, she measured the cognitive components in the SDT. Hunter's (1991) results were significant in supporting SDT theory that verbal cognitive ability is evident in visual talents.

A group of Brazilian art therapists and psychologists translated the SDT into Portuguese and standardized it on 2,000 children, adolescents, and adults (Allessandrini, et al. 1998). The therapists also examined possible differences in scores on the SDT due to gender, grade level, and type of school (public or private). ANOVA results were presented for age and grade levels and compared to U.S. norms. Interrater reliability was reported to be strong, .94, .95., and .95 for SDT scores. Irrespective of gender, they found that cognitive scores were dependent on age and level of education. No significant differences were found in emotional content.

Dhanachitsiriphong (1999) used the SDT with a population of male adolescents in a detention agency in Thailand. Twelve boys were split between a control and experimental groups. Dhanachitsiriphong (1999) used the SDT as a pre and posttest to measure the effectiveness of a new art therapy program. The control group participated in regular center activities. Significantly higher scores were found after the conclusion of the three-month art therapy program on cognitive and emotional scores.

Kopytin (2002), a psychiatrist in St. Petersburg, Russia, translated the SDT into Russian and standardized on a representative sample of 702 children, adolescents, and adults living in Russia and Estonia. Only the scores of the Russian participants were included in the normative data. The normative sample included 642 children, adolescents, and adults. The children and adolescents ranged in age from 5 to 19 with 350 females and 294 males. The adult sample ranged in age from 19–48 with 36 women and 22 men. The SDT was administered by 11 psychologists who interpreted the results and developed the norms. Most of the psychologists attended an art therapy training program, which included a workshop on the SDT. Kopytin (2002) found that cognitive scores increased with age. In comparison with United States adult norms, no significant differences were found. They did note that

Russian children and adolescents scored higher on the predictive drawing, drawing from observation, and total test scores as compared to American children. On the other hand, Russian children's scores were lower in the drawing from imagination. No significant differences were found between children with or without language impairment. Females showed significantly more positive themes than males on the emotional content scale. Also females showed more positive self-images as compared to males, opposite of the American norms. The correlation of the SDT and the FEATS will be discussed in more detail in Chapter 16 of this book.

The SDT has been used in research studies in the United States as well. For instance, Marshall (1988) used the SDT with a population of children with learning disabilities. Specifically, she developed a program designed to promote the cognitive skills of learning disabled children. At the conclusion of the 14-week developmental program, the mean scores for the younger children (7 to 10 years of age) increased from 16.24 to 21.90 with the largest gain in the drawing form imagination task. The second group of adolescents (13-14 years of age) showed little improvement in total scores.

Henn (1990) used the STD with multiply handicapped adolescents. Specifically, Henn (1990) was interested in the impact of an integrated approach to teaching on the understanding of horizontal, vertical, and depth relationships of a group for 24 racially mixed students who ranged in age from 16 to 21. The population of students had a below average IQ. Additionally, some of these students were nonverbal. Henn (1990) and a movement therapist led the sessions. An art therapist and Henn (1990), both blind to the participants, scored the STDs. Interscorer reliability was reported to be .95 for horizontal relationships, .86 for vertical relationships, and .84 for depth relationships, generating an overall coefficient of .92. After the conclusion of the group, the post-test scores were significantly higher.

Hiscox (1990) examined the use of the SDT with a learning disabled population. Using a sample of 14 children with learning disabilities, 14 children with dyslexia, and a control group of 14 children with no known disabilities, she compared the SDT scores with scores on the California Achievement Test Verbal, Quantitative and Nonverbal Batteries (CAT). Hiscox (1990) found that SDT assesses cognitive skills not measured. Further, the results suggest that the SDT may be a useful assessment for identifying cognitive strengths in children with learning disabilities.

Foster (1990) used the SDT to measure the impact of a five-month art program that focused on visual perception, using a sample of 22 third grade public school students. At the conclusion of the group, posttest scores were higher in 19 out of the 22 students. When she compared SDT scores to scores on the Comprehensive Test of Basic Skills (CTBS), Foster (1990) found that lower scores on the SDT correlated with lower scores on the CTBS.

Additionally, Foster (1990) reported that children participating in the art program demonstrated rapid progress in reading.

DESIRABLE FEATURES

The SDT can be used with children, adults, and nonreaders. The test can be administered in group settings or individually. "Its brevity is useful for subjects with histories of limited attention span" (Horovitz, 1985, p. 44). In addition, it provided a breakdown of cognitive skills into three different areas: sequential concepts, spatial concepts, and association and formation of concepts. The latter half of the manual was devoted to scoring examples that were helpful to the administrator.

UNDESIRABLE FEATURES

Although Silver (2002) provided guidelines for scoring the SDT, additional training may be required. A particularly complicated section of the test, drawing from observation received the lowest correlation coefficients on tests of interscorer reliability; therefore, it would be better understood in the form of a lecture and practice sessions for interpretation prior to administration. Although the research studies are clearly delineated, those without a strong background in statistical analysis may find these studies confusing.

OVERALL EVALUATION

There are gender differences with respect to the SDT. Silver (2002) noted that American males drew more assaultive relationships compared to girls. Also, Silver (2002) noted that females depicted more caring relationships in the emotional content of their drawings compared to males. Kopytin (2002) found that Russian females demonstrated more positive self-images and emotional content on the SDT. Allessandrini and colleagues (1999) found that Brazilian males had higher scores in predictive drawings as compared to females. Also, Hunter (1992) found that Australian women had higher scores on the drawing from imagination and the drawing from observation subtests.

The expanded norms strengthened the confidence in the SDT and countered some of the concerns stated in the first edition of this book (Brooke, 1996) as well as those mentioned by Crehan (1989). The validity evidence for the drawing from observation subscale remains weak.

It is not certain if the SDT can be used adequately with hearing impaired populations. Eccarius (2001), an instructor in Deaf Education at the University of Nebraska-Lincoln, shared this concern, but she stated that this would be a concern for professionals or parents working with hearing impaired children. She asserted, and I agree, that trained art therapists would have little difficulty using this assessment with the hearing impaired and would find the tool clinically valuable.

I agree with previous reviewers (Crehan, 1989; Chase, 1989; and Mealor, 1989) that the SDT is a creative attempt to measure cognitive skills in a non-verbal approach. The new manual includes demographic information, which was needed to establish additional reliability and validity data for this instrument. The STD has been widely used as a pre and posttest measure. Further, it is being used not only in the United States, but abroad. It is an excellent tool for assessing children's cognitive abilities and emotional capacities. This assessment has been translated, standardized, and published in Brazil and in Russia, where art therapists are now also using and translating DRAW A STORY (DAS). Please see the next chapter for more information on the DAS.

REFERENCES

American Educational Research Association, American Psychological Association, & National Council on Measurement in Education. (1985). *Standards for educational and psychological testing.* Washington, DC: American Psychological Association.

Allessandrini, C.D., Duarte, J.L., Dupas, M.A., Bianco, M.R. (1998). SDT: The Brazilian standardization of the Silver Drawing Test of Cognition and Emotion. *Art Therapy: Journal of the American Art Therapy Association, 15*(2), 107–115.

Anderson, V. (2001). *A study of the correlations between the SDT Drawing from Imagination Subtest and the Gates-MacGinitie Reading Comprehension Test with middle school students.* Unpublished masters' degree thesis, MCP Hahnemann University, Philadelphia.

Brooke, S.L. (1996). *A therapist's guide to art therapy assessments: Tools of the trade.* Springfield, IL: Charles C Thomas Publishers.

Chase, C.I. (1989). Review of the Silver Drawing Test of Cognitive and Creative Skills. *Mental Measurements 1989 book.* (10: 745). Lincoln, NE: Burrs Institute of Mental Measurements.

Crehan, K.D. (1989). Review of the Silver Drawing Test of Cognitive Skills and Adjustment. *Mental Measurements 1989 book.* (10 333). Lincoln, NE: Burrs Institute of Mental Measurements.

Dhanachitsiriphong, P. (1999). *The effects of art therapy and rational art therapy on cognition and emotion development of male adolescents in Barn Katrina Training School of the Central Observation and Protection Center.* Unpublished thesis, Burapha University, Thailand.

Eccarius, M. (2001; Summer). Three art assessments: The Silver Drawing Test of Cognition and Emotion; Draw a Story; Screening for Depression: and Stimulus Drawings and Techniques. *Volta Review, 103*(3), 203–205.

Foster, E. (1990). *Art therapy conference follow-up project.* Unpublished manuscript, Kearney State College, Kearney, NE.

Hayes, K. (1978). *The relationship between drawing ability and reading scores.* Unpublished master's thesis, Buffalo State College, New York.

Henn, K. (1990). *The effects of an integrated arts curriculum on the representation of spatial relationships.* Unpublished master's thesis, Buffalo State College, New York.

Hiscox, A.R. (1990). *An alternative to language oriented IQ tests for learning disabled children.* Unpublished master's thesis, College of Notre Dame, Belmont, California.

Horovitz, E.G. (1985; March). Silver Drawing Test of Cognitive and Creative Skills. *Art Therapy, March,* p. 44.

Hunter, G. (1992). *An examination of some individual differences in information process, personality, and motivation with respect to some dimension of spatial thinking or problem solve in TAFE students.* Unpublished thesis, The University of New England, School of Professional Studies, Arnidale, Australia.

Kopytin, A. (2002). The Silver Drawing Test of Cognition and Emotion: Standardization in Russia. *American Journal of Art Therapy, 40,* 223–237.

Marshall, S.B. (1988). *The use of art therapy to foster cognitive skills with learning disabled children.* Unpublished master's thesis, Pratt Institute, School for Arts and Design, Brooklyn, New York.

Mealor, D.J. (1989). Review of the Silver Drawing Test of Cognitive and Creative Skills. *Mental Measurements 1989 book 10.* 10:747). Lincoln, NE: Burrs Institute of Mental Measurements.

Moser, J. (1980). *Drawing and painting and learning disabilities.* Unpublished Doctoral dissertation, New York University, New York.

Silver, R. (1990). *Silver Drawing Test of Cognitive Skills and Adjustment.* Sarasota, FL: Ablin Press.

Silver, R. (2002). *Three Art Assessments: The Silver Drawing Test of Cognition and Emotion; Draw a Story: Screening for Depression; and Stimulus Drawing and Techniques.* New York: Brunner-Routledge.

Silver, R. (2003). Cultural differences and similarities in responses to the Silver Drawing Test in the USA, Brazil, Russia, Estonia, Thailand, and Australia. *Art Therapy: Journal of the American Art Therapy Association, 20*(1), 16-20.

Silver, R. (2004). Personal communication on February 12, 2004.

Chapter 10

DRAW A STORY TEST

TITLE: Draw a Story Test (DAS)
AGE: Ages five and over
YEAR: 2002
PURPOSE: designed to screen for depression
SCORES: scores are rated on a 5-point Likert scale with 1 representing highly negative themes and 5 representing highly positive themes. Lower scores indicate a higher risk for depression.
MANUAL: manual (315 pages); profile (27 pages); DAS reliability data and validity data (9 pages)
TIME LIMIT: 10-20 minutes for administration
COST: $34.95 for book containing all three of Silver's assessments (SDT; DAS; SDT); in *Three Art Assessments* (Silver, 2002)
Free download from
www.routledge-ny.com/testmaterials.cfm
AUTHOR: Silver, Rawley; Rawled@aol.com
PUBLISHER: Brunner-Routledge, 29 West 35th Street, New York, NY 10001

INTRODUCTION

When Silver (2002) was creating the norms for the STD, she was curious about whether the drawing from imagination subtask could be used as a screen for depression. In her work with children, she noted some cases where children drew images of suicide or annihilation.

Because childhood depression can be masked by fantasies about death or violence, Draw A Story began as an attempt to screen for depression. It is based on the premise that strongly negative or morbid responses to the drawing task, particularly by children, may reflect depressive illness, and that follow up would be appropriate. (Silver, 2002, p. 133)

Silver (2002) stated that art therapists have used the DAS with children who were abused, brain injured, depressed, or emotionally disturbed. Further, it was used with nonclinical populations of children and adults.

PURPOSE AND RECOMMENDED USE

The primary purpose of the DAS is to screen for depression. Silver (2002) commented that the DAS emerged out of her work with children and the STD. The DAS is recommended for children or adolescents considered at risk for depression.

DIMENSIONS THAT THE TEST PURPORTS TO MEASURE

The DAS measures negative and positive themes in an artist's response to selecting images. Specifically, Silver (2002) reported that the DAS assesses the emotional content of the responses to the drawing task as opposed to their formal pictorial attributes. Her reliability and validity studies were designed to address whether strongly negative emotional content is linked to depression.

ADMINISTRATION

With the DAS, the artist is asked to choose two subjects from an array of stimulus drawings, similar to the drawing from imagination task on the STD, and then imagine something happening between the images they select. Silver (2004) noted that the themes in an artist's response to the DAS set of stimulus drawings differs from the set used in the SDT. The artist will use these images to create a story. When the drawing is complete, the administrator will ask the artist to describe the story.

NORM GROUPS

Silver (2002) reported that 1,028 children, adolescents, and adults completed the DAS. Art therapists volunteered to administer the DAS. The artist population included 446 people with no known disability and 449 people with emotional disturbances, clinical depression, delinquency, or learning disabilities. The participants came from several states throughout the country. Additionally, Silver (2004) noted that most of the DAS responses can be found in the archives of the American Art Therapy Association and includes 1,000 DAS drawings.

INTERPRETATION OF SCORES

Responses to the task are rated on a 5-point Likert scale. A score of one point indicates strongly negative themes or fantasies about the images selected. With a score of one, subjects are depicted as sad, helpless, suicidal, or in life-threatening situations. According to Silver (2002), "this score is based on definitions and observations of depressive illness by clinicians" (p. 161). A score of two points is used for moderately negative images about the subjects or the relationships portrayed. For a score of three points, the drawing contains responses that are both positive and negative, ambivalent, ambiguous or unemotional. The score of four points indicates moderately positive themes. A score of five points, according to Silver (2002), is used for drawings showing strongly positive themes or fantasies of the images or relationships depicted. The lower the score, the higher the risk of depression.

SOURCE OF ITEMS

There are 14 images from which an artist can select two and create a response to the DAS. There are two forms for the DAS. Form A has 14 stimulus drawings that were selected from the SDT because they elicited negative themes. Form B offsets the negativity of Form A. For research purposes, Form A should be used as the pretest/posttest measure (Silver, 2002). Form B can be used through the course of the therapeutic relationship in order to clarify responses or for diagnostic purposes.

The DAS is based on DSM-IV criteria for depressive illness: feelings of sadness, worthlessness, and hopelessness. Recurrent thoughts of death or suicide are also characteristic of depression. Further, Silver (2002) based her work on research supporting the prevalence of violence, aggressive behavior, as well as death fantasies in depressed children (McKnew, Cytryn, and

Yahries, 1983). Further, Wadeson (1980), who wrote the forward to the first edition of this book (Brooke, 1996), noted that depressed patients will use less color, invest less effort, and depict less affect or more depressive affect, even to the point of harming others in their drawings. Further, Gantt (1990) observed that artists diagnosed with depression differed from other diagnostic groups in their representation of problem-solving skill and use of logic.

RELIABILTY AS DETERMINED BY THE AUTHOR

Scorer reliability was measured using Form A of 20 unidentified responses to the DAS. Three registered art therapists scored these assessments blindly and independently. According to Silver (2002), the drawings were randomly selected from five clinical and nonclinical groups of children and adolescents. The art therapists attended a one-hour meeting to discuss the scoring procedures. Silver (2002) reported the correlations significant at the point .001 level: .81 Judges A & B; .80 Judges A & C, and .82 Judges B and C.

Test-retest reliability was measured with a group of 24 third grade students using Form A. The qualifications of the administrators were not discussed. Levels of significance and coefficients were not reported, but Silver (2002) did state that of the first 12 students pretested, 7 received the same scores on the posttest after a one-month interval. After a two-year interval, the other 12 children were posttested and 11 drawings received the same score. This suggests reliability of the DAS over longer periods of time with children. Based on these reliability studies, Silver (2002) reported that there is a link between depressive illness and strongly negative responses.

> Although strongly negative responses do not necessarily indicate depression and, conversely, positive responses do not exclude depression, they suggest that a child or adolescent scoring 1 point may be at risk for depression. The findings also indicated that negative feelings persisted over time, suggesting that they reflected characteristic attitudes rather than passing moods. (Silver, 2002, 163)

Silver (2002) noted that many of the learning disabled students scored "1" and no significant differences emerged between their scores and those diagnosed with depression.

In another study of test-retest reliability, three registered art therapists administered Form A of the DAS to a group of children and adults. After a one-week interval, one art therapist administered the DAS to eight children with emotional disturbance. No time interval was reported for the second art therapist, who administered the DAS to six mentally disturbed adolescents.

The third art therapist administered the DAS to 17 adults who volunteered to participate. Silver (2002) combined the numbers and reported a significant correlation (.70262, p < 0.000) for the 31 subjects. Correlation for the eight children was reported (0.93277, p < 0.000) and for the adolescents and adults combined (.45095, p < .05).

The test-retest reliability for Form B was also examined using a sample of 33 children, adolescents, and adults. The sample included normal individuals and those previously diagnosed as depressed, emotionally disturbed, attention deficit, and learning disabled. Two judges rated the drawings independently. Inter-scorer correlations were significant (.80806, p < 0.000).

Form B was examined again using a sample of 34 children, adolescents, and adults. Seventeen graduate art therapy students administered and scored the DAS. The inter-scorer reliability was .59 (children), .63 (adolescents), and .60 (adults). No other demographic information on the sample was presented.

VALIDITY AS DETERMINED BY THE AUTHOR

Silver's (2002) manual reports on three studies, which examined the validity of the DAS as a screen for depression. In the first study, 254 children and adolescents, ranging in age from 8 to 21, were administered the SDT. From this study, the 14 stimulus drawings for the DAS were selected. Of the sample, 21 had clinical depression, 61 had emotional disturbances with nondepressive symptoms, 31 had learning disabilities, and 24 were nondepressed children who responded to the drawing from imagination task from the SDT. Nineteen art therapists, counselors, and teachers volunteered to administer and/or score the drawings. Silver (2002) reported that 56% of the participants with depression responded with strongly negative themes compared to 11% of the normal participants, 21% of the mentally disturbed, and 32% of the learning disabled participants. Using a chi-square analysis, significantly more participants with depression scored one point compared to those who were not diagnosed with depression (27.63, p. < .001). The proportion of participants with depression scoring one point was not significantly greater than the participants with learning disabilities scoring one point (3.269, p < .05). Further testing with these two populations using the DAS is needed.

In a second study, 24 art therapists, counselors, and teachers volunteered to administer and score the DAS from a population of 350 children and adolescents. Of this sample, 35 children and adolescents were diagnosed with depression, 15 adults had depression, 117 were normal children and adolescents, 74 children and adolescents had emotional disturbance with nondepressive symptoms, 64 adolescents had learning disabilities, 18 children and adolescents had hearing impairment, and 27 were older adults. Silver (2002) found that 63% of the children and adolescents with depression responded with strongly negative themes (a score of 1 point) compared to 10% of the nondepressed children and adolescents. The results were significant at the .0005 level using a chi-square analysis. The results were also significant compared to learning disabled, emotionally disturbed, hearing impaired, and adult populations. Silver (2002) concluded that the DAS could be a useful first step in identifying some, but not all children and adolescents with depression. Additionally, Silver (2002) found that the DAS did not significantly discriminate adults with depression.

The third DAS study examined age and gender differences in response to the drawing task. The depressed sample included patients hospitalized for depression, 18 females aged 12–69, and 23 males, aged 17–53. The nondepressed sample came from a nursing home and also included undergraduate university students (34 females, 19–72 and 26 males, 20–77). It is not clear if this sample was screened for depression. Using an analysis of variance for depression and the use of space and detail, no significant differences emerged for the depressed groups. There were gender differences in that depressed females used significantly less detail than depressed males.

It seems that the use of the DAS as a screen for depression with adolescents and adults is unclear. Silver (2002) admitted that combining the adult and adolescent samples may have exacerbated the issue. Borderline results were found with depressed men and the depiction of negative themes whereas no significant differences were found with the depressed women and the DAS. Silver (2002) concluded that depression in women may be associated with ambivalent or ambiguous themes. I tend to agree from my work with sexual abuse survivors who were previously diagnosed as clinically depressed (Brooke, 1997). They tended to have these ambivalent themes in their artwork, as seen in the case study in Chapter 19 of this book, as well as verbalizing ambiguous or ambivalent content.

RESEARCH USING THE TEST

Silver outlined the goals of the DAS as follows: (1) to identify depressed individuals; (2) to provide access for therapeutic dialogue; and (3) to increase understanding of depressive illness. Silver selected 14 stimulus drawings from 65 drawings used in two previous instruments. How the drawings were selected and who was involved in the selection process remained unclear.

As with the Drawing from Imagination subtest of the SDT, the participant was asked to select two images and make a drawing that tells a story for the DAS. Silver (1988) reported that group and individual administration was possible with this test. Inter-scorer reliability was reported to be .80 which was significant at the .001 level. Silver (1988) reported that the DAS was a reliable measure yet did not present statistical information. Out of a class of 24 third grade students, she chose 12 to be retested since they responded with negative fantasies. A few questions arose when reading the section on reliability. Why not retest the entire group? How long was the retest interval? What are the demographic characteristics of this population?

Silver (1988) conducted a final study to determine if the DAS can be used as a screening device for depression. A score of one point on the DAS indicated strongly negative themes such as hopelessness and sadness. Silver's (1988) hypothesis was that depressed individuals would score one point on the DAS. Although the participants were not randomly selected, Silver (1988) did include some demographic information. When she tested her hypothesis, she found that only depressed children and adolescents typically scored one point. The results were not significant for depressed adults.

Silver (2002) included a discussion of several research studies that utilized the DAS. This assessment was used with clinical and nonclinical populations as well as children, adolescents, and adults.

Using Form A, a sample of 95 adolescents (13–17), diagnosed as emotionally disturbed completed the DAS. This was compared to a control sample of 68 nondisturbed adolescents. The four subgroups included: 60 boys with disturbances, 35 girls with disturbances, 42 control girls, and 26 control boys. Thirteen art therapists or teachers administered the DAS to the experimental group while six art therapists or teachers administered the DAS to the control groups. The adolescents in the control group came from four public schools and one private school. There were significant differences between the groups in that few emotionally disturbed adolescents drew pictures with positive themes. The group of normal girls had the most positive scores (43%) followed by the boys with disturbances (26%), normal boys (16%), and the girls with disturbances (14%). In negative responses to the DAS, boys in the control group had most of the extreme negative scores.

Another study focused on age and gender differences in attitudes toward self and others. DAS drawings from 360 subjects (children, adolescents, and adults) were separated into drawings about solitary objects and drawings about relationships. The participant demographics were clearly delineated by gender and age group. They were assigned to age and gender groups and scored on the rating scale. The researcher hypothesized that males would focus on independence and competition and females would center on relationships and caring for others. For the sample of 56 children, 32 were classified as emotionally disturbed or learning disabled, 14 were hospitalized as clinically depressed, and 9 were considered normal. Of the 147 younger adolescents (13-16), 13 were hospitalized with depression, 78 had been designed as emotionally disturbed or learning disabled, and 56 were not impaired. Of the 68 older adolescents (17–19), 1 was hospitalized for clinical depression, 27 diagnosed as emotionally disturbed or learning disabled, and 40 were not impaired. Of the sample of 79 adults (21–64), 7 were hospitalized women with depression, 53 nondepressed women, and 19 were men. Thirteen art therapists in 10 different states administered the DAS. There were no significant differences found in the drawings about solitary subjects. In the drawing about relationships, there were significant gender differences with males responses tending to be more negative. More positive relationships appeared in the drawings by older women than any other age or gender group. More adolescent girls than any other female age group drew images that were sad, helpless, or drew isolated subjects which earned a score of one. Silver (2002) concluded that gender differences emerged with respect to the emotional content of the drawings. Overall, males portrayed negative relationships and females positive relationships. Further, females tend to focus on relationships and responsibility toward others whereas males focused in independence and detachment.

Turner (1993) used the DAS as a screening device for abused adolescents. This was one of a battery of assessments used to gather information on the client's abuse history. According to Silver, "She [Turner] found it useful in assessing the extent of abuse, the meaning attached to abuse, and the effects of abuse on her clients' defenses, coping skills, sense of self, relationships, and world view" (pp. 180–181). The DAS Form A was the last assessment Turner (1993) used in the battery of assessments given to her clients. The DAS provided information about self-protective abilities, trust, self-value, and community attachments. These topics were discussed in the assessment interviews.

Wilson (1993), a registered art therapist, used the DAS Form A with a population of brain injured people. The participants were inpatients and outpatients of a facility dealing with brain injuries resulting from accidents, assaults, strokes, or aneurysms. Wilson (1993) was interested in her patient's ability to combine subjects, organize images, establish relationships, and problem solve. The DAS was helpful in revealing inner emotional states and revealed low self-esteem, depression, and adjustment concerns with respect to their disability. In an earlier study, Wilson (1990) used the DAS with adolescents who had suicidal ideation or attempted suicide. She used this as a pre and posttest measure to determine the image of changes during the hospitalization for depression and suicide. Twelve out of 13 adolescents drew pictures about negative or frightening events. Only one DAS had a positive theme. Wilson (1990) used the DAS to determine her client's emotional state and perception of their current situation.

In 1994, Dunn-Snow, a board certified registered art therapist, used Form

A of the DAS to determine the needs of students diagnosed with severe emotional disturbance in public school settings. "I have found the Silver Draw-A-Story Assessment to be a beneficial art therapy tool for assessing needs and promoting the creative and therapeutic process in my work as an art therapist with severely emotionally disturbed students in both elementary and secondary grades in a large urban school district" (Dunn-Snow, 1994, p. 35). In one case study, strongly negative themes emerged which correlated with this student's high school records for depression. She varied the instructions of the DAS to use it as a group therapeutic technique to create structure and promote relationship building. Dunn-Snow (1994) found that the use of the assessment was helpful in working with anxious students by providing them with structured art tasks. Dunn-Snow (1994) discussed her case approaches and provided illustrations.

Brandt (1995) used the DAS with depressed adolescents, those who committed sex offenses, and typical adolescents. She found that adolescent males committing sex offenses were less likely to be depressed or perceive themselves or their environment negatively through the responses on the DAS.

In 1995, Silver and Ellison conducted a study using the DAS with delinquent adolescents. Specifically, they wanted to see the benefits of using the DAS to provide a rapid assessment of incarcerated males. It was hoped that the DAS would provide more accurate and timely referrals for mental health services. Using Form B, the DAS was administered to 53 boys ranging in age from 13 to 18 in a residential detention facility, who identified their self-images after responding. Ellison administered the DAS and scored them. Silver scored the same drawings but was blind to the artists who drew them. Interrater reliability was checked using a third independent, and blind rater. Further, 10 of the 53 drawings were selected at random and scored by three art therapists and five social workers. Interscorer agreements ranged from 72% to 93% with the higher ratings occurring among the art therapists. Silver (2002) concluded that although discussing procedures helps with the scoring of the DAS, it is not essential. Discussions can be bypassed to expedite screening in cases where time is of the essence. The article also presents six case studies, which assist practitioners in discovering the underlying dynamics of conduct disordered individuals.

Building on this study, Silver (1996) examined gender differences in the fantasies of adolescents who were delinquent and those were not delinquent. The sample included 64 adolescents in a detention center and 74 normal students attending schools along the East Coast. This included 82 males (53 were delinquent, 29 were controls) and 56 females (11 were delinquent, and 45 were controls). The drawing responses were divided into four groups: gender, delinquency, drawings about solitary objects, and drawings about relationships. No significant differences were found with respect to gender or delinquency and self-image scores. Significant gender differences occurred in drawings of both solitary and assaultive content. Males significantly drew more pictures about assaultive relationships. Females significantly drew more pictures of solitary subjects as compared to males. Further, control participants significantly drew more solitary objects than did the delinquent participants.

DESIRABLE FEATURES

There are several case examples for each of the five-point rating criteria. The test is easy to administer and does not require much time for completion. The projective nature of this assessment has the potential to yield affective information about the artist's emotional state. It is always interesting to see how other researchers and therapists use an assessment, and Silver (2002) included such research right in the test manual.

UNDESIRABLE FEATURES

The assessment does not utilize color, which may be a useful indicator of depression (Wadeson, 1980; Gantt, 1998). It would be helpful if a rating scale could be created, if not by Silver then another researcher, to discuss other characteristics such as line pressure and quality, use of space, and possibly incorporate the use of color. Learning disabled students seem to score low on this assessment, resembling students who are depressed. Further research is needed to ascertain if the DAS can be used reliably with learning disabled people.

OVERALL EVALUATION

This is an interesting assessment, which potentially yields information about the artist's affective state. Interscorer reliability is high for art therapists. Some training may be required for others outside of the field of art therapy to reliably score the DAS.

Future research may want to focus using the DAS with an assessment of emotional intelligence. Goleman (1995) describes emotional intelligence as the ability to monitor one's own and others' emotions, to make distinctions among them, and to use the information as a reference to guide behavior. Typically, people with low emotional intelligence suffer from anxiety and depression.

The validity evidence suggests that it may be a screen for depression for children. Additional research is needed to state the DAS accurately screens for depression in adolescents or adults. It would be interesting to see more research with these populations, especially, to see the relationship between women with depression and the occurrence with ambivalent and ambiguous themes. Although some researchers have used the DAS (Cohene & Cohene, 1989) with hearing impaired children, additional research is needed with this population as well.

REFERENCES

Brandt, M. (1995). *Visual stories: A comparison study utilizing the Silver art therapy assessment with adolescent sex offenders.* Unpublished master's thesis. Ursuline College, Pepper Pike, Ohio.

Brooke, S.L. (1996). *Tools of the trade: A therapist's guide to art therapy assessments.* Springfield, IL: Charles C Thomas Publishers.

Brooke, S.L. (1997). *Art therapy with sexual abuse survivors.* Springfield, IL: Charles C Thomas, Publisher.

Cohene, S. & Cohene, L.S. (1989). Art therapy and writing with deaf children. *Journal of Independent Social Work, 42*(2), 21–46.

Dunn-Snow, P. (1994). Adapting the Silver Draw A story Assessment: Art therapy Techniques with children and adolescents. *American Journal of Art Therapy, 33,* 35–36.

Gantt, L. (1998). A discussion of art therapy as a science. *Art Therapy: Journal of the American Art Therapy Association, 15*(1): 3–12.

Goleman, D. (1995). *Emotional intelligence.* New York: Bantam Books.

McKnew, H., Cytryn, L., & Yahries, H. (1983). *Why isn't Johnny crying?* New York: Norton.

Silver, R. (1988). *Draw-a-Story: Screening for depression and emotional needs.* Mamaroneck, NY: Abalone Press.

Silver, R. (1996). Sex differences in the solitary and assaultive fantasies of Delinquents and nondeliquent adolescents. *Adolescence, 31*(123), 543–552.

Silver, R. (2002). *Three Art Assessments: The Silver Drawing Test of Cognition and Emotion; Draw a Story: Screening for Depression; and Stimulus Drawing and Techniques.* New York: Brunner-Routledge.

Silver, R. (2004). Personal communication on February 12, 2004.

Silver, R., & Ellison, J. (1995). Identifying and assessing self-images in drawings by delinquent adolescents. *The Arts in Psychotherapy, 22*(4), 339–352, ERIC EJ: 545–763.

Turner, C. (1993). *The Draw S Story in assessment of abuse.* Preconference course at the 1993 Conference of the American Art Therapy Association, Atlanta, GA.

Wadeson, H. (1980). *Art psychotherapy.* New York: NY: John Wiley & Sons.

Wilson, M.F. (1993). *Assessment of brain injury patients with the Draw A Story Instrument.*

Preconference course presentation at the 1993 Conference of the American Art Therapy Association, Atlanta, GA.

Wilson, M.F. (1990). *Art therapy as an adjective treatment modality with depressed hospitalized adolescents.* Unpublished master's degree thesis, Ursuline College, Pepper Pike, Ohio.

Chapter 11

DRAW A PERSON TEST

TITLE: Draw a Person Test: Screening Procedure for Emotional Disturbance (DAP: SPED)

AGE: For children and adolescents (6 to 17 years)

YEAR: 1991

PURPOSE: designed to identify individuals who have emotional problems and are in need of further evaluation

SCORES: yields a standard score, which is used to determine if further assessment is (1) not indicated, (2) indicated, or (3) strongly indicated

MANUAL: manual (71 pages); illustrations (14 pages); profile (4 pages); reliability data (2 pages); validity data (5 pages)

TIME LIMIT: maximum time limit of 15 minutes for administration

COST: $45.00 for testing manual; $40.00 for (50) record forms; $99.00 for complete kit

http://www.proedinc.com/store/index.php?mode=product_detail&id=10695

AUTHOR: Naglieri, Jack A., McNeish, Timothy J., and Bardos, Achilles N.

PUBLISHER: PRO-ED, 8700 Shoal Creek Boulevard, Austin, TX, 78758-6897.

INTRODUCTION

The Draw a Person Screening Procedure for Emotional Disturbance (DAP: SPED; Naglieri, et al. 1991) was developed to serve as an aid in the identification of children or adolescents who may be behaviorally or emotionally disordered. The authors of the DAP: SPED designed a quantitative scoring system that would distinguish between behaviorally disordered and normal populations. In addition, the instrument ensued from the Draw A Person: A Quantitative Scoring System (DAP: QSS; Naglieri, 1988), which assessed cognition. Using the DAP: SPED, emotional status and cognitive development can be assessed.

PURPOSE AND RECOMMENDED USE

The DAP: SPED was planned as a screening procedure used to identify individuals in need of evaluation for emotional problems. The authors reported that the test may be useful in identifying children who suffer from behavioral problems. Additionally, school counselors may use the instrument to identify students in need of individual or group counseling. The authors suggested that the DAP: SPED can be incorporated into the regular psychoeducational assessment battery. Further the DAP: SPED may be used during initial interviews or initial family assessments. The authors recommended that the DAP: SPED be followed by additional testing and/or referrals to professional agencies.

DIMENSIONS THAT THE TEST PURPORTS TO MEASURE

The scores of the DAP: SPED were grouped into three categories based on need of additional assessment that (1) is not indicated, (2) is indicated, or (3) is strongly indicated. For example, if a child received a score of less than 55 points, further evaluation for emotional problems was not indicated. If a child received a score of 55 to 64, additional evaluation was indicated. Should a child receive a score of 65 or above, further evaluation was strongly indicated. It was not clear how these cutoff scores were determined. The authors recommended that the cutoff scores should not be rigidly applied.

> Additionally, because we recognize the limitations of any screening approach, we suggest that the users may cautiously apply other criteria depending upon their setting and goals. When doing so, the nature of the DAP: SPED as a screening instrument and the issues involved with setting a cutoff score should be carefully considered. (Naglieri et al., 1991, p. 63)

Forms for rating the cognitive development of the client were included in a separate assessment (DAP: QSS, Naglieri, 1988). The same drawings for the DAP: SPED can be used to rate cognitive development. For additional information on scoring cognition, please refer to the DAP: QSS (Naglieri, 1988).

ADMINISTRATION

The authors required users of the DAP: SPED to have training and experience in test theory and development, including individual and group assessment procedures. Although qualifications and titles vary from state to state, the authors stated that psychologists, school psychologists, counselors, diagnosticians, behavior specialists, special educational personnel, learning specialists, speech and language specialists, rehabilitation professions, physicians, and social workers have the training to administer, score and interpret the DAP: SPED.

The DAP: SPED required strict adherence to administration guidelines. The examiner should allow a maximum of five minutes for completion of each drawing. Should the individual finish before five minutes, the examiner should proceed to the next drawing. The following directions were outlined for individual administration:

> I'd like you to draw some pictures for me. First I'd like you to draw a picture of a man. Make the very best picture you can. Take your time and work very carefully, and I'll tell you when to stop. Remember, be sure to draw the whole man. Please begin. (Allow five minutes.)

> This time I want you to draw a picture of a woman. Make the very best picture you can. Take your time and work very carefully, and I'll tell you when to stop. Be sure to draw the whole woman. Please begin. (Allow five minutes.)

> Now I'd like you to draw a picture of yourself. Be sure to draw the very best picture you can. Take your time and work very carefully, and I'll tell you when to stop. Be sure to draw your whole self. Please begin.

The directions for group administration were similar and included the same time constraints. Each examinee should have a pencil with an eraser and a DAP: SPED Record Form. The examiner was responsible for completing the demographic information on the front of the Record Form.

NORM GROUPS

The DAP: SPED standardization sample was drawn from a population of 4,468 children aged 5 to 17 years. They were the same individuals used to standardize the DAP: QSS (Naglieri, 1988). Using the 1980 census data as a guide, a sample representative of the population in terms of age, gender, geographic, race, socioeconomic status, and ethnicity was identified. The authors provided tables on the demographic characteristics of the samples including breakdowns by age, gender, geographic region, etc. The authors did an excellent job of providing information on the standardization sample. The resulting sample included 2,260 students from 6 to 17 years of age.

INTERPRETATION OF SCORES

The scoring system was comprised of two types of items. First, the DAP: SPED included items dealing with figure dimensions. Templates were used for scoring these items. Three sets of three templates, one for each age group 6 to 8, 9 to 12, and 13 to 17 years, were used for items one through eight. The templates were used to determine the size of the figure, the slant of the figure, and placement on the page. The manual contained clear directions and illustrations that aided in the scoring of these items.

The second group of items dealt with rating the content of the drawing to detect items such as shading, frowning mouth, and erasures. One point was given for each item that met the criteria outlined in the manual. For instance, a baseline was scored if the child drew a ground line, and grass. The manual included detailed descriptions of the criteria considered.

SOURCE OF ITEMS

Item development contained an exhaustive review of the literature on indicators of emotional disturbance. Additionally, items were considered indicators if they occurred infrequently in normal populations and showed appropriate psychometric properties. Items were initially categorized by figure size, placement on the page, stance, integrations, omissions, shading, and more. Independent raters were used to review the items, modify them, and eliminate ambiguities in the scoring system. Following a pilot study, the authors found that the DAP: SPED had good interrater and intrarater reliability. In addition, it was an effective device for discriminating normal from emotionally disturbed populations.

VALIDITY AS DETERMINED BY THE AUTHORS

The discriminant validity of the DAP: SPED was examined with a group of 81 students placed in a special educational setting matched to 81 well-adjusted students from the standardization sample. Every special education student was diagnosed as having a severe behavioral handicap, which included children with learning disabilities and emotional problems. The DAP:

SPED significantly discriminated between the two groups.

Another study examined 49 adolescents (16 females and 33 males) attending a psychiatric residential treatment facility for the seriously emotionally disturbed. More than 85% of the sample was labeled as conduct disordered. The sample was matched to the standardization sample based on age, gender, race, and geographic region. All students were administered the DAP: SPED in a group setting. Again, the authors found that the assessment significantly discriminated between the two groups in that the residential students earned higher scores.

A third study involved 58 children and adolescents (8 females and 50 males) in special education placements. This sample was predominantly white and was matched according to age, gender, race, and geographic region. The special education group earned significantly higher scores on the DAP: SPED than the standard group. The results again demonstrated the discriminant validity of the DAP: SPED.

In a fourth study, 54 children and adolescents attending a day treatment facility for the emotionally disturbed were matched to the standardization sample. Naglieri and Pfeiffer (1992) found that the day treatment individuals earned significantly higher scores on the DAP: SPED than the standardization sample. "The present findings, therefore, suggest that the DAP: SPED system, because of its objective and uniform scoring rules, nationally representative standardization sample, and good reliability, may be relatively more useful for evaluating human figure drawings and may be shown to hold promise as a screening test" (Naglieri & Pfeiffer, 1992, p. 158).

Although some human figure drawing tests have been used as indicators of intelligence, the authors sought to prove that the DAP: SPED was unrelated to intellectual functioning. Using the MAT-SF (Matrix Anologies Test–Short Form) test (Naglieri, 1985) scores of the standardization sample, the authors found very low, nonsignificant correlations with the DAP: SPED. The MAT-SF test, a nonverbal test, used the progressive matrix format to measure intelligence.

The authors examined the standardization sample for cultural differences. No significant differences were found between black and white students. Additionally, no differences were found between Hispanic and non-Hispanic students. "These findings, like the analyses of race differences, however should be considered tentative until additional investigations are conducted" (Naglieri et al., 1991, p. 20).

RELIABILITY AS DETERMINED BY THE AUTHORS

Using the scores obtained from the standardization sample, the authors provided internal consistency and standard errors of measurement for each age group. They found that the DAP: SPED had an appropriate level of internal reliability for screening purposes (range of .67 to .78).

An earlier scoring system was used to determine interrater and intrarater reliability data. Twenty-five drawings were scored two times by the same rater, and then the drawings were scored by different raters. The qualifications of the raters were not discussed. Interrater reliability was reported to be .91 and intrarater reliability was reported to be .94. Another study examined the interrater reliability of the DAP: SPED. Interrater reliability was reported to be .84 and intrarater reliability, using a one month interval, was reported to be .83.

A sample of 67 students attending a school for learning problems (learning disabilities, emotional, behavioral problems, and brain injury) were used to examine the stability of the DAP: SPED. Other demographic characteristics of the sample were not discussed. Using a one-week interval, no significant differences in scores were found, providing some support for the stability of the DAP: SPED.

RESEARCH USING THE DAP

Much of the research conducted to date was on the DAP: QSS. Since the DAP: SPED stated that the drawings obtained can be used to determine cognitive functions, research on the DAP: QSS will be briefly reviewed. Neisworth and Butler (1990) wrote a test review on the DAP: QSS. They stated that the manual was comprehensive, clear, and concise. Administration and interpretation guidelines were well-outlined. "The inclusion of the self-instruction competency test is an excellent way to learn how to administer the DAP and to be assured that when one is scoring the test, the best possible results will be obtained" (Neisworth & Butler, 1990, p. 190). The scoring system covered detail, proportion, and parts of the body. As with the DAP: SPED, raw scores were converted to standard scores. The manual used the same normative sample as the DAP: SPED. Test-retest reliability ranged from .60 to .89 for the total score and from .58 to .70 for individual scores. Interrater reliability was reported to be .86 to .95. Intrarater reliability ranged from .89 to .98. Construct validity was provided in that children's scores increased with age. Concurrent validity evidence was provided by comparing the assessment to the Goodenough-Harris scoring system (r = .77). Since the DAP correlated higher with the MAT-SF than with the MAS math and reading, the reviewers concluded that the DAP was measuring something other than achievement. Other studies found no scoring differences across race or gender. Although the reviewers found the DAP: QSS an improvement over other assessments, they stated that "construct validity is arguable and treatment utility is questionable" (Neisworth & Butler, 1990, p. 194).

Kamphause and Pleiss (1991) reached a similar conclusion when reviewing the DAP: QSS. "While the DAP is the best drawing technique available, its concurrent validly evidence does not support the use of such instruments as measures on intelligence" (p. 395). The authors stressed that the DAP: QSS was not a valid or reliable measure of intelligence or a screener for intelligence. Motta and colleagues (1993) agreed that the DAP: QSS offered little evidence in support of concurrent and predictive validity. For additional information on the DAP: QSS, please refer to the following authors (Naglieri, 1988; Prewett et al., 1989; Wisniewski & Naglieri, 1989).

Naglieri (1993) responded to these authors by stating that Motta et al. (1993) "have missed the point that DAP: SPED offers a significant improvement in the use of the draw a person technique as a means of evaluating the presence of emotional problems" (p. 171). Further, Naglieri (1993) argued that simple behavioral observations were not sufficient to correctly classify students. In support of Naglieri (1993), Bardos (1993) contended that Motta et al. (1993) neglected to comment on the extensive and representative standardization sample used in the DAP: SPED. Additionally, Bardos (1993) asserted that it was valid to investigate previously labeled, emotionally disturbed children. This was done to provide discriminant validity evidence. "Could it be possible that some of them find it impossible or extremely difficult to conduct a behavioral assessment for every student in their system as the authors recommend" (Bardos, 1993, p. 180)?

Over the years, there has been much controversy concerning the validity and reliability of human figure drawing tests. Motta and colleagues (1993) reviewed the DAP: SPED. They asked: "Why anyone would use figure drawings to identify such an obviously disturbed group when simple behavioral observation would suffice, is left to the reader's imagination" (Motta et al. 1993, p. 165). They reported that Naglieri and Pfeiffer's (1992) study identified less than half of the emotionally disturbed group. In other words, 48.15% of the clinical sample was identified as in need of further evaluation. Since the majority of the sample was not identified, the authors criticized the accuracy rate of the scoring procedure. "These sad data speak for themselves" (Motta et al., 1993, p. 165).

Wessel (1993) examined the use of the DAP: SPED with a population of emotionally disturbed, learning disabled, and cognitively impaired children. Of this sample, 31 students came from as small town in southern Wisconsin and 39 came from an urban area in eastern Wisconsin. The participants ranged in age from 7 to 14 years. There were no significant differences based on age, race, or geographical density. Wessel (1993) found that the DAP:

SPED significantly discriminated between emotionally disturbed and learning disabled but not emotionally disturbed and cognitively impaired children. She concluded that the DAP: SPED may not be a reliable instrument for distinguishing emotionally disturbed children from other special populations.

Briccetti (1994) used the DAP: SPED with a group of deaf children, aged 9 through 12. Participants had severe to profound hearing loss and were at least low average intelligence. The children were separated into two groups: emotionally disturbed and those showing no disturbances. The DAP: SPED scores did not significantly distinguish between these two groups. Briccetti (1994) noticed that the children showing no disturbance had more indicators of pathology in the DAP: SPED. Briccetti (1994) concluded that the DAP: SPED is not a valid instrument for evaluating hearing impaired children.

Bruening, Wagner, and Johnson (1997) examined inter rater knowledge of sexually abused and nonabused girls' scores on the DAP: SPED. Twenty sexually abused girls, receiving services at a university outpatient clinic and 20 nonabused girls completed the DAP: SPED. The drawings were then randomly assigned to one of two case descriptions: (1) actual–raters knew the girls' actual abuse status or (2) pretend–raters were told that the girl's status was opposite from what it actually was. Three raters, graduate students, independently scored the DAP: SPED drawings. Bruening, Wagner, and Johnson (1977) found no significant results for the effect of the knowledge of the girls' status. They concluded that the DAP: SPED is significantly objective enough to withstand extraneous influences of varying case descriptions.

Matto (2001) examined the clinical utility of the DAP: SPED with a population of high-risk youth. She wanted to see if the DAP: SPED significantly predicted emotional and behavioral functioning of a population of youth, 6–12 years of age, receiving counseling services at outpatient and residential treatment facilities in Maryland. Participant functioning constructs included behavior, psychosocial adjustment, and self-esteem. The results showed that the total DAP:SPED score was a significant predictor in explaining behavioral disturbance and two psychosocial adjustment domains, hostility and productivity, even after statistically controlling for prominent demographic variables. The DAP: SPED self-drawing and the woman alone were significant predictors of behavior and self-esteem whereas the DAP: SPED man alone drawing significantly predicted productivity. Matto (2001) concluded that this information could be used to determine service decisions and takes as little as 10 minutes to score.

Matto (2002) conducted a validity study using the DAP: SPED with high-risk youth. Specifically, Matto (2002) was interested in determining if the DAP: SPED was a significant predictor of behavioral functioning of a group of 68 latency-age children, 6 to 12 years of age, receiving outpatient services or participating in a residential treatment facility. Two-thirds of the sample were males and a majority were Caucasian with the remaining participants of African American or biracial descent. The results significantly predicted behavioral disturbance. After controlling for the Child and Adolescent, Adjustment Profile parent report, the DAP:SPED moderately predicted behavioral disturbance with this age group. "Along with the empirical significance shown in this study, the DAP: SPED contributes to this measurement base in gathering behavioral information from the child himself or herself, offering a supplemental source to existing parent self-report and another source in environments in which it is difficult to obtain information from a parent" (Matto, 2002, p. 224). Matto (2002) concluded that her results provided preliminary support that the DAP: SPED yields information about a child's behavioral functioning.

DESIRABLE FEATURES

The DAP: SPED manual was clear and concise. Administration and scoring guidelines were outlined in detail. The assessment required little time for administration. The templates were helpful when scoring the drawings. Case examples were clearly structured and demonstrated the scoring system adequately.

UNDESIRABLE FEATURES

The fact that the directions read "I would like you to draw for me" may promote transference issues with the examiner if the child already has a pretesting relationship. If the directions were changed to read " Draw a picture . . . ," it would avoid any extraneous influences on the drawing itself. There was a performance demand in the way the directions read. Since the child has only five minutes to complete the drawing, this may prove to be very frustrating. In addition, to make the best picture you can, a child may need more than five minutes. It was not clear from the instructions if the child was aware that she only has five minutes to complete the drawing. If children are not aware, they may become upset and have difficulty completing the assessment.

OVERALL EVALUATION

The DAP: SPED is perhaps the most psychometrically advanced figure drawing assessment available. The test designers provided an excellent standardization sample that outlined demographic characteristics clearly and completely. The manual was easy to read. Instructions for administration, scoring, and interpretation were very detailed; yet, clear. Trevisan (1996) reviewed the rigorous validity and reliability studies on the DAP: SPED and concluded that it is a useful instrument for making a preliminary determination of whether a child or adolescent may be suffering from emotional problems.

> These studies and their positive results clearly set this measure apart from most other projective techniques. With good test user practice and clinical caution, I recommend giving serious consideration to using the DAP:SPED. (Trevisan, 1996, p. 229)

Construct validity evidence was weak. This was a general complaint about most human figure drawing tests. Discriminant validity evidence was moderate to strong. The DAP: SPED appeared to discriminate between normal populations and special populations. One criticism was that the special populations included a number of individuals, some with learning disabilities, others with emotional problems. Since not all children with learning disabilities such as dyslexia have emotional problems, additional research is needed to determine exactly what the DAP: SPED is screening.

Reliability evidence appeared strong. No significant differences were found after a one-week interval, indicating the stability of the instrument. Future studies may vary the length of this interval provided that it does not exceed six months (Anastasi, 1988). The authors could have provided more information on the qualifications of the raters. It was not clear if the test designers also served as raters in the studies cited.

Although the manual stated that the drawings could be used as measures of intellectual functioning, there was no evidence provided. The manual refers the reader to the DAP: QSS manual for scoring information. It appeared from the research conducted to date that the DAP cannot be used as a measure of intellectual functioning since predictive and concurrent validity evidence was lacking.

REFERENCES

Anastasi, A. (1988). *Psychological testing.* 6th ed. New York: Macmillian Publishing Company.

Bardos, A.N. (1993). Human figure drawings: Abusing the abused. *School Psychology Quarterly, 8*(3), 177–181.

Briccetti, K.A. (1994). Emotional indicators of deaf children on the Draw-A-Person test. *American Annals of the Deaf, 139*(5), 500–505.

Bruening, C.C., Wagner, W.G., & Johnson, J.T. (1997). Impact of rater knowledge on sexually abused and nonabused girls' scores on the Draw-A-Person: Screening Procedure for Emotional Disturbance (DAP: SPED). *Journal of Personality Assessment, 68*(3), 665–667.

Kamphause, R.W., & Pleiss, K.L. (1991). Draw-a-Person techniques: Tests in search of a construct. *Journal of School Psychology, 29,* 395–401.

Matto, H.C. (2001). Investigating the clinical utility of the Draw-a-Person: Screening Procedure for Emotional Disturbance (DAP:SPED) projective test in assessment of high-risk youth. A measurement validation study. *Dissertation Abstracts International: Section A: Humanities & Social Sciences, 61*(7-A), 2920.

Matto, H.C. (2002). Investigating the validity of the Draw-A-Person: Screening for Emotional Disturbance: A measurement validation study with high-risk youth. *Psychological Assessment, 14*(2), 221–225.

Motta, R.W., Little, S.G., & Tobin, M.I. (1993). The use and abuse of human figure drawings. *School Psychology Quarterly, 8*(3), 162–169.

Naglieri, J.A. (1985). *Matrix Analogies Test–Short Form.* New York: Psychological Corporation.

Naglieri, J.A. (1988). *Draw a Person: A quantitative scoring system.* New York: Psychological Corporation.

Naglieri, J.A. (1993). Human figure drawings in perspective. *School Psychology Quarterly, 8*(3), 170–176.

Naglieri, J.A., McNeish, T.J., & Bardos, A.N. (1991). *Draw a Person: Screening Procedure for Emotional Disturbance.* Austin, TX: Pro-Ed.

Naglieri, J.A., & Pfeiffer, S.I. (1992). Performance of disruptive behavior disordered and normal samples on the Draw A Person: Screening Procedure for Emotional Disturbance. *Psychological Assessment, 4*(2), 156–159.

Neisworth, J.T., & Butler, R.J. (1990). Test review: Draw a Person: A quantitative scoring system. *Journal of Psychoeducational Assessment, 8,* 190–194.

Prewett, P.N., Bardos, A.N., & Naglieri, J.A. (1989). Assessment of mentally retarded children with the Matrix Analogies Test-Short Form, Draw A Person: A Quantitative Scoring System, and the Kaufman Test of Education Achievement. *Psychology in the Schools, 26,* p. 254–260.

Trevisan, M.S. (1996). Review of the Draw a Person. The Screening Procedure for Emotional Disturbance. *Measurement and Evaluation in Counseling and Development, 28*(4), 225–229.

Wessel, J. (1993). Use of the DAP:SPED with a Sample of Students Enrolled in ED, CD, and LD Public School Programs. Paper presented at the Annual Convention of the National Association of School Psychologists (25th, Washington, DC, April 13-17, 1993).

Wisniewski, J.J., & Naglieri, J.A. (1989). Validity of the Draw A Person: A quantitative scoring system with the WISC-R. *Journal of Psychoeducational Assessment, 7,* 346–351.

Chapter 12

MAGAZINE PHOTO COLLAGE

TITLE: Magazine Photo Collage (MPC)
AGE: Age limit not presented
YEAR: 1993
PURPOSE: designed to reveal client's conflicts, defense mecha-
                nisms, and styles of functioning; interpretation based on
                the client's procedural approach to the task, pictorial
                content, and free associations
SCORES: based on guidelines for interpretation
MANUAL: manual (183 pages); illustrations (93 pages); profile (21
                pages); reliability data (none reported); validity data
                (none reported)
TIME LIMIT: to be completed in one session (time limit not otherwise
                defined)
COST: $20.00–$40.00 for testing manual
AUTHOR: Landgarten, Helen B
                http://search.tandf.co.uk/bookscatalogue
PUBLISHER: Brunner/Mazel, Inc., 19 Union Square, New York, NY,
                10003.
                http://www.brunner-routledge.co.uk/

INTRODUCTION

The Magazine Photo Collage (MPC: Langarten, 1993) was designed for multicultural assessment and treatment. Rather than using a standardized test, such as the Thematic Apperception Test (TAT) that represents only one race, the MPC may be standardized by the therapist to fit specialized populations. Depending on the therapist's population of interest and expertise, he/she may provide images varying in age, gender, and race. As with the

TAT (Murray, 1943), the focus of the MPC was on content. Unlike other projective assessments, the materials used for administration may vary from one therapist to the next. The box of photo images continuously changes. As a result, the MPC was an empowering process:

> Because clients choose their own collage images, they are provided with a rich symbolic vocabulary for self-expression, and one that is individualized to suit their own needs. The opportunity to exercise some control over the selection process can lessen inhibitions and resistant factors for many clients. This facet also encourages the positive transference and hastens the establishment of a therapeutic alliance. (Landgarten, 1993, p. 2)

Completed collages allowed the therapist to confront the meaning of the images, make an intervention, offer an interpretation, or simply note the content before going on to the next phase of the assessment.

Since 1967, Landgarten has been addressing the problems of cross-cultural counseling. Monocultural assumptions of mental health, derogatory stereotypes of minorities, and limited knowledge of cultural groups result in inappropriate and ineffective counseling approaches (Sue & Sue, 1990). Additionally, cultural values, class values, and language variables also limit counseling effectiveness. By trying to select images that match the client's culture, Landgarten (1993) hoped to resolve some of the problems of cross-cultural counseling. As a result, she found that therapy progressed at a faster pace. This in turn, fostered positive transference and a stronger relationship with her clients. In her book on the MPC, Landgarten (1993) presented case examples of Asian, Black, Hispanic, and Caucasian clients' work on several types of issues: School phobia, anorexia nervosa, loss, suicidal ideation, and posttraumatic stress disorder to name a few. The MPC also had the capability of addressing individuals who come from two or more racial groups. This was particularly valuable when dealing with racial identity issues.

PURPOSE AND RECOMMENDED USE

The MPC was designed to generate information about client conflicts, defense mechanisms, and styles of functioning (Landgarten, 1993). It may be used with any cultural group provided that the therapist can include photos that relate to the client's cultural background. In addition, it may be incorporated into the treatment process by including tasks that have a thematic orientation or offer free choice. "Regardless of the way in which the clinician proceeds, the client's collage becomes the document that gains access to conscious as well as unconscious material" (Landgarten, 1993, p. 3). Age limit and the possibility of group administration were not discussed.

DIMENSIONS THAT THE TEST PURPORTS TO MEASURE

The First Task of the MPC involved a free choice collage of miscellaneous images. According to Landgarten (1993), this task will convey information on how the collage was constructed. For instance, the therapist may note how the images were handled, glued, and placed on the page. Additionally, the counselor may observe the document for specific messages or themes.

Involving a collage of people images, the Second Task was said to indicate the client's perception of trust within self, significant others, or the therapist. It explored the connection between action and cognition by writing what each image was thinking and saying. This facet of the task may reveal congruencies and disparities. The Second Task was a measure of the client's self-image and generated information about the transference relationship. How this task indicated transference was unclear.

For the Third Task, the client was asked to pick out pictures of people or miscellaneous items that stand for something good and something bad. This task revealed images that the client associated with positive feelings and negative emotions. The therapist may consider the use of only people images, only miscellaneous images, or a combination of the two groups. Landgarten (1993) purported that the use of humorous images and miscellaneous images was a distancing mechanism.

In the Fourth Task, the client was presented with a restriction: Selecting only one picture from the people box. This task measured the person's positive or negative outlook on life. "This will illuminate the individual's attitude, coping mechanisms, and whether or not problem-solving through alternatives is part of his/her life-style" (Landgarten, 1993, p. 11). Since Landgarten (1993) did not expand further on this statement, the exact nature of determining the client's attitude remained unclear.

ADMINISTRATION

Landgarten (1993) recommended that all four MPC tasks be completed in one session (length of session was not discussed), beginning with Task One and ending with Task Four. It was the administrator's choice whether or not to set a time limit. If one was set, then the therapist should consider pressure factors when doing the assessment. Qualifications of the administrator were not discussed.

Collages were completed on newsprint or white paper, 16" x 20".

After the assessment phase, the therapist had the option of using colored construction paper. The following tools were required: A thin black marker, medium black marker, ball-point pen, round-tip scissors, and a lead pencil. In order to observe handling, Landgarten (1993) stressed that liquid glue should be used during the assessment. After the assessment phase was complete, the client may use a glue stick. Overall, Landgarten (1993) was very clear in the types of materials required and the manner in which the MPC may be administered.

NORM GROUPS

The MPC was not standardized on a population. It included case examples representing various cultural groups. The manner in which these cases were selected was unclear. Although the cases denoted various cultural groups and both genders, very few children were included. It may be that Landgarten (1993) felt that the MPC was more appropriate for adolescents and adult populations.

INTERPRETATION OF SCORES

The assessment process was divided into three parts: process, content, and free associations. Landgarten (1993) endorsed an analytical approach in that each process must be viewed separately as opposed to the whole. In the first part of the assessment, the therapist viewed how the client approached the task. Landgarten (1993) outlined seven components of this process. One component was the way that the client looked through the box of pictures. Landgarten (1993) expressed that the demeanor may be categorized as follows: lackadaisical, serious, casual, disdainful, angry, anxious, and so forth. Additionally, she maintained that clients who were extremely cautious in any of the categories may have one or more of the following problems: passivity, depression, ambivalence, inability to deal with emotion, problems with decision-making, or obsessive-compulsive characteristics. Also, clients who recklessly completed the collage and were characterized as having problems with boundaries may have serious psychopathology such as bipolar depression, borderline personality disorder, drug addiction or psychosis. According to Landgarten (1993), functioning individuals will look through many images, take a reasonable amount of time, use appropriate glue, and have some white space surrounding their images. She then furnished examples that illustrated the first part of the assessment process.

The second part of the MPC concerned evaluation of the pictorial content. The therapist observed inclusions and exclusions. For the people pictures, Landgarten (1993) designed a list of eight questions. For example, "Are all the photographs either of men or women, or boys or girls" (p. 20)? The client's free associations were taken into account. Projections about self, significant others, and transference issues were considered. According to Landgarten (1993), the Miscellaneous images "may disclose the person's value system, attitude toward life, concerns, fears, wishes" (Landgarten, 1993, p. 20). Also, the images may reveal the client's developmental level. Images that should alert the therapist included a looped rope, crashed cars, wrecked homes, broken glass, weapons, or pills.

The third part of the assessment involved free associations. Any verbal response was acceptable. Landgarten (1993) claimed that the client's verbal associations were critical to validate the therapist's hypotheses about the client.

SOURCE OF ITEMS

The MPC consisted of black and white and color magazine images that were culturally homogeneous to the client's population. These images were selected by the counselor and divided into two categories: people and miscellaneous items. Printed words were removed from the images. In addition, the images were NOT carefully cut in order to provide more information about the manner in which the client completed the collage. The images for the People box comprised some of the following: people from different cultures, reality oriented (avoiding glamorous images), showing movement as well as static positions, and included different environments. Males and females of various ages and facial expressions were included. Miscellaneous items generally came from ads and encompassed a variety of inanimate objects such as trucks, jewelry, tools, furniture, and houses.

How Landgarten (1993) selected these four particular tasks was unclear. If the tasks had a theoretical foundation in art therapy or psychotherapy, it was not presented in the manual. Additional information was needed on the historical development of the tasks.

VALIDITY AND RELIABILITY AS
DETERMINED BY THE AUTHOR

Landgarten (1993) openly admitted that she did not investigate the reliability or validity of this instrument.

> Suggestions or interpretations are based on my many years of clinical practice. This book does not lay claim to the exact meanings for particular images. In fact, images can represent different meanings to different clients. (Landgarten, 1993, p. 2)

Establishing reliability evidence for the MPC may be possible. Landgarten's assessment factors can be incorporated into a scoring sheet used to rate the client's demeanor as well as the pictorial content. Interrater reliability can be checked in this manner. Since the historical development and theoretical background of the MPC were not discussed, it was difficult to project a possible study of validity.

RESEARCH USING THE MPC

To date, there was no research on the MPC. Instead, the literature contained a few articles on the use of collage in general. For instance, Katz (1987) used photo collage as a treatment modality for working with a group of eight-year-old females.

> the affective and cognitive arenas of the preconscious are allowed to surface, with one's picture providing a safe distance for looking at one's self. The inspiration which one feels at this moment combines spontaneous ideas, visions, social and personal desires, all of which describe the individual. (Katz, 1987, p. 83)

Katz (1987) asserted that through photo collage, clients were able to cultivate an empathic connection with others, ventilate personal concerns, and master skills and aesthetic development. In working with young girls, Katz (1987) found that ego functions were strengthened. Frustration tolerance increased and impulsiveness decreased. The purpose of her work was to foster conflict resolution skills. "This issue of identity, in relation to one's individuation and the struggle toward more mature realization of one's unique potentials, is a major theme explored through this modality, and highly congruent with the purposes of social group work" (Katz, 1987, p. 89). The changes in the group were observed by the researcher and were not in relation to measured changes in demeanor.

Another article focused on a secondary school teacher's use of photo collage in her classroom. Jones (1990) instructed her students to trace a silhouette of a partner's face. Students then pasted images into their own silhouette. Next, they worked on the space around the silhouette. In the surrounding area, some students represented one of the four elements and others created symbols of their Zodiac sign. Overall, Jones (1990) found that this activity was very pleasurable for the students.

Reissman (1992) used collage work with students to increase multicultural awareness. By breaking the students into groups, she had them look for one particular racial group in the daily newspapers. They were asked to make predictions about how many news items would be devoted to the ethnic group and what section of the newspaper would contain stories about the group. Collages were created out of the articles found in the papers. "These students found that through selection of images, the news media could perpetuate, create, or defuse stereotypes" (Reissman, 1992, p. 52).

Although these articles were interesting, they represented only a qualitative approach to collage work. There is a need to see empirical studies that evaluated the effectiveness of collages, specifically the MPC, by examining self-esteem, social reticence, or depression. This information would strengthen the rationale of photo collage work in general as well as the use of the MPC as a therapeutic assessment.

DESIRABLE FEATURES

The MPC process was empowering because the client had control over the selection of magazine images. Landgarten (1993) designed a four-task assessment protocol, which was simple to administer and fit into the treatment process easily. It avoided the cookbook approach to art therapy assessment in that interpretation was primarily based on the client's free associations and the therapist's observation of the manner in which the collage was completed. Collage work was less threatening for some clients who may feel intimidated when drawing, painting, or sculpting. Landgarten (1993) presented clear guidelines for the administration of the MPC, materials needed, and case examples that illustrated the interpretation of the assessment. Also, the MPC appeared to counter some of the problems inherent in cross-cultural counseling by taking into consideration images familiar to clients with diverse backgrounds.

UNDESIRABLE FEATURES

The assessment used only images of people and inanimate objects. This limited the scope of the assessment in that animal and nature images were not included. In my experience, animal images were often used in collages and drawings. Clients seemed to identify with them. Important information may be neglected if the client was not able to select nature images.

The fact that the MPC was to be completed in one session was confining.

The time period for a session may vary from one therapist to the next. When following Landgarten's (1993) guidelines and using a 50-minute time limit, I found that clients were rushing through the assessment in order to complete the four tasks. Naturally, this interfered with the interpretation of the assessment. I varied Landgarten's (1993) approach by allowing the client to take as much time as needed to complete the MPC. Another weakness of the MPC was that the tasks were viewed separately. With an assessment of this nature, common themes among the tasks should be considered.

Interpretation of the tasks may be difficult. The exact nature of how the collage measured transference and countertransference issues was unclear. The same holds true for the interpretation of the client's attitude from one particular image. Additional information was needed to on the interpretation of the collage tasks.

OVERALL EVALUATION

Although researchers continue to use collage work and collage therapy in research (Sato, 1998, 1999; Williams, 2000; Ireland, 2002; Sato, 2002; Takata, 2002), there has been no direct use of the MPC in research. To date, only two book reviews have been published on the MPC (Phillips, 1995; Orr, 1996).

> As an art therapist in the 90s, however, I missed reference to the creative process, to the "spirit and soul" of the work of using imagery for self-expression. I took issue with the repeated view that clients were "resistant" rather than justifiably defended. I wanted color reproductions instead of the black-and-white ones, which seemed to reinforce a general emphasis on content; more guidelines for assessing client strengths as well as pathology. I also wanted more discussion of Landgarten's verbal interventions and a guide to new techniques for using *collage* as a creative process. (Orr, 1996, p. 84)

On a positive note, Orr (1996) stated that the MPC surmounts racial and cultural biases; thereby advancing the course of therapy.

Since Landgarten (1993) has been working with collages for over 30 years, it would have been helpful to include information on the historical development of the MPC. Additionally, it would have been interesting to learn how these four tasks were selected to comprise the MPC. A reference list including other people's work with collages would be practical. Further, a list of other possible collage tasks to guide therapy would have been useful to ongoing treatment.

The lack of validity and reliability information was regretful but it is not impossible to obtain. A scoring guide can be constructed to record information on the assessment. This would be beneficial in the collection of inter-rater reliability evidence. Another interesting study that would promote validity would be to examine the variation in time when completing the MPC: a single session versus as many sessions as the client requires. Since Landgarten (1993) claimed that the MPC was a multicultural assessment, research should be completed to sanction this point.

The use of the case method appeared to be the approach of choice with this art therapy assessment. Although the case method fosters insight on the use of art therapy, it has several limitations. First, case studies are not representative samples. Additionally, the observers are not blind and therefore, may not be objective. Lastly, the case method does not utilize a comparison group. These are important considerations when reviewing any type of assessment that utilizes a case approach.

Overall, the MPC is an empowering approach when working with clients. It offered the client a choice in selecting images and providing his/her own interpretation of the collage. Additionally, it reduced the possibility of cultural bias by including images consistent with a client's cultural background. I have attempted to promote client autonomy and responsibility by requiring people to contribute images to the collection boxes for the MPC. Also, I have encouraged the use of animal, tree, and water images. In conclusion, the MPC may increase a client's awareness of self by yielding information about inner conflicts and relationships with others.

REFERENCES

Ireland, M.S. (2002). From fragments to wholeness: Collage, the kinesthetic art of Jane Lang. *American Journal of Art Therapy, 40*(3), 211–213.

Jones, L. (1990). In your element: Students often "fill their heads' with all kinds of ideas. *School Arts, January,* 36–37.

Katz, S.L. (1987). Photocollage as a therapeutic modality for working with groups. *Social Work with Groups, 10*(4), 83–89.

Landgarten, H. B. (1993). *Magazine Photo Collage.* New York, NY: Brunner Mazel Publishers.

Murray, H.A. (1943). *Thematic Apperception Test.* Cambridge, MA: Harvard University Press.

Orr, S. (1996). Book reviews. *American Journal of Art Therapy, 34*(3), 83–84.

Phillips, T.H. (1995). Book reviews. *Pastoral Psychology, 44*(2), 131–133.

Reissman, R. (1992). Multicultural awareness collages. *Educational Leadership, December-January,* 51–52.

Sato, S. (1998). Collage therapy and analysis of production process in collage work. *Shinrigaku kenkyu. The Japanese Journal of Psychology, 69*(4), 287–294.

Sato, S. (1999). Analysis of the structure in the material pictures of collage work.

Shinrigaku kenkyu. The Japanese Journal of Psychology, 70(2), 120–127.

Sato, S. (2002). Collage work characteristics and personality. *Shinrigaku kenkyu. The Japanese Journal of Psychology,* 72(2), 192–196.

Sue, D. W. & Sue, D. (1990). *Counseling the culturally different.* New York: John Wiley & Sons.

Takata, Y. (2002). Supporting a nurse teaching in a school infirmary using collage Therapy. *Psychiatry and Clinical Neurosciences, 56*(4), 371–379.

Williams, B. (2000). Collage work as a medium for guided reflection in the clinical supervision relationship. *Nurse Education Today, 20*(4), 273–278.

Chapter 13

BELIEF ART THERAPY ASSESSMENT

TITLE:	Belief Art Therapy Assessment (BATA)
AGE:	Age limit not presented
YEAR:	2002
PURPOSE:	designed to understand the spiritual dimensions of a client; interpretation based on the client's developmental level, subject matter, formal qualities of artwork, and client attitude
SCORES:	based on interpretation guidelines
MANUAL:	manual (195 pages); illustrations (47 pages); profile (64 pages); reliability data (none reported); validity data (none reported)
TIME LIMIT:	no time limit for administration
COST:	$34.95–$51.95 for testing manual http://www.ccthomas.com/details.cfm?P_ISBN=0398073139
AUTHOR:	Horovitz, Ellen G.
PUBLISHER:	Charles C Thomas Publishers, 2600 South First Street, Springfield, IL, 62794–9265. http://www.ccthomas.com/

INTRODUCTION

The Belief Art Therapy Assessment (BATA: Horovitz, 2002) emanated from the exploration of mourning and loss issues. "Beginning with these losses reconnects the patient to his very origin of dis-ease (e.g., symptomatic discomfort) and sets the stage for inclusion of the spiritual dimension" (Horovitz, 2002, p. 14). While many professionals in the field have equated the pursuit of religion with poor mental health, Horovitz (2002) stated that investigating spirituality was motivated by a search for meaning in one's life. This sense of purpose served to connect the client to society or community. She endorsed McNiff's (1992) concept of art as healing, a mystical experience that fostered integration. As McNiff (1992), she confronted client pain and suffering as a method of moving the client toward growth.

Since the field of art therapy was just beginning to explore spirituality, Horovitz (1994, 2002) developed the BATA. This assessment was fashioned to explore the client's belief systems as it related to personal and familial functioning.

> In fact, I ardently maintain that families can be instructed how to care for themselves within a brief time frame. The argument stems from the fact that they have been caring for themselves all along, even when doing it badly. All the more reason to tap into a client's belief system; for in doing so, the therapist can empower the identified patient yet align with the hierarchical powers. (Horovitz, 1994, p. 27)

As Ellison (1991), Horovitz perceived that religious beliefs may affect the client's coping skills and ability to deal with stress. Additionally, exploration of religious symbols and beliefs may provide an avenue through which the client can understand and integrate life experiences. Corsini and Wedding (1989) defined religion as the "expression of an archetypal need to endow our human existence with meaning" (p. 140). As Horovitz (2002), they purport that analyzing religious imagery may help the client contend with his/her inner resources and serve to empower him/her.

PURPOSE AND RECOMMENDED USE

Horovitz (2002) recommended that the BATA be used only when the client had questions about his/her spirituality. Horovitz (2002) warned that for clients who are emotionally disturbed or psychotic, the BATA may not be appropriate in that it may exacerbate their condition. The BATA began with an interview intended to gather information on the client's past and present religious beliefs. Next, the client was given two directives and asked to make art products in response to each. Since Horovitz (2002) had difficulty conducting the BATA in public school settings, it may not be appropriate for school psychologists to administer this assessment. From reading the manual, it appeared that the BATA can be used by private practitioners in the event that a client expresses a need to explore spiritual dimensions. It may be used with religious individuals as well as agnostics or atheists (see the first edition of this book, the case of Lee; Brooke, 1996). The BATA may be utilized to elicit information on client issues as well as determine the course of treatment.

DIMENSIONS THAT THE TEST PURPORTS TO MEASURE

The BATA was created to provide an indication of a client's spiritual belief system. The assessment consisted of two directives. The first directive was stated as follows:

> Have you ever thought about how the universe was created and who or what was responsible for our creation? . . . . Many people have a belief in God; if you also have a belief in God, would you draw, paint, or sculpt what God means to you. (Horovitz, 1994, pp. 30-31)

For people who did not believe in God, the administrator may ask what beliefs the client supports. As in the case of Lee in the first edition of this book, his spirituality emanated from his belief in dragons (Brooke, 1996). Should the client state that he/she believes in nothing, the administrator may request that the client represent that idea using art media. After the first directive, the client was given a postassessment interview. These questions attempted to ascertain what the client made and what it meant to him/her. The second directive was stipulated as follows:

> Some people believe that there is an opposite of God. If you believe there is an opposite force, could you also draw, paint or sculpt the meaning of that? (Horovitz, 1994, p. 32)

Next, the postassessment interview was administered again.

ADMINISTRATION

Horovitz (2002) enumerated a series of media that may be used for the BATA. The list included two-dimensional drafting media, two-dimensional painting media, three-dimensional media, and types of paper. This was one of the few assessments that offered a wide variety of media. The administrator conducted the interview first. Since clinicians vary in their skills as interviewers, Horovitz (2002) furnished some general questions for the query. She offered the administrator the option of adding or deleting questions depending on the client's personality and psychological parameters. Next, the client was given the first directive followed by a postassessment interrogation. The

BATA concluded with the second directive followed by another post-assessment interrogation. The qualifications of the administrator were not discussed.

NORM GROUPS

The BATA was not standardized on a population. Instead, the manual contained a series of case examples that comprised members of the clergy, adult artists, emotionally disturbed children and adolescents, and a suicidal, bulimic anorectic. The case examples were thorough compared to some authors (Burns & Kaufman, 1972; Burns, 1987) who only provided minimal information on the client background. Horovitz (2002) depicted genograms, timelines, and photographs in the case examples.

INTERPRETATION OF SCORES

Interpretation of the BATA was based on developmental level, formal qualities of the artwork, subject matter, and client attitude. Development was determined by Lowenfeld and Brittain's (1987) stages of cognitive development. Horovitz (2002) outlined a series of parameters to guide the reader in the interpretation of the art products. For instance, formal qualities of the artwork considered the creation or lack of creating a product. If a client was unable to produce a product, it may indicate withdrawal, playful experimentation, destructive behavior, extreme duress or anxiety due to nature of the topic, or resistance (Horovitz, 2002). Subject matter deliberated common themes and blatant contradictions. Attitude was the client's demeanor as the product was created. Response to specific media, avoidance of materials, gratification, and self-perceptions were other considerations relating to client attitude.

Horovitz (2002) cited a model invented by Fowler (1981) that was used in the interpretation of the BATA. Fowler (1981) constructed a stage theory for spiritual development, similar to Kohlberg's (1981) theory of moral development. This six-stage theory was clearly outlined in Horovitz's (2002) work. In the second edition of this text (2002), a table of comparative norms comparing Erikson, Piaget, Kohlbeg, Lowenfeld and Brittain and Fowler, Horovitz, (2002) aids the clinician in examining the results of the BATA in terms of previous developmental constructs from cognition to moral development (pp. 176–177).

SOURCE OF ITEMS

The creation of the BATA originated from Horovitz's (1994) "conviction that people's belief systems were indigenous to their operational and systems functioning" (p. 28). Looking back on the work of Coles (1990), who asked children to draw a picture of God, Horovitz (2002) decided that some religious factions might take offense to this request. She redesigned the directive to provide an indication of the "meaning" of God as opposed to the representation of God. Additionally, she expanded Coles' (1990) two-dimensional drawing request to include a myriad of two and three dimensional art media.

VALIDITY AND RELIABILITY AS DETERMINED BY THE AUTHOR

Horovitz (2002) did not investigate the validity or reliability of the BATA and indeed directly stated that this was not her aim. To date, no published research has examined the BATA. "Although the data could be analyzed, categorized, and converted into mathematical computation, my precise desire was to create a battery that recognized the spiritual dimension of a person and contribute pertinent information in order to effect treatment" (Horovitz, 1994, p. 27). Horovitz (2003), in a personal communication with me, stated that the BATA has now been used with 300 students attending Nazareth College in Rochester, New York.

DESIRABLE FEATURES

The BATA offered a free choice of art media. Given that some clients may be anxious about exploring spiritual issues, this was a valuable improvement over other art therapy assessments that were limited to using only pencil drawings. Also, the BATA can be used with agnostics or atheists. Horovitz (2002) supplied a list of questions and suggestions when working with these individuals. The manual was very descriptive and included several case examples that demonstrated the use of the BATA.

UNDESIRABLE FEATURES

A form for recording the interview, postassessment interrogations, formal qualities of the artwork, and client attitude would have been helpful.

Creating a checklist may be a first step in furnishing reliability information for the BATA. Since examiner qualifications were not discussed, guidelines for interpretation could have been more detailed. Individuals with little clinical experience or training in art therapy may find the BATA difficult to interpret.

OVERALL EVALUATION

Farely-Hansen (1996) describes the BATA as a courageous piece of work. She was impressed with the use of the BATA with diverse populations and the incorporation of three-dimensional media into the assessment process.

> On the other hand, it was hard for us, as clinicians in private practice to imagine asking clients the author's 10 questions as written; they seemed somehow too formal and too theistic. Our custom has been to inform potential clients of our transpersonal perspective in an initial interview, then to integrate questions like Horovitz-Darby's more broadly into treatment. (Farrely-Hansen, 1996, p. 84)

Horovitz (2002) included several case examples in the manual. Although she described Fowler's (1981) theory of spiritual development in detail, it would have helped the reader to see it applied in the case examples. This may be the key to providing validity evidence for the BATA. Creating a checklist that outlined spiritual development (Fowler, 1981), cognitive development (Lowenfeld & Brittain, 1987), and qualitative interpretations of the artwork may serve as the foundation for providing both reliability and validity evidence. Additionally, Horovitz-Darby (1988) created the Cognitive Art Therapy Assessment (CATA) in which she clearly detailed the interpretation of paint, clay, and drawing media. Incorporating these guidelines for interpretation would have been worthwhile when interpreting the BATA. Additional information on the reliability and validity of the BATA was needed.

To date, the BATA was the only assessment in art therapy that explored a client's spiritual development. Since spirituality was an important facet of many people's life, this assessment was long overdue. Additionally, the client was offered a wide variety of media in order to complete the assessment. Most art therapy tests were limited to paper and pencil drawings. Another important feature of this assessment was that it can be used with atheists or agnostics; it was not restricted to individuals who subscribe to the traditional Christian religions.

There is a great deal of interested in exploring spirituality in conjunction with art therapy, with children and adults (Pfund, 2000; Furguson, 2001; Fehlner, 2002; Pendelton et al., 2002; Breslin et al., 2003). The BATA is an assessment that considers the spiritual side of a client. Although the BATA may not be appropriate for all individuals, it did offer an option to those clients who were ready to explore their spiritual nature.

REFERENCES

Breslin, K.T., Reed, M.R., & Malone, S.B. (2003). A holistic approach to substance abuse treatment. *Journal of Psychoactive Drugs, 35*(2), 247–251.

Brooke, S.L. (1996). *A therapist's guide to art therapy assessments: Tools of the trade.* Springfield, IL: Charles C Thomas Publishers.

Burns, R.C. (1987). *Kinetic-House-Tree-Person-Drawings: An interpretive manual.* New York, NY: Brunner/Mazel Publishers.

Burns, R.C., & Kaufman, S.H. (1972). *Actions, styles, and symbols in Kinetic Family Drawings (K-F-D): An interpretive manual.* New York: Brunner/Mazel.

Coles, R. (1990). *The spiritual life of children.* Boston, MA: Houghton-Mifflin.

Corsini, R. J. & Wedding, D. (1989). *Current psychotherapies.* Itasca, IL: F.E. Peacock Publishers, Inc.

Ellison, C.G. (1991). Religious involvement and subjective well-being. *Journal of Health and Social Behavior, 32*(1), 80–99.

Farely-Hansen, M. (1996). Book reviews. *American Journal of Art Therapy, 34*(3), 84–85.

Fehlner, J. (2002). Bridging spiritual direction and relational psychotherapy through Spontaneous artwork. *Canadian Art Therapy Association Journal, 15*(1), 29–44.

Fowler, J.W. (1981). *Stages of faith: The psychology of human development and the quest for meaning.* San Fransciso, CA: Harper.

Furguson, E.R. (2001). Health and spirituality. Cancer recovery: mind-body techniques. *Alternative Medicine, 43,* 106–109.

Horovitz-Darby, E.G. (1988). Art therapy assessment of a minimally language skilled deaf child. Chapter 11 in *Mental Health Assessment of Deaf Clients: Special Conditions.* Proceedings from the 1988 University of California's Center on Deafness Conference, ADARA, 115–127.

Horovitz, E.G. (2002). *Spiritual art therapy: An alternate path,* second edition. Springfield, IL: Charles C Thomas Publisher.

Horovitz, E.G. (1994). *Spiritual art therapy: An alternate path.* Springfield, IL: Charles C Thomas Publisher.

Kohlberg, L. (1981). *The philosophy of moral development.* New York: Harper & Row.

Lowenfeld, V., & Brittain, W.L. (1987). *Creative and mental growth.* 8th edition. New York: Macmillan.

McNiff, S. (1992). *Art as medicine: Creating a therapy of the imagination.* Boston, MA: Shambhala.

Pendelton, S.M., Cavalli, K.S., Pargament, K.I., & Nasr, S.Z. (2002). Religious/spiritual coping in childhood cystic-fibrosis: A qualitative study. *Pediatrics, 109*(1), E8.

Pfund, R. (2000). Nurturing a child's spirituality. *Journal of Child Health Care: For Professionals Working with Children in the Hospital and Community, 4*(4), 143–148.

Chapter 14

ART THERAPY DREAM ASSESSMENT

TITLE: Art Therapy Dream Assessment
AGE: children and adults
YEAR: 1999
PURPOSE: Dream interpretation
SCORES: No formal scores
MANUAL: No formal test manual
TIME LIMIT: No time limit for administration
COST: No cost
AUTHOR: Horovitz, E.
PUBLISHER: Ellen Horovitz—For more information on the ATDA you can email Ellen Horovitz: ehorovit@rochester.rr.com and eghorovi@naz.edu

INTRODUCTION

> This process of the dream guide mirroring back the exact words scripted by the dreamer is a powerful, medicinal uptake in itself. But the process of honing down the contents of the script to a final sentence (each time repeated verbatim by the dream guide) an equally startling discovery can be made. (Horovitz, 2004)

Dream interpretation, in the field of psychology, began with the work of Sigmund Freud. In 1900, Freud published his work on dream analysis (Hull, 1974). *The Interpretation of Dreams* is probably one of his best know works. Freud viewed dreams as a need for wish fulfillment. Additionally, he paved the way as far as noting the significance of dream content and Jung carried the interpretations of dream symbols forward. Jung was a novice artist himself and felt the healing power of art. Whereas Freud's contribution to art therapy was in the latent content of dreams, Jung's was in treating such images as communications from the psyche that could be understood on a number of levels (Edwards, 1987). Both Freud and Jung asserted that art symbols revealed emotional content (Munster, 2000). Thus, it seems that art would be a natural method for working with dream symbols and exploring their affective content.

Dream analysis entails determining the meaning of dreams through decoding symbols, myths, and memories. Ekhardt (1997) commented on the process of dream work:

> I love working with dreams, as they show most clearly in imagery the direction in which the patient's energy is being mobilized. . . . Dreams show us the battleground with ourselves and with others and are the best point of departure for revealing the past, present and future. Obviously I zero in on spirit and energy." (p. 270)

Freud used free association as a process of dream analysis, creating a link to semantic memory. Given that dreams have emotional content as noted by both Freud and Jung, combining dream analysis with art therapy is logical in that art therapy engages the right side of the brain which can be helpful in uncovering emotions and aiding the healing process.

PURPOSE AND RECOMMENDED USE

Horovitz (2004) recommended the ATDA for clients who want to get at the root of what is troubling them. It is a particularly valuable tool for clients plagued by recurring dreams. She also recommended this assessment as a tool for strengthening the therapeutic relationship.

DIMENSIONS THAT THE TEST PURPORTS TO MEASURE

According to Horovitz (2004), dreams can represent unrecognized aspects of self. The symbols in the dream are unique to the dreamer; thus, there is not one standard method for dream interpretation. It unfolds in a dialogue between the therapist and client.

ADMINISTRATION

The administrator asks the client to draw any dream that he or she has had, a recurring or a recent dream. Using oil pastels, pastels, drawing media, paint, clay, or other three-dimensional material, the client then illustrates the dream. Next, the client will write a paragraph to describe the dream, a dream script.

NORM GROUPS

Horovitz (2004) utilized a case approach in her development of ATDA and presented this in form of a power point slide lecture to her students attending the art therapy program at Nazareth College.

INTERPRETATION OF SCORES

The ADTA is not formally scored. Interpretation is based on the written script that the client creates in response to the art process. Clinical experience with art and dream work is needed to interpret the ATDA.

After writing the paragraph, the client reads the script back to the therapist. Next, the therapist reads the written work back to the client. By underlining the text, the client chooses those words which captures the crux of the dream. After underlining the key words, the client reads the cluster. Next, the therapist reads the underlined words back to the client.

The process continues by then reducing the cluster of words to eight words that stand out. Again, the client reads the eight words to the therapist and then the therapist will in turn read the words back to the client.

Last, the client is requested to take the remaining eight words and combine them into a single sentence. The client reads the sentence and then the therapist, in turn, reads it back to the client. Horovitz (2004) calls this process dream guide mirroring. She felt that this is a power and medicinal process that leads to amazing discoveries (Horovitz, 2004).

SOURCE OF ITEMS

Horivitz (2004) attended an art therapy conference, which required writing a dream text in response to a drawing of a dream. Horovitz (2004) felt the text can be critical in the interpretation of the dream. Richmond (2003) talks about the importance of dream text.

To use dream material clinically, we need to realize that we never use the dream itself. . . . All you can do is put the dream into words in an imperfect attempt to describe what you experienced. So, in the end, to talk about the dream you really talk about the *text of your perception of the dream.* http://www.guidetopsychology.com/dreams.htm

In essence, Richmond (2003) asserted that the text is a form of interpretation of the raw dream experience. Client's attempts to make sense of those images is revealing of his or her psychological processes.

VALIDITY AND RELIABILITY AS DETERMINED BY THE AUTHOR

Given that this is a newly developed assessment, reliability and validity studies have yet to be conducted using the ATDA. Additional research using the ATDA is needed. Please look for the book by Horovitz titled, *"A Leap of Faith: The Call to Art,"* which will provide additional information on the assessment.

ART THERAPY RESEARCH AND DREAMS

Dissuno (1999) conducted a qualitative study that examined children's dream stories within the context of an art therapy setting. Together, the children and their therapist use the dream stories as artistic metaphors. Dissuno's (1999) work documents the therapy processes of two children as they play, make art, and talk about their dreams. The article discussed how the children with their therapist used metaphors shared in play, art, and dreams. The therapist uses this information to help the child with real life issues. The combined efforts of the child and therapist in looking at the dream presented a view of the child's reality for both the child and therapist. Dissuno (1999) described children's dreams as creative symbolic processes reflecting the children's developmental struggles, their creative capacities, and their emotional vulnerabilities.

Hale (1990) used the creative modalities, including dream exploration, to help stimulate childhood memories, bringing them to the surface, and dealing with the content through expressive therapy. Music and guided imagery were used to help awaken the images. Hale (1990) noted that art therapy provided a sensory experience which may stimulate memory; therefore; therapists must use caution when using this approach and be sensitive to the client's resistance when facing potentially threatening memories. Her case method illustrates the use of art therapy in conjunction with dream work and guided imagery.

DESIRABLE FEATURES

Most clients enjoy talking about dreams. The ATDA is a simple process and can be used to decipher a dream. Often, the process of dream interpretation will lend itself to information, which may not be revealed in any other fashion. "It is also a very powerful tool in terms of jump-starting the therapeutic relationship" (Horovitz, 2004). One of the nice features of this assessment is the free range of art media that can be used to complete the ATDA. Many of the assessments reviewed in this book are two-dimensional and many of those do not even use color. This is one of the very few assessments that can use three-dimensional art. Additionally, the client has a choice of media, freeing up expression and creativity to the assessment directive.

UNDESIRABLE FEATURES

This is a new assessment, which does not have a formal test manual. As with the FSA (Betts, 2003), the ATDA needs additional research to provide support for test validity and reliability. Given that there are no formal guidelines for the assessment, clinical experience is required for interpretation of the ATDA. There is a strong verbal component to this assessment, one that requires the client to read and write. This should be considered when working with children and may have to be modified when working with special populations.

OVERALL EVALUATION

According to Langs (1988), dreams occur because they are meant to be analyzed. Further, he asserts that just the process of remembering a dream promotes emotional stability. "Remembering dreams seems to diminish the likelihood for acting blindly because of unrealized pressures for inner emotions and unconscious experience and needs (Langs, 1988, p. 68).

Dreams and the graphic depiction of them can help reveal unconscious processes and can be instrumental in the course of therapy (Muff, 1996). The use of art therapy to explore dreams is not new. Research has focused on the usefulness of depicting dreams in recovering memories, understanding self in relation to groups, and exploring feelings (Leuschner & Hau, 1995; Buckner,

1996; Chiaia, 1999; Grand, 1999).

The study of dreams is what led me from majoring in architecture to beginning my long journey in the field of psychology. I have long felt that dreams are messages from our unconscious. What we are too busy to pay attention to in our waking life comes through as messages in our dreams. Using an assessment such as the ATDA, therapists can help clients give meaning to dream content and bring to awareness those unconscious elements, increase self-awareness, and at the same time, open creative potential. Evans (1983) considers dreams as landscapes of the night that are keys to creativity.

The ATDA is simple and easy to administer. Given that the assessment does not have scoring criteria or guidelines for interpretation, clinical experience with dream interpretation and art will be necessary to interpret the ATDA. The process of dream interpretation is imaginative in itself, and through the ATDA, it becomes poetic and artistic. Psychologists have long realized the importance of dreams to physical, emotional, and mental well-being, leading to the development of dream therapy and a growing application of dream art. The ATDA is one of the first assessments to combine dream analysis and art therapy.

REFERENCES

Betts, D.J. (2003). Developing projective drawing test: Experiences with the Face Stimulus Assessment (FSA). *Art Therapy: Journal of the American Art Therapy Association, 20*(2), 77–82.

Buckner, S. (1996). Dreaming and waking in Russia. *Art Therapy: Journal of the American Art Therapy Association, 13*(4), 297–306.

Chiaia, M.E. (1999). Imagination in dialogue: A collaborative method of self-inquiry. *Dissertation Abstracts International: Section B: The Sciences & Engineering, 59*(10-B), 5572.

Dissuno, R.E. (1999). Working with children's dream stories in an art therapy setting. *Dissertation Abstracts International Section A: Humanities & Social Sciences, 60*(1-A), p. 65.

Eckhardt, M.H. (1997). Reflections. *American Journal of Psychoanalysis, 57*(3). 270.

Edwards, M. (1987). *Jungian analytic art therapy. In Judith Rubin's, Approaches to art therapy: Theory and technique.* Philadelphia, PA,: Brunner/Mazel, Inc. pp. 92–113.

Evans, C. (1983). *Landscapes of the night: How and why we dream.* New York: Viking Press.

Grand, I.J. (1999). Collaboration and creativity: An interdisciplinary study. *Dissertation Abstracts International: Section B: The Sciences & Engineering, 60*(3-B), 1349.

Hale, S.E. (1990). Sitting on memory's lap. *Arts in Psychotherapy, 17*(3), 269–274.

Horovitz, E. (2004, January 21). Personal communication.

Hull, E.C. (1974). *C.G. Jung: Dreams.* New Jersey: Princeton University Press.

Langs, R. (1988). *Decoding your dreams: A revolutionary technique for understanding your dreams.* New York: Henry Holt and Company.

Leuschner, W., & Hau, S. (1995). Artistic dream reconstructions of the Wolf Man in the light of experimental findings. *Psyche, 49*(7), 609–632.

Muff, J. (1996). Images of life on the verge of death: Dreams and drawings of people with AIDS. *Perspectives in Psychiatric Care, 32*(3), 10–21.

Muster, N.J. (2002). *Cult survivor's handbook: How to live in the material world again.* [Online article]. http://surrealist.org/norimuster/handbook6.html

Richmond, R.L. (2003). Dream interpretation. [Online article]. http://www.guideto psychology.com/dreams.htm

Chapter 15

FACE STIMULUS ASSESSMENT

TITLE: Face Stimulus Assessment (FSA)
AGE: children, adolescents, and adults
YEAR: 2001
PURPOSE: designed to be used with clients who are nonverbal or
                have communication disorders; especially for use with
                multicultural populations.
SCORES: N/A
MANUAL: FSA guidelines (3 pages); reliability data (none report-
                ed); validity data (none reported)
TIME LIMIT: 50-minute time
COST: Clinician's Packet: $10. Includes: Assessment
                Templates, Handbook, Rating Guidelines, Reference
                List. Researcher's Packet: $10. Includes: Assessment
                Templates, Handbook, Rating Guidelines, Reference
                List, researcher number, sample informed consent form.
AUTHOR: Betts, Donna, J.
PUBLISHER: Donna J. Betts; 2060 E Park Avenue, Tallahassee, FL,
                32301; DonnaBettsATR@aol.com; for more information
                visit: http://www.art-therapy.us/FSA.htm

INTRODUCTION

Inspired by the work of Silver (1976) and Stalmatelos and Mott (1985), Betts (2003) wanted to develop an assessment that would allow her to work with clients who were nonverbal. At the time the FSA was developed, Betts (2003) was working in a culturally diverse metropolitan school setting. Her clients were primarily nonverbal and had cognitive impairments, which made it difficult for them to follow directions. Further, she noted that it was difficult for them to draw unless they were motivated by a visual stimulus. Betts (2003) began using a stimulus of a face as a means to promote problem solving and provide the client with the opportunity to project his/her own concepts onto the picture.

PURPOSE AND RECOMMENDED USE

According to Betts (2003), the purpose of the FSA is to better understand the creative capabilities, cognitive functioning, and developmental levels displayed by the artist. Specifically, Betts (2003) was interested in ascertaining the strengths of the artist. She designed the assessment to work with people experiencing developmental delays. Betts (2003) stated that this projective assessment can be used with children and adolescents with multiple disabilities, particularly those experiencing communication difficulty.

DIMENSIONS THAT THE TEST PURPORTS TO MEASURE

Betts (2003) asserted that the use of the three face stimulus drawings provides a method to reveal the artist's capacity for memory and visual retention. Further, it allowed for the assessment of the client's ability to organize the elements of the human face.

ADMINISTRATION

The FSA can be administered individually or in a group format. Betts (2003) recommends the following materials:

- Standard packet of 8 Crayola markers.
- Packet of 8 Crayola Multicultural markers.
- Stimulus picture #1: one 8 1/2″ x 11″ sheet of white Xerox paper depicting the complete face stimulus.
- Stimulus picture #2: one 8 1/2″ x 11″ sheet of white Xerox paper depicting the outline of the face and neck.
- Stimulus picture #3: one 8 1/2″ x 11″ sheet of blank white Xerox paper.

There is a 50-minute time limitation for completing all three pictures. The standardized face drawing is presented to the client with the following request "Use the markers and this piece of paper." When completed, the first drawing is removed from the artist's view and he/she is presented with picture two, an outline of a face, followed by picture three, free drawing of a face.

NORM GROUPS

The FSA was not normed on a population. Norms predicting client abilities as well as disabilities have yet to be established. Initial impressions of the assessment are presented in Bett's (2003) article. This article does not provide an in-depth analysis of the cases presented.

INTERPRETATION OF SCORES

In her guidelines, Betts (2001) provided an informal rating procedure, which is based on her clinical experience. For the first picture, Betts (2001) suggested that the following points be addressed:

- Whether or not the client's motor skills permit him or her to color inside the lines.
- Client's ability to use natural colors (realism), and evidence of recognition that the picture is of a human face.
- Addition of other elements (such as hair and jewelry).
- Whether the client adjusts the face to look like the client himself/herself (and what this might indicate with respect to self-perception)—consider race and gender factors.
- Use of picture space—whether the client fills in the background or not, and whether there is color differentiation between the face and background.

For the second picture, the therapist should determine if the client ignores the fact that it is a shape of a human face by scribbling over it to make it another object rather than a face. If the client does make the drawing a face, use the indications that were mentioned for the first picture. If the object is not a face, the therapist should evaluate use of line, color, and other relevant features. For the third picture, the therapist must determine if the client completes a face out of compliance. Further, the therapist should compare this face to the previous two face drawings. If the client does not draw a face, the therapist should try to ascertain the reason why (rebellion or creativity). Page orientation, line, and color usage are some other recommended elements to consider when viewing the drawings.

SOURCE OF ITEMS

Research on face recognition led Betts (2003) to develop the FSA. There is a great deal of research interest in face recognition. In 1961, Fantz's research revealed that newborns preferred to look at patterned stimuli, such as a drawing of human face compared to plain stimuli. At one month of age, infants will limit their visual exploration to the border of a human face drawing and stare at the hairline or chin. Then at about two months scanning abilities improve and infants will begin exploring the internal features of the patterns (Bronson, 1991). Newborns track face-like patterns longer (Easterbrook et al. 1998; Johnson, 1999) which leads researchers to believe that there is an innate capacity for infants to recognize human faces (Morton, 1993; Mondlock et al. 1999). Even weeks after birth, the human face is a powerful stimulus which draws and holds our attention (Alley, 1988; Dannemiller & Stephens, 1988).

Since the face is such a powerful stimulus and the primary source for perceiving and conveying emotion, Betts (2003) began to research the use of face drawings in the literature. For instance, Gair (1975) used self-portraits to determine the impact of experimental treatments. The Draw a Face Test (DAF; Burns & Zweig, 1980), is an assessment that contains a series of pictures of children playing games and other scenes. The artist is to draw in the faces of the children that are most similar to him/herself.

Betts (2003) began to experiment with her own face drawing and developed a series of three pictures. This was predicated on the work of other art therapists who value sequence-drawing procedures (Ulman, 1965; Cohen, 1985).

RELIABILITY AND VALIDITY AS DETERMINED BY THE AUTHOR

Given that this is a newly developed assessment, reliability and validity studies have yet to be conducted using the FSA. There is no normative sample for the FSA to date.

RESEARCH USING THE ASSESSMENT

Robb (2002) used the FSA with a group of Russian children from orphanages attending a six-week day camp in the United States. She used the FSA as a pre and postassessment. Robb (2002) stated that only seven children completed the pre and postassessments due to the lack of structure in the design of the program; therefore, it was not used as an indicator of the children's progress in the camp. Overall, Robb (2002) found that the use of art therapy helped address the issues causing the children anxiety, such as immersion in the American culture and adjusting to the adoption process. She did not offer suggestions about the use of the FSA in future research.

DESIRABLE FEATURES

As in some of the previously mentioned art therapy assessments, the FSA does not require the administrator to observe the drawing process. It can be administered individually or in a group setting. This tool is directly applicable to multicultural populations: The face stimulus is gender-neutral and represents a variety of cultures, and Crayola Multicultural markers are used. It shows promise as an assessment that will reveal information about the artist's body image. It can also be used informally as a drawing technique.

UNDESIRABLE FEATURES

Only those individuals who have a great deal of clinical experience in art therapy assessments should use the FSA. According to Betts (2004), "The FSA can also be used by any art therapist as a drawing technique, which does not necessarily need to be rated or used as a formal evaluation. I have colleagues whose students are using the FSA in this way." It has not been used extensively with different populations. The exact nature of what the FSA measures has to be established through additional research.

OVERALL EVALUATION

This is a new art therapy assessment. Normative research and information on reliability and validity have to be established. Further, the guidelines for interpretation need to be formalized so people other than experienced art therapists will be able to use the assessment.

Betts (2003) suggested that a rating scale be developed for the FSA. "In order to develop a valid and reliable rating method for the FSA, researchers would need to establish a method to rate those elements in the drawings that graphically demonstrate the identified concept, ability, or skill, such as the role of color, figural and size differentiation, drawing systems, compositional strategies, the incidence of bizarre or unconventional elements, and the use of pictorial space" (Betts, 2003, p. 80).

Given that the assessment originated out of work with children who were developmentally delayed, additional research is needed with this population. Correlations with emotional disturbance and or developmental delays or communication problems should be established. Since FSA seems to reveal information about the artists' self concept, it can be paired with standardized measures such as Battle's Culture Free Self-Esteem Inventory (cited in Brooke, 1995) or the Coopersmith Self-Esteem Inventory (1967). The realm of possibilities is wide open with this new assessment.

REFERENCES

Alley, T.R. (1988). *Social and applied aspects of perceiving faces.* Hillsdale, NJ: Lawrence Erbaum Associates.

Betts, D.J. (2004, January). *Personal communication.*

Betts, D.J. (2003). Developing projective drawing test: Experiences with the Face Stimulus Assessment (FSA). *Art Therapy: Journal of the American Art Therapy Association, 20*(2), 77–82.

Betts, D.J. (2001). *Projective drawing research: Assessing the abilities of children and adolescents with multiple disabilities.* 32nd Annual Conference of the American Art Therapy Association, Albuquerque, NM.

Bronson, G.W. (1991). Infant differences in ate of visual encoding. *Child Development, 62,* 44–54.

Brooke, S.L. (1995, January). A critical review of Battle's Culture-Free Self-Esteem Inventory. *Measurement and Evaluation in Counseling and Development, 27* (4), 248–252.

Burns, W.J. &, Zweig, A.R. (1980). Self-concepts of chronically ill children. *Journal of Genetic Psychology, 137,* 179–190.

Cohen, B.M. (Ed.), (1985). *The Diagnostic Drawing Series Handbook.* Alexandria, VA.

Coopersmith, S. (1967). *The antecedents of self-esteem.* San Francisco, CA: W.H. Freeman.

Dannemiller, J.L., & Stephens, B.R. (1988). Critical test of infant pattern preference models. *Child Development, 59,* 210–216.

Easterbrook, M.A., Kisilevsky, B.S., Muir, D.W., & LaPlante, D.P. (1999). Newborns discriminate schematic faces from scrambled faces. *Canadian Journal of Experimental Psychology, 53,* 231–241.

Fantz, R.L. (1961, May). The origin of form perception. *Scientific American, 204*(5), 66–72.

Gair, S.B. (1975). An art-based remediation program for children with learning disabilities. *Studies in Art Education, 17*(1), 55–67.

Johnson, M.S. (1998). The neural basis of cognitive development. In D.Kuhn & R.S. Spiegler (Eds.), *Handbook of child psychology: Vol, 2. Cognition, perception and language* (5th ed, pp. 1–49.). New York: Wiley.

Mondlock, C.J., Leis, T., Budreau, D.R., Maurer, D., Dannemiller, J.L., Stephens,

B.R., & Kleiner-Gathercoal, K.A. (1999). Face perception during early infancy. *Psychological Science, 10,* 419–422.

Morton, J. (1993). Mechanisms in infant face processing. In B. de Boysson-Bardies, P. McNeilage, & J. Morton (Eds.), *Developmental neurocognition: Speech and face processing in the first year of life* (pp. 93–102). Londong: Kluwer.

Robb, M. (2002). Beyond the orphanages: Art therapy with Russian children. *Art Therapy: Journal of the American Art Therapy Association, 19*(4), 146–150.

Silver, R.A. (1976). Using art to evaluate and develop cognitive skills. *American Journal of Art Therapy, 16,* 11–19.

Stamatelos, T., & Mott, D.W. (1985). Creative potential among persons labeled developmentally delayed. *The Arts in Psychotherapy, 12,* 101–113.

Ulman, E. (1965). A new use of art in psychiatric diagnosis. *Bulletin of Art Therapy, 4,* 91–116.

Chapter 16

FORMAL ELEMENTS ART THERAPY SCALE (FEATS)

TITLE:	Formal Elements Art Therapy Scale (FEATS)
AGE:	children, adolescents, adults
YEAR:	1990
PURPOSE:	designed to correlate with psychiatric symptoms
SCORES:	scoring is based on graphic equivalents of psychiatric symptoms; the 14 scales include the following: prominence of color; color fit; implied energy; space; integration; logic realism; problem solving; developmental level; details of objects and environment; line quality; person; rotation; and perseveration; it is manually scored;
MANUAL:	manual (70 pages); illustrations (14 pages); reliability data (2 pages); validity data (2 pages)
TIME LIMIT:	no time limit
COST:	$50 (plus $7 shipping and handling)
AUTHOR:	Gantt, Linda, & Carmello Tabone
PUBLISHER:	Gargoyle Press; 314 Scott Avenue, Suite 1000, Morgantown, West Virginia, 26508, gargoylepress@aol.com

INTRODUCTION

This chapter will combine the assessment along with the rating scale designed to accompany the assessment rather than considering each separately. Gantt and Tabone (1998) developed The Formal Elements Art Therapy Scale (FEATS) based on the Person Picking an Apple from Tree (PPAT) assessment. The PPAT is a single picture assessment, which was standardized by Gantt (1990, 2000). Both the rating scale and the assessment have evolved over the past ten years. The Formal Elements Art Therapy

Scale (FEATS) is based on the concepts of pattern matching and the graphic equivalent of psychiatric symptoms. The test authors hoped to develop a research tool which is credible and would add to the field of art therapy by creating a standardized art therapy assessment.

PURPOSE AND RECOMMENDED USE

The FEATS manual was created for several purposes. First, Gantt and Tabone (1998) intended to provide a method for understanding and examining the nonsymbolic aspects of art. Second, they wanted to demonstrate how structural characteristics of a drawing furnishes information on a person's clinical state and their psychiatric diagnosis based on *DSM-IV* criteria. Specifically, Gantt (2000) stated that FEATS measures the following: (1) changes in clinical states; (2) changes in children's drawings as they mature; and (3) differences between two or more groups (such as ethnic or cultural groups) (p. 44). The intent was to provide a clearer picture of possible graphic indicators of psychiatric conditions such as depression and schizophrenia. Additionally, the test authors described these elements in a manner that is in line with an art therapist's way of thinking. The purpose of the FEATS was to focus on how people draw rather than the content of their drawing, an often overlooked part of the assessment process. Gantt and Tabone (1998) intended to address those features of the drawing that do not necessarily have to be explained by the artist.

DIMENSIONS THAT THE TEST PURPORTS TO MEASURE

Graphic equivalents of symptoms were described as those attributes found in the formal characteristics, not the symbolic content of drawings. FEATS was comprised of 14 scales. I will provide a brief description of each of these scales.

Scale 1–Prominence of color, focuses on how much color the artist uses in the drawing. Gantt and Tabone (1998) asserted that color relates to affect, which is supported in the literature (Lehmann & Risquez, 1953; Hammer, 1958; Groth-Marant, 1990; Brooke, 1997). *Scale 2*–Color fit determines the object color fit. Color choice is the discretion of the artist; therefore, the scale may indicate possible schizophrenia by bizarre color choices or other peculiarities displayed by people with brain injury. *Scale 3*–Implied energy focuses on the amount of effort invested by the artist to make the drawing. The test authors suggest a curvilinear relationship between invested energy and manic activity by the artist (Gantt & Tabone, 1998). *Scale 4*–Space measures the amount of area used in the drawing. This is correlated with the amount of energy invested by the artist. Depressed individuals tend to use less space (Wadeson, 1980; Dawson, 1984). On the other hand, brain injured people tend to avoid empty spaces (Reitman, 1947). *Scale 5*–Integration, views the objects (person, tree, and apple) in relation to one another. In other words, integration measures "the degree to which the items in the picture are balanced into a cohesive whole" (Gantt & Tabone, 1998, p. 34). Disintegration often characterizes the work of schizophrenic patients (Reitman, 1948; Pickford 1967; Wadeson, 1980). *Scale 6*–Logic, measures illogical responses to the drawing assignment. Again, the test authors mention the bizarre and abstract forms drawn by schizophrenic patients. *Scale 7*–Realism, ascertains whether the elements drawn are realistic or not.

> We do not expect that the people with whom we are working will be trained artists. But we do expect that the average nonpatient of average intelligence will be able to draw recognizable trees and people. (Gantt & Tabone, 1998, p. 36)

In order to measure this scale, the interpreter of the FEATS must recognize at least one element–the tree, person, or apple. *Scale 8*–Problem solving, focuses on how the artist draws the person getting the apple out of the tree. According to validity studies conducted by Gantt (1990; 1993), this scale significantly distinguished four diagnostic categories; schizophrenic, depressed, bipolar, and organic brain injured groups from the control group. *Scale 9*–Developmental level, is based on Lowenfeld's (1947) work on the developmental stages in children's artwork. Adult's work is compared to children's developmental artistic stages. *Scale 10*–Details of objects and environment, quantifies the amount of elements put into the components of the drawing. For instance, depressed individuals will tend to neglect details or not finish drawings (Hammer, 1958; Wadeson, 1980). This holds true for schizophrenics patients as well (Goldworth, 1950). *Scale 11*–Line quality, indicates the amount of control the person has on the myriad of lines used in the drawing. Lines will have different lengths and weights. Consistency in line quality characterizes normal drawings according to the test authors (Gantt & Tabone, 1998). People meeting diagnostic criteria will often draw disconnected or sketchy lines (Cronin & Werblowsky, 1979; Wadeson, 1980) or agitated lines as in the case of manic patients (Wadeson, 1980). *Scale 12*–Person, may reflect the body image of the artist. Problems of body image may be indicative of artists with depression (Gantt & Tabone, 1998), as well a sexual abuse survivors suffering from post-traumatic stress disorder (Brooke, 1997). *Scale 13*–Rotation, measures the tilt of the tree and person in the drawing. People with organic disorders will demonstrate extremes and or errors in rotation (Lynn, 1971). *Scale 14*–Perseveration, is the continuation of a response beyond what is reasonably expected. When I was working with a developmentally delayed, emotionally disturbed eight-year-old, I found that many of her drawings were marked by perseveration–for instance, using the pencil to stab the picture repeatedly to fill up space.

ADMINISTRATION

The assessment is given individually, with no limit on age. Drawings are completed on white paper (12″ x 18″) using a choice of 12 colors of felt tip markers (red, orange, blue, turquoise, green, dark green, hot pink, magenta, purple, brown, yellow, and black). The authors require "Mr. Sketch"™ watercolor markers. The administrator hands the paper to the artist, who decides the direction of the paper. The artist is given the following directive: "Draw a person picking an apple from a tree." There is no time restriction for the drawing. The test authors recommend collecting the PPAT in the initial session with a patient or client so progress can be determined by using the PPAT again at the conclusion of therapy.

NORM GROUPS

A breakdown of the demographic characteristics of the norm group was not presented in the manual. "We have not determined norms yet, that is our next project. Our comparison group was people who were not in the psychiatric hospital at the time the drawings were collected" (Gantt, 2004). Gantt and Tabone (1998) did discuss the limitations of their sample. For instance, the sample contained very few minority group participants. Also, many of the drawings were obtained from nonpatients. Further, the authors noted that many of the people participating in the control group were associated with a university or hospital, indicating a higher level of education as well as other differences in demographics. Due to the limitations of the sample, Gantt and Tabone (1998) are cautious about generalizing the results of their findings.

INTERPRETATION OF SCORES

The authors stated that symbolic interpretation of the PPAT is not the aim of their work. Rather, they viewed the drawings as a method of providing information about the artist's clinical state of mind at the time of the drawing. This is not a dictionary or cookbook approach to interpretation (Brooke, 1996). Gantt and Tabone (1998) noted that the following elements are essential for understanding drawings (p. 54):

- No sign is pathognomonic
- Context is vital
- The timing of collection is crucial
- Symbols may have multiple and contradictory meanings
- Form is information

When they refer to pathogomonic elements, Gantt and Tabone (1998) mean that there is no one single element of a drawing that will be indicative a psychiatric condition.

SOURCE OF ITEMS

Gantt and Tabone (1998) constructed each scale "so that it would be isomorphic with the clinical symptoms that were distinctive features of the specific diagnostic groups and would measure the relative magnitude of the variable" (p. 24). Each of the 14 FEATS scales is based on the following sources (pp. 24–25):

- Symptoms from the DSM that could have graphic equivalents;
- The art therapy and psychological literature on both spontaneous art and the directed drawings; and
- The test author's clinical observations of PPATs done by adult psychiatric patients.

Each scale is rated on a 0–5 Likert scale, which allows for the assessment of gradual changes and these changes can be measured quantitatively.

VALIDITY AS DETERMINED BY THE AUTHOR

Using a hospital setting, the test authors searched records to find patients who met strict diagnostic criteria. They obtained a sample of 25 people, five in each diagnostic group and five in the control group. People who had more than one Axis I disorder, substantially different Axis I disorders during different hospital stays, and any Axis II disorders were eliminated from consideration. The raters achieved acceptable interrater reliability on 10 scales (all but the energy, line quality, perserveration, and rotation scales). Using an analysis of variance, the test authors found that 10 of the 12 scales distinguished between two or more groups. No other statistical information was presented. The scales that did distinguish at least one group from another at the $p < .05$ level were: energy, integration, logic, realism, problem solving, developmental level, details, and person (Gantt, 2004).

RELIABILITY AS DETERMINED BY THE AUTHOR

Gantt and Tabone (1998) used 37 raters to rate 30 drawings from their pilot sample. Interrater reliability was reported to be .90 and higher for most scales. A breakdown of the reliabilities for each scale was not reported in the manual. The authors did report a breakdown on the 14 scales on a subsequent reliability study using three art therapists, three social work students, and three recreation therapy students. Aside from the perseveration scale with moderate correlations of .57, .74, and .52, all other scales were .74 and higher.

RESEARCH USING THE TEST

Gantt (1993) examined the correlation of psychiatric diagnoses with FEATS. The diagnoses were based on *DSM-III-R* criteria. Using records from 1989, Gantt found that 547 adults were treated on the inpatient unit where the drawings were collected. From this population, 205 patients were selected if they had one of the following discharge diagnoses: Schizophrenia, Major Depression, Bipolar Disorder, or Organic Mental Disorder. This group was further screened. Those with more than one Axis I disorder during their stay, including substance abuse disorders, those with substantially different Axis I disorders during different hospital stays, those with severe psychotic symptoms, those with Axis II disorders, those with a history of stroke or seizure disorder, and those over 70 years of age were dropped from the study. The remaining sample consisted of 36 people. The control group contained students, visitors, and family members associated with the hospital. Most were women. This is not a representative control group given that they could not rule out possible psychiatric conditions in this population. The controls ranged in age from 18 to 70 years. The raters of the study were blind to the hypotheses. All three had their M.S. degree in art therapy with experience ranging from 1–15 years. Gantt (1993) found that there was a statistical difference, at the .05 level, between the groups on 10 of the 14 FEATS scales. Perseveration, line quality, and energy showed the lowest intraclass correlations.

Normal drawings were described as having colors appropriate to the subject matter, logical, well integrated, showing developmental features common to adolescent drawings, having a reasonable amount of detail, color, and energy, depicting a realistic person, and showing a practical way of getting the apple out of the tree (Gantt, 1993). Drawings by people diagnosed with organic mental disorders showed relatively little color and the color did not fit the object. Additionally, there were few details, little energy, and little use of space. The drawings were not well integrated, were illogical, demonstrated little problem-solving skill or realism, showed a low developmental level, and the person was not recognizable.

On the other hand, there were no statistically significant differences between the drawings by participants diagnosed with depression and those of the control group on any of the scales. The drawings of depressed people could be distinguished from the organic mental disorder group by the increased energy, greater integration, greater use of logic, better problem solving, higher development level, and the depiction of a more recognizable person. Overall, the drawings by the depressed group showed less color, fewer details, and less use of space (Gantt, 1993).

The PPATs of the schizophrenic group were distinguished from those of both the controls and people diagnosed as depressed by a statistically significant lower mean score on problem solving. These drawings were similar to the organic group by their lack of detail, prominence of color, and color fit. The mean scores of the manic and schizophrenic groups were identical on prominence of color and space, and similar on seven other scales (Gantt, 1993).

A later pilot study (Williams, Agell, Gantt, & Goodman, 1996) demonstrated that raters could scan PPATs and correctly assign them to different diagnostic groups based on the drawings alone. Gantt (2002) noted that no information was given on the age or sex of the people creating the PPATs other than they were at least 18 years of age. "The surprising result was that the pictures themselves provided enough information so that the raters could make global judgments that were right more times than they were wrong" (Gantt, 2002, p. 44).

Munley (2002) conducted a pilot study to determine if children with AD/HD reasoned differently to art directives compared to children with no learning or behavioral problems. Using a population of young boys, 6-11 years of age, Munley (2002) compared the PPATs of boys diagnosed with AD/HD to a matched control group that had no known behavioral or learning difficulties. Five raters blind to the hypotheses used FEATS to rate the drawings. At the .05 level of significance, Munley (2002) found that three FEATS categories significantly predicted artists in the AD/HD group: color prominence, details of objects and environment, and line quality.

Munley (2002) selected the PPAT/FEATS because the media could easily be manipulated by children diagnosed with AD/HD. Additionally, Munley (2002) felt that FEATS provides a valid and reliable rating method to evaluate the global characteristics of the drawing. Additionally, there is a strong relationship between the rating scales and AD/HD symptoms. Last, Munley (2002) noted that only one drawing was necessary.

Munley (2002) found five participants, between the ages of 5 and 12, who were not being medicated for their AD/HD diagnosis. All participants came from a behavioral health system in a suburban Midwestern industrial town. All participants were Caucasian. The control population came from a Midwest urban parochial school and contained 13 males with no known behavior or learning problems. They ranged in age from 5 to 10 years of age. None of the matched pairs was more than 6 months apart in age according to Munley (2002).

The five raters were described as people with a strong interest in art and extensive experience with children. They included an architect, a nurse, an art historian, an interior designer, and a businessman (four women and one man). The raters were blind to the study's hypotheses. Receiving two hours of training, the raters then rated the 10 drawings for the study using FEATS. The rating of the drawings took just under two hours. Munley (2002) stated that a strong interrater correlation was confirmed. A logical regression analysis revealed high reliability coefficients for prominence of color (88.25%), details of objects and environment (77.98%), and line quality (66.81). These three elements significantly predicted membership in the AD/HD group. No statistical differences were found on the actual energy and implied energy scales. Munley (2002) was surprised by this given the hyperactivity that is associated with AD/HD. Munley (2002) did observe that when making the drawing, the boys in the AD/HD group were easily distracted and impulsive in their physical movements. The boys in the control group were more focused and took a longer amount of time to complete the drawing. The results of the study were limited by the small sample size and lack of a representative sample.

Kopytin (2002), a Russian psychiatrist, used the PPAT and FEATS with a sample of 78 Russian children and adults. The PPAT and FEATS were translated into Russian. Specifically, the scores on the FEATS were correlated with the SDT (Silver, 1990). Overall, the correlations between these two assessments were strong with the exception of the following scales: color fit, logic, line quality, rotation, and perseveration. The strongest correlations were between the SDT scores and space, integration, realism, developmental level, and person. Koptyn (2002) asserted that the results suggest that the SDT and many of the FEATS scales tap similar abilities as well as assess similar constructs.

DESIRABLE FEATURES

The test authors provided a detailed rating manual as well as pictures describing the 14 scales. Gantt and Tabone (1998) provided clear descriptions of people diagnosed as a nonpatient, schizophrenic, organic mental disordered, bipolar, and major depressive person. Further, they furnished ratings for people in those categories. The criteria for each scale is clearly delineated and included example drawings with ratings. The content tally sheet was also a useful tool and clearly explained.

UNDESIRABLE FEATURES

Gantt and Tabone (1998) stated that the assessment can be used for any age group, yet, the manual only depicted drawings done by adults. "We are in the process of writing our children's manual and will illustrate this with children's drawings. However, we have rated children's drawings using the illustrations for the adults and have had no problems" (Gantt, 2004). How does developmental level influence the PPAT? For those working with children, the ratings may be more difficult to complete. The drawings have to be collected at the time a person has their peak symptoms if one would want to measure clinical states using this assessment. Timing is critical to the interpretation of drawing. Also, it is not known from FEATS manual or research conducted to date if there are cultural differences with the PPAT. Most participants in these studies were Caucasian.

OVERALL EVALUATION

There has been a great deal of research interest in regard to graphic indicators of psychiatric symptoms (Maclay et al., 1938; Schube & Cowell, 1939; Antasasi & Foley, 1940; Anastasi & Foley, 1941; Anatasi & Foley, 1944; Zimmerman & Garfinkle, 1942; Goldworth, 1950; Robertson, 1952; Dax, 1953; Lewinsohn, 1964; Pianetti et al. 1964; Handler & Reyher, 1965; Kahn & Jones, 1965; Roback & Webersin, 1966; Pickford, 1967; Salzman & Harway, 1967; Sandman et al., 1968; Gravitz, 1969; Prinzhorn, 1972; Ulman & Levy; 1974; Harrower et al., 1975; Wadeson & Carpenter, 1976; Russell-Lacey et al., 1979; Wadeson, 1980; Amos, 1982; Holmes & Wiederholt, 1982; Bergland & Gonzalez, 1993; Gantt, 1993; Jamison, 1993; Williams et al., 1996). The PPAT and FEATS attempts to link psychiatric symptoms to graphic indicators. Unfortunately, the sample sizes of the study in the manual and for Gantt's follow-up research using FEATS were small. Also, it is not certain if psychiatric conditions were present in the control groups. The participants in the manual also represented a rather homogenous group. It would be interesting to see if there are cultural differences with the PPAT. It is not known if the PPAT/FEATS can be used effectively with children; however, Gantt (2004) is currently working on developing a normative sample of children's work on the PPAT using FEATS.

The FEATS is an excellent quantitative assessment. The rating criteria are clearly outlined with example drawings for the scales. FEATS show a great deal of promise as a research tool. Clearly, it does distinguish between groups with psychiatric diagnoses. Additional validity studies using the PPAT and FEATS are needed, particularly to determine if there are cultural differences.

REFERENCES

Amos, S. (1982). The diagnostic, prognostic, and therapeutic implications of schizophrenic art. *The Arts in Psychotherapy, 9,* 131-143.

Anastasi, A, & Foley, J. (1940). A survey of the literature on artistic behavior in the abnormal: III. Spontaneous productions. *Psychological Monographs, 52,* 1–71.

Anastasi, A., & Foley, J. (1944). An experimental study of the drawing behavior of adult psychotics in comparison with that of a normal control group. *Journal of Experimental Psychology, 34,* 169–194.

Bergland, C., & Gonzalez, R. (1993). Art and madness: Can the interface be quantified? *American Journal of Art Therapy, 31,* 81–90.

Brooke, S.L. (1996). *A therapist's guide to art therapy assessments: Tools of the trade.* Springfield, IL: Charles C Thomas Publishers.

Brooke, S.L. (1997). *Art therapy with sexual abuse survivors.* Springfield, IL: Charles C Thomas Publishers.

Cronin, S., & Werblowsky, J. (1979). Early signs of organicity in art work. *Art Psychotherapy, 6,* 103–108.

Dawson, C. (1984). *A study of selected style and content variables in the drawings of depressed and nondepressed adults.* Unpublished doctoral dissertation, University of North Dakota, Grand Forks, ND.

Dax, E. (1953). *Experimental studies in psychiatric art.* London: Faber & Faber.

Gantt, L. (2004, January 22). Personal communication.

Gantt, L. (2001). The Formal Elements Art Therapy Scale: A measurement system for global variables in art. *Art Therapy: Journal of the American Art Therapy Association, 18,* (1): 51–56.

Gantt, L. (2000). Assessments in the creative art therapies: Learning from each other. *Music Therapy Perspectives, 18,* 41–46.

Gantt, L. (1993). In *Current research in arts medicine: A compendium of the MedArt International 1992 World Congress on Arts and Medicine.* Bejani, F.J. (Ed). Cappella Books.

Gantt, L. (1990). *A validity study of the Formal Elements Art Therapy Scale (FEATS) for diagnostic information in patients' drawings.* Unpublished doctoral dissertation, University of Pittsburgh, Pittsburgh, PA.

Gantt, L., & Tabone, C. (1998). *Formal elements art therapy scale: The rating manual.* Morgantown, WV: Gargoyle Press.

Goldworth, S. (1950). *A comparative study of the drawings of a man and a woman done by normal, neurotic, schizophrenic, and brain damaged individuals.* Unpublished doctoral dissertation, University of Pittsburgh, Pittsburgh, PA.

Gravitz, M. (1969). Figure size as an index of depression and MMPI scores in normal adults. *Journal of Clinical Psychology, 7,* 143–144.

Groth-Marant, G. (1990). *Handbook of psychological assessment.* New York, NY: John Wiley & Sons.

Hammer, E. (1958). *The clinical application of projective drawings.* Springfield, IL: Charles C Thomas.

Handler, L., & Reyher, J. (1965). Figure drawing anxiety indices: A review of the literature. *Journal of Projective Techniques and Personality Assessment, 29,* 305–313.

Harrower, M., Thomas, C. & Qaltoman, A. (1975). Human figure drawings in a prospective study of six disorders: Hypertension, coronary heart disease, malignant tumor, suicide, mental illness, and emotional disturbance. *Journal of Nervous and Mental Disease, 161,* 191–199.

Holmes, C, & Wiederholt, J. (1982). Depression and figure size on the Draw a Person test. *Perceptual and Motor Skills, 55*(3), 825–826.

Jamison, K. (1993). *Touched with fire: Manic depressive illness and the artistic temperament.* New York, NY: The Free Press.

Kahn, M., & Jones, N. (1965). Human figure drawings as predictors of admission to a psychiatric hospital. *Journal of Projective Techniques and Personality Assessment, 29,* 319–322.

Kopytin, A. (2002). The Silver Drawing Test of Cognition and Emotion: Standardization in Russia. *American Journal of Art Therapy, 40,* 223–237.

Lehmann, H., & Risquez, F. (1953). The use of figure paintings in the clinical evaluation of psychotic conditions. A quantitative and qualitative approach. *Journal of Mental Science, 99,* 763–777.

Lewinsohn, P. (1964). Relationship between height of figure drawings and depression in psychiatric patients. *Journal of Consulting Psychology, 28,* 380–381.

Lowenfeld, V. (1947). *Creative and mental growth.* New York: NY: Macmillan.

Lynn, B. (1971). *Potential of the H-T-P Test for diagnosing organicity and retardation.* Unpublished doctoral dissertation, Illinois Institute of Technology, Chicago, IL.

Maclay, W., Guttmann, E., & Mayer-Gross, W. (1938). Spontaneous drawings as an approach to some problems of pathology. *Proceedings of the Royal Medical Society, 31,* 1337–1350.

Munley, M. (2002) Comparing the PPAT drawings of boys with AD/HD and age matched controls using the Formal Elements Art Therapy Scale. *Art Therapy: Journal of the American Art Therapy Association, 19*(2), 66–76.

Pianetti, C., Palacios, M., & Elliott, L. (1964). Significance of color in the drawings of chronic schizophrenics. *American Journal of Occupational Therapy, 18,* 137–140.

Pickford, R. (1967). *Studies in psychiatric art.* Springfield, IL: Charles C Thomas.

Prinzhorn, H. (1972). Artistry of the mentally ill. New York, NY: Springer-Verlag.

Reitman, F. (1947). The "creative spell" of schizophrenics after leucotomy. *Journal of Mental Science, 93,* 55–61.

Reitman, F. (1948). Dynamics of creative activity. *Journal of Mental Science, 94,* 314–320.

Roback, H., & Webersin, A. (1966). The size of human figure drawings of depressed psychiatric patients. *Journal of Abnormal Psychology, 71,* 416.

Robertson, J. (1952). The use of color in the painting of psychotics. *Journal of Mental Science: The British Journal of Psychiatry, XCVIII, 410,* 174–184.

Russell-Lacy, S. Robinson, V., Benson, J., & Cranage, J. (1979). An experimental study of pictures produced by acute schizophrenic subjects. *British Journal of Psychiatry, 134,* 195–200.

Salzman, L., & Harway, N. (1967). Size of figure drawings of psychotically depressed patients. *Journal of Abnormal Psychology, 72,* 205–207.

Sandman, C., Cauthen, N., Kilpatrick, D., & Deabler, H. (1968). Size of figure drawings in relation to depression. *Perceptual and Motor Skills, 27,* 945–946.

Schube, P.L., & Cowell, J. (1939). Art of psychotic persons. *Archives of Neurology and Psychiatry, 41,* 707–728.

Silver, R. (1990). *Silver Drawing Test of Cognitive Skills and Adjustment.* Sarasota, FL: Ablin Press.

Ulman, E., & Levy, B. (1974). The effect of training on judging psychopathology from painting. *American Journal of Art Therapy, 14,* 35–38.

Wadeson, H. (1980). *Art psychotherapy.* New York: NY: John Wiley & Sons.

Wadeson, H., & Carpenter, W. (1976). A comparison of art expression in schizophrenic manic-depressive bipolar, and depressive unipolar patients. *Journal of Nervous and Mental Disease, 162,* 334–344.

Williams, K., Agell, G., Gantt, L., & Goodman, R. (1996). Art-based diagnosis: Fact or Fantasy? *American Journal of Art Therapy, 35,* 9–31.

Zimmerman, J., & Garfinkle, L. (1942). Preliminary study of the art productions of the adult psychotic. *Psychiatric Quarterly, 16,* 313–318.

Chapter 17

THE LEVICK EMOTIONAL AND COGNITIVE ART THERAPY ASSESSMENT

TITLE:	Levick Emotional and Cognitive Art Therapy Assessment (LECATA)
AGE:	3–11 years of age
YEAR:	2001
PURPOSE:	Measures the normal emotional and cognitive development of children.
SCORES:	Scores are based on age and indicate cognitive and emotional criteria (these are also basis—not indicators); The LECATA yields two quantitative scores: Average Cognitive Level and Average Emotional Level.
MANUAL:	LECATA Test administration/scoring manual (26 pages); procedures manual (200 pages); reliability and validity data (3 pages)
TIME LIMIT:	approximately one hour for all drawing asks; this is not a rigid time limit and may be adjusted by the clinician
COST:	$60 for both manuals, plus postage.
AUTHOR:	Levick, Myra F.
PUBLISHER:	Myra F. Levick, Ph.D., ATR-BC, HLM: myralevick@adelphia.net 19730 Dinner Key Drive, Boca Raton, FL 33498 (561) 482-0114

INTRODUCTION

Myra Levick is well renowned in the field of art therapy. As many pioneers in the field, her career flowed from her early creative art expression (Feen-Calligan & Sands-Goldstein, 1996). The LECATA was developed in 1986 at the request of Janet Bush, then Director of the Miami-Dade Clinical Art Therapy Program for Exceptional Children. It is based on Levick's (1983) original work in, *They Could Not Talk and So They Drew.* Because the Miami-Dade clinical program was growing, there was a need to turn to consistent a standardized procedure for art therapy assessment. Thus, the LECATA was born.

Specifically, the LECATA centers on the cognitive and emotional functioning of the artist. It can provide an overview of the child's developmental level. The assessment is designed to measure "normal" art ability manifesting cognitive and emotional development with children at least three years of age and older. "With the LECATA, the art therapist can make a specialized contribution to the treatment team, providing information that has been gathered from drawings, creating access to understanding inner often hidden aspects of the individual's world, particularly when the individual is resistant, nonverbal, or highly defended" (Levick, 2001-a, p. 3).

PURPOSE AND RECOMMENDED USE

The LECATA was designed to measure normal emotional and cognitive development of children. Further, it provided emotional indicators, which identify defense mechanisms of the ego. The assessment can be used to contribute information to the treatment team that may not be available by other means. Additionally, Levick stated that the LECATA can be used to identify children before there are overt indicators of problems in behavior or school performance. Further, the LECATA can be used as a tool to identify dysfunctional family systems (Levick, 2001-a).

DIMENSIONS THAT THE TEST PURPORTS TO MEASURE

The LECATA yielded two scores, one cognitive and emotional development respectively. "It provides the significant indicators of cognitive and emotional development and it is designed to provide unique and important information to a treatment team with the understanding of the developmental level an individual is functioning at, may regress to, or has the potential to achieve" (Levick, 2001-a, p. 3). Cognitive indicators were based on Piagetian and artistic constructs. Emotional indicators were determined by graphic representations of defense mechanisms of the ego.

ADMINISTRATION

Levick (2001-a) noted that although the LECATA was designed to be used specifically by art therapists, other therapists can be qualified to administer the LECATA provided that qualified LECATA instructors train them. According to Levick (2004), other clinicians with comparable credentials to an art therapist and some background in art can be trained in administering the test. Weekend seminars have been conducted in the past years by Dr. Levick and colleague, Ms. Bush, and they continue to provide private one or two-day individual training at the South Florida Art Psychotherapy Institute. In both situations, the trainee is required to have supervision until such time as the trainee and trainer are satisfied with the competency of the new administrator. A certificate of completion is provided (Levick, 2004).

To administer the LECATA, the following materials will be required: a box of 16 assorted colors of craypas, 12″ x ˋ8″ white drawing paper, pencil and eraser available upon request. Levick (2001-b) stated that there should be as much consistency throughout the drawing process as possible. For instance, if the administrator uses an easel for the first drawing, it should be used for all the drawing tasks.

Levick (2001-b) provided scripts for the introduction and the drawing tasks. Here is the introduction script (Levick, 2001-b, p. 2):

My name is _____. My task here today is to learn more about you. I know that you have probably had some tests here before and that you may have some more tests. What you will do today is like a regular test but there are no grades and no rights or wrongs. You will have one hour to do five drawings using craypas and this paper. When you are finished with each drawing, please write a title on the paper. While you are talking about your pictures, I will be writing down what you say about each one. Do you have any questions? When we finish today, I will put your name, today's date and the number of each drawing on the back of your paper. If there are no more questions, we will begin.

Similar scripts were provided for the remaining drawing tasks. Additionally, Levick (2001-b) listed guidelines for the administrator, which were helpful in prompting the artist. Levick (2001-b) also suggested a closing script.

Children will complete the following tasks (Levick, 2001-b):

1. A free art task and story about the complete image
2. A drawing of the self
3. A scribble with one color and picture created from the scribble
4. A place you would like to be (3–5 years of age). A place that is important to you (6–11+ years of age).
5. A family

The scribble drawing is not scored, rather the picture created from it is scored and titled.

NORM GROUPS

According to Levick (2004), normative has been collected since 1998. Normative data on 331 children, kindergarten through sixth grade, from Palm Beach School District have been collected, recorded, and analyzed. Interpretation of data is in process and expected to be published in September of 2004.

INTERPRETATION OF SCORES

The scoring system for the LECATA is based on Correlation of Developmental Lines of Cognitive, Artistic, Psychosexual Sequences, and Defense Mechanisms of the Ego Appropriate for those Periods of Development (Levick, 1983) and Definitions and Criteria for Identifying Defenses Manifested in Graphic Productions (Levick, 1983). A scoring sheet was provided for each of the five tasks and indicated emotional and cognitive development based on age. Levick (2001-b) provided detailed notes on the cognitive and emotional criteria for the LECATA.

Task one, the free drawing and story is designed to elicit a variety of emotional responses from enthusiasm to resentment and hostility (Levick (2001-a). As with the PPAT, this drawing served as the baseline and gave an overall view on the child's psychological state at the time of the assessment. The story helped glean information about the child's habitual ways of responding and defensive postures.

The second task, drawing of the self was very similar to the interpretation of the DAP and HFD drawing tasks. As Levick (2001-a) outlined in her manual, this drawing tasks provides the therapist with information about how the artist perceives him or herself. This drawing has the potential of stimulating feelings about body image and self-concept (Levick, 2001-a).

Scribble drawings have always been interesting to me as an art therapist. Levick (2001-a) used the scribble drawing task to provide information on the artist's ability to resist regression as well as ascertain his or her ability to symbolize and use abstract thinking.

The fourth task, draw a place that you would like to be, was designed to measure how the artist relates to the environment. For older children, this drawing task may reveal information about their internalized value system (2001-a).

The last task is the family drawing. As the KFD, this drawing provided information on the family system and interaction between members. Further, it revealed the artist's attitude toward family members and perceptions of roles within the family system.

SOURCE OF ITEMS

The LECATA evolved out of Levick's doctoral dissertation called, "Resistance: Developmental Image of Ego Defenses, Manifestations of Adaptive and Maladaptive Defenses in Children's Drawings (Levick, 1983). The LECATA was based on Piaget's cognitive developmental stages (Piaget, 1962) and Anna Freud's psychosexual developmental theories (Freud, 1966). Specifically, the LECATA was founded on following theoretical concepts: Piagetian cognitive developmental theory; artistic developmental theory (Lowenfeld, 1957; Kellogg & O'Dell, 1967; Gardner, 1973; Rubin, 1978); psychoanalytic theory (Freud, 1962; Erikson, Feldman, & Steiner, 1997; Cooper, 1998); and chronological defense mechanisms development (Freud, 1936, 1937; Cramer, 1991; Dorpat, 1993; Hatcher, 1994). These theoretical constructs provide information on the artist's cognitive and emotional functioning levels.

VALIDITY AND RELIABLITY AS
DETERMINED BY THE AUTHOR

Levick (2001-b) stated that there is a need for field-testing and standardizing for reliability and validity of the assessment, which will provide a more solid foundation for the LECATA's clinical use. "There are reliability studies in the notebook and in the back of my textbook, which are the first reliability and validity studies, plus the current research noted above" (Levick, 2004).

RESEARCH USING THE TEST

To date, there is little research that documents the use of the assessment as a clinical tool. Although the LECATA may seem similar to tree drawings, family drawings, and free drawings, Levick (2004) did not intend to reinvent the wheel. "The scribble is from Naumburg originally and had emotional significance for her. Making something out of it is Kwiatowka, as is the idea of the first free drawing. The family drawing is neither a portrait nor a KFD–

but totally open ended" (Levick, 2004).

In looking at children's developmental art abilities, scribble drawings are often the first to emerge and will serve as an indicator of the child's cognitive capacity (Matthews, 1989). Historically, the use of the scribble drawings emerged out of evaluation procedures with families (Kwiatkowka, 1967; Garcia, 1975). Based on Rhoda Kellog's interpretation of scribbles for evaluation, Kiendle and colleagues (1997) used scribble drawings to help empower a group of children with disabilities. Hanes (1995) used Florence Cane's (1983) scribble technique with an adult population in a psychiatric hospital. This article evaluated the scribble technique and provided example drawings.

It would be interesting to see the LECATA used with special populations. For instance, children suffering from posttraumatic stress have cognitive and emotional deficits. In addition to dealing with depression and anxiety, children with PTSD hold cognitions of self-reproach and poor self-image. In general, art therapy shows promise when working with children with PTSD, specifically by working on emotional issues and problem solving (Mallay, 2002). Further, Silver (2001) has shown that cognitive skills can be assessed and developed through art.

DESIRABLE FEATURES

The LECATA has the advantage of being used with preschoolers as well as adolescents and even adults. The directions for administration are easy to understand. Scoring procedures are clearly outlined. The LECATA can be completed in a few hours. It gives an overview of the individual's developmental level on cognitive and emotional levels. Thus, a child that is at risk or comes from a dysfunctional family system can be identified early and the treatment team can make the necessary intervention.

Another desirable feature is that the procedural manual contains a comprehensive chapter on psychological testing, what it entails, and different types of assessments. Further, Levick (2001-a) provided information on reliability and different types of validity with respect to conducting psychological assessment research. A glossary of measurement terms was also included.

Levick (2001-a) furnished extensive theoretical information as it related to the assessment. This included information about basic Piagetian concepts and cognitive developmental stages. Additionally, basic information on psychoanalytic theory and ego mechanism of defense was included.

UNDESIRABLE FEATURES

The reference to the word, "test," in the opening script may cause anxiety in some children. Further, although the therapist stated that he or she will be writing down information, this may also be anxiety provoking for the child. It may be more advantageous to audiotape the session, but this does deviate from the instructions as outlined by Levick. In response to this, Levick (2004) stated:

> In 15 years, just saying there is no marking for this test immediately alleviated anxiety. In 40 years of practice, I have always written down what patients say and always offer them the freedom to read what I say. Interesting to note that rarely does anyone want to see what I wrote unless I request that they do so for a therapeutic purpose.

The LECATA was not standardized on a population of children; therefore, a standard of comparison is not yet available for practitioners using the LECATA. Additionally, limited reliability and validity information is noted in the manual. More research is required to determine the consistency in the results of the LECATA, consistency in the way it is interpreted, and validation of what the assessment yields.

Preferably, you have to be a trained art therapist to administer and interpret the LECATA. The alternative to this is to be trained by a LECATA instructor. Certification for training is provided.

OVERALL EVALUATION

Both manuals were detailed and easy to read. Specific guidelines were established for administration procedures, scoring, and interpretation. Particularly valuable were the appendixes in the test administration and scoring manual. Broken down by age, Levick (2001-b) described cognitive, artistic, psychosexual, and defensive development of children. Additionally, she listed the major defenses, defined them, and provided a list of graphic indicators. Scoring guidelines were clearly outlined and conversion tables were easy to use. Levick (2001-b) also provided a generic sample report form.

The largest weakness was the lack of a norm population. Levick (2004) noted that these norms are currently being developed and should be available in September, 2004. There is some reliability; yet more research is needed on this assessment. Rater reliability, internal consistency, content validity, criterion-related validity, and construct validity have yet to be established for this assessment.

There is a great deal of research potential using this tool. For instance how does the LECATA correlate with assessments such as the DAP, KFD, and DDS? These assessments can be correlated specifically with different drawing tasks: DDS–task one; DAP–task two, and DDS–task five. Does the LECATA adequately discriminate between "normal" children and those children diagnosed with cognitive and or emotional deficits? Can therapists generate the same scores for an artist's work based on the scoring criteria in the manual or is further training necessary? All these questions must be addressed to establish credibility that this assessment is a reliable and valid instrument for assessment cognitive and emotional development in children. Levick (2004) commented that the Rorschach and the TAT are the major projective assessments that the LECATA can be correlated with.

Of all the assessments that I have reviewed to date, the LECATA is the most comprehensive in terms of explaining the theoretical constructs upon which the assessment was based. Artistic, cognitive, and emotional criteria were clearly explained and examples provided. Scoring and reporting procedures were clear and easy to follow Articles on art therapy and a list of art therapy resources was also included in the procedural manual.

REFERENCES

Cooper, S.H. (1998). Changing notions of defense within psychoanalytic theory. *Journal of Personality, 66,* 94–964.

Cramer, P. (1991). *The development of defense mechanisms: Theory, research, and assessment.* NY: Springer-Verlag.

Dorpat, T.L. (1993). Review of the developmental of defense mechanisms: Theory, research and assessment, *Psychoanalytic Books, 4:*405–407.

Erikson, S., Feldman, S.S., & Steiner, H. (1997). Defense reactions and coping strategies in normal adolescents. *Child Psychiatry and Human Development, 28,* 45–56.

Feen-Calligan, H., & Sands-Goldstein, M. (1996). A picture of our beginnings: The artwork of art therapy pioneers. *American Journal of art Therapy, 35*(2), 43–60.

Freud, A. (1936). The mechanism of defense. *Writings, 2:*2–53.

Freud, A. (1937). *The ego and the mechanisms of defense* (International Psychoanalytic Library), London, England: Hogarth Press.

Freud, A. (1946). *The ego and the mechanism of defense.* American Edition, NY: International University Press.

Garcia, V.L. (1975). Case study: Family art evaluation in a Brazilian guidance clinic. *American Journal of Art Therapy, 14*(4), 132–139.

Gardner, H. (1973). *The arts and human development.* NY: John Wiley and Sons.

Goleman, D.P. (1995). *Emotional intelligence.* NY: Bantam Books.

Hanes, M.J. (1995). Clinical application of the scribble technique with adults in an acute inpatient psychiatric hospital. *Art Therapy: Journal of the American Art Therapy*

Association, 12(2), 111–117.

Hatcher, R. (1994). Review of ego mechanisms of defense: A guide of clinicians and researchers. *International Journal of Psychoanalysis, 75,* 170–172.

Ihilevich, D., & Gleser, G. (1986). *Defense mechanisms: Their classification, correlate and measurement with the Defense Mechanism Inventory.* Owosso, MI: DMI Associates.

Kellogg, R., & O'Dell. (1967). *The psychology of children's art.* CRM-Random House.

Kiendle, C., Hooyenga, K., & Trenn, E. (1997). Empowered to scribble. *Art Therapy: Journal of the American Art Therapy Association, 14*(1), 37–43.

Kwiatkowka, H. (1967). Family art therapy. *Family Process, 6*(1), 37–55.

Levick, M.F. (1983). *They could not talk and so they drew.* Springfield, IL: Charles C Thomas.

Levick, M.F. (1983). Resistance: Developmental image of ego defenses, manifestations of adaptive and maladaptive defenses in children/s drawings. *Dissertation Abstracts International, 42*(10).

Levick, M.F. (1997). *See what I'm saying: What children tell us through their art.* Springfield, IL: Charles C Thomas.

Levick, M.F. (2001-a). *The Levick Emotional and Cognitive Art Therapy Assessment (LECATA): Procedures.* Florida: Myra F. Levick.

Levick, M.F. (2001-b). *The Levick Emotional and Cognitive Art Therapy Assessment (LECATA): Test administrationn and scoring manual.* Florida: Myra F. Levick.

Levick, M.F. (2004). Personal communication, February 7, 2004.

Lowenfeld, V. (1957). *Creative and mental growth.* NY: McMillan.

Mallay, J.N. (2002). Art therapy, an effective intervention with traumatized children with suspected acquired brain injury. *Arts in Psychotherapy, 29*(3), 159–172.

Matthews, J. (1989). How young children give meaning to drawing. In A. Gilroy & T. Dalley (Eds). *Pictures at an exhibition: Selected essays on art and art therapy.* New York, NY: Tavistock/Routeldge, p. 127–142.

Piaget, I. (1962). *Play, dreams and imitation in childhood.* Translated by C. Grattengo, and F.M. Hodgson. NY: W. W. Norton.

Rubin, J. (1978). *Child art therapy.* NY: Van Nostrand, Reinhold.

Silver, R. (2001). Assessing and developing cognitive skills through art. In J.A. Rubin (Ed); *Approaches to art therapy: Theory and technique.* New York: Brunner-Routledge, 241–253.

Chapter 18

RECOMMENDATIONS

Considering the findings in the previous chapters of this book, this section will summarize the strengths and weaknesses of the art therapy assessments reviewed. Recommendations will be made based on the assessment's reliability and validity evidence as well as the desirable and undesirable features. Additionally, the clinical usefulness of the assessment will be evaluated based upon research to date and my clinical experience.

HUMAN FIGURE DRAWING TEST (1968)

Koppitz (1968) conducted thorough research to provide evidence for the usefulness of the HFD. She clearly described developmental items and emotional indicators of human figure drawings by utilizing case studies. Mental development, school achievement, organic conditions, and personality characteristics were a few of the areas reviewed using human figure drawings. Unfortunately, interpretations of the HFDs were based on these case studies. Additionally, quantitative scoring procedures were not demonstrated in the case examples.

Koppitz' (1968) HFD did show some discriminant validity, particularly with high achievers compared to low achievers. Although she demonstrated that the HFD could discriminate between shy and aggressive children, other researchers were unable to produce the same results (Lingren, 1971; Norford & Barakat, 1990). Discriminant validity for the HFD was lacking: The HFD did not discriminate sexually abused, learning disabled, or aggressive children from well-adjusted populations. I agree with Motta et al. (1993) who argued that the HFD was not a reliable or valid instrument for assessing intelligence. Information on the reliability of the HFD needs to be examined. Since the standardization sample was selected over 30 years ago, future research should focus on reestablishing norms for the HFD. Clinicians may use the HFD in conjunction with other assessments in order to provide information on client issues. In my work with sexual abuse survivors, omission of body parts was a common feature of HFDs. Additionally, sexual abuse survivors typically only draw the head and neglect the lower part of the body (Brooke, 1997). This assessment does require clinical experience when interpreting drawings. It is recommended that the HFD not be used as a measure of intelligence; rather, as a tool to illuminate client concerns and self-perceptions.

KINETIC FAMILY DRAWINGS (1972)

Burns and Kaufman (1972) added a kinetic component to traditional family drawings to create the KFD. The case examples were helpful in understanding how the authors intended the KFD to be used. Overall, the KFD potentially yielded valuable information about familial relationships as well as self-concept. The authors created a grid to quantify information about the KFD; yet, they did not present guidelines for the interpretation of measurements.

There was very little information on how the test was developed. Additionally, no information was given on who was able to administer the KFD and their qualifications. Interpretation may be difficult given the ambiguity in the test terms and lack of examples for the grid information. Objective scoring systems have been developed for the KFD (Cummings, 1980; Mostkoff & Lazarus, 1983). With training, inter rater reliability has been established (McPhee & Wegner, 1976). Test-retest reliability evidence was weak suggesting that the KFD may be sensitive to mood changes. Validity evidence was also mixed. Studies that examined the KFD as a possible screening device had mixed results. Research indicated that cultural differences as well as sex differences were found when using the KFD (Cabacungan, 1985). The exact nature of what the KFD measured was not clear.

Despite these limitations, the KFD showed promise as a tool that yielded information about a child's personality state. Research indicated that the KFD was a particularly useful instrument when evaluating children who were suspected sexual abuse survivors. Further evidence was needed to determine whether or not the KFD can adequately distinguish between other groups such as emotionally disturbed versus well-adjusted children. It is recommended that the KFD be used as a tool to gather information about a child's view of self in relationship to family members.

KINETIC SCHOOL DRAWING (1985)

The Kinetic Drawing System (Knoff and Prout, 1985) was comprised of the KFD as well as a new assessment, the Kinetic School Drawing. The KSD measured the child's self-concept, peer relations, and academic potential. The manual included several case examples that were helpful when interpreting drawings. Overall, the manual was easy to read and clear. Interpretation of the KSD may be difficult. Normative information was lacking. The authors did not provide guidelines for interpreting the drawings completed by special populations.

The reliability of the KSD was not established in the manual. Andrews and Janzen (1988) did create a scoring guide, reference sheet, and rating scale that demonstrated some reliability. Additional information regarding the stability of this assessment was needed. Overall, the KSD did demonstrate some concurrent validity with achievement measures. Discriminant validity information was lacking. As opposed to Neale and Rosal's (1993) findings, this author did not agree that the KSD was a valid instrument. There was not enough information on the KSD to validate its use within the school or counseling settings; therefore, I recommend caution when using the KSD in these settings.

DIAGNOSTIC DRAWING SERIES (1986)

The DDS (Cohen, 1985) measured behavioral and affective states of the client through structured and unstructured drawing tasks. It is one of the few assessments that utilize color for the drawing tasks. One advantage of using the DDS was that three drawings are obtained in one session. Interpretation of the DDS may be difficult. Other than noting the presence or absence of pictorial characteristics, the handbook and rating guide did not provide information related to diagnostic categories. Another possible limitation was the time factor. The pressure of completing a drawing in 15 minutes may cause stress and anxiety in some people.

Research on the DDS, to date, has shown that it can distinguish between clinical populations and well-adjusted individuals. People with adjustment disorders, depression, dysthymia, schizophrenia, and organic syndromes had drawing styles characteristically different than well-adjusted individuals. Overall, the DDS showed promise as tool to provide information on clinical diagnoses. More important, Cohen (1985) established reliability and validity of the DDS. The assessment is currently used in research in the United States and abroad, showing interest in establishing additional reliability and validity evidence for the DDS. I highly recommend the DDS when determining the status of individuals in need of clinical evaluations.

HOUSE-TREE-PERSON TEST (1987)

This test was designed to provide information on personality characteristics and interpersonal relationships. The HTP, (Buck, 1987) utilized chromatic as well as achromatic drawings. Guidelines for interpretation were clearly outlined. Buck (1987) furnished case examples that illustrated the quantitative and qualitative scoring methods. The manual was very detailed in its approach to design, administration, scoring, and interpretation. The quantitative method of the test was complex and required additional time in determining scores. Given that the administrator was tracking a myriad of issues, the use of a stopwatch to time the client may be awkward.

Reliability and validity evidence has yet to be established for the HTP. Some interrater reliability evidence was provided by a few researchers (Marzolf & Kirchner, 1972). Validity evidence was mixed. Buck (1987) recommended that the HTP be used as a screening device to measure maladjustment, appraise personality integration, and identify common personality characteristics of a specific population; yet, he did not provide evidence that the HTP was a valid device for screening in these areas. Additionally, he stated that the HTP can be used for employment and placement purposes. If the HTP was to be used to determine job classification decisions, evidence of differential prediction among job positions should be documented. Since the standardization sample was questionable, caution should be taken when using the HTP as a measure of intellectual functioning.

Buck (1987) was very thorough when outlining the administration and scoring sections of the manual. The case illustrations were helpful in providing insight on the use of the HTP. Another positive function of this assessment was that it incorporated color, a factor neglected by some art therapy tests. Validity and reliability evidence needs to be established. It is recommended that the HTP be used as a tool to gather information on client issues rather than as a measure of intellectual functioning

KINETIC HOUSE-TREE-PERSON TEST (1987)

Burns (1987) added a kinetic component to the HTP when designing the KHTP. He found that moving figures yielded more information about client issues as compared to static figures. Additionally, combining the house, tree, and person all on one page provided more information than when viewed separately. The manual was easy to read and contained several case examples to assist the therapist with interpretation. Another desirable feature of the KHTP was the incorporation of Maslow's (1954) theory to create a developmental model for the assessment. Burns (1987) modified Maslow's approach to interpret the items on the KHTP.

The KHTP may be difficult to interpret when a symbol occurs that was not included in the case examples or the summary tables. Although Burns (1987) provided a table for the scoring of attachments, he did not include scoring information when presenting the case examples. Despite the limitations, KHTP generated some valuable information about the client's perception of self, the environment, and the family. The kinetic component was a valuable addition to the HTP. The interaction of the items as well as the developmental model were a strong improvement over the HTP. Overall, the manual was clear and the test was easy to administer. Although validity and reliability evidence has yet to be established, the KHTP may be a particularly useful test when working with new clients. In one drawing, the therapist will gain knowledge of the client's view of self in relationship to the environment. I have found this as a valuable tool when working with sexual abuse survivors (Brooke, 1997).

FAMILY CENTERED CIRCLE DRAWINGS (1990)

Burns (1990) developed the FCCD to furnish information on parent-self relationships. Symbol systems were utilized to understand the nature of the drawings. It differed from the KFD in that the therapist was able to see the client's relationship with one parent at a time and focused in on one particular symbol. This assessment seemed to be more helpful in uncovering the barriers in the client's past relationship with their parents as opposed to discovering or getting in touch with their inner parents.

Reliability and validity of the FCCD was not examined. Interpretation of the FCCD was limited. It focused only on the drawing and neglected other aspects of the assessment domain. The FCCD was an interesting approach that generated information about the client's relationship with self and family; yet, the assessment lacked important data regarding administration requirements, interpretation, and information on a norm population. Guidelines for special populations such as learning disabled, hearing impaired, and culturally diverse individuals were not discussed. Overall, the FCCD had great potential as an art therapy assessment. With additional research information, the FCCD may be a valuable tool when viewing the client's relationship to self and family. The FCCD may be helpful in cases where the client has conflict with one or both parents.

SILVER DRAWING TEST (2002)

The SDT (Silver, 2002) was designed to assess cognitive abilities in three areas: sequential concepts, spatial concepts, and concept formation. The SDT was a creative attempt to measure cognitive skills in a nonverbal manner. There have been many improvements in the SDT manual as well as additional research that supports SDT reliability and validity.

The expanded norms strengthened the confidence in the SDT and countered some of the concerns stated in the first edition of this book (Brooke, 1996) as well as those mentioned by Crehan (1989). The validity evidence for the drawing from observation subscale remains weak.

The SDT is a creative attempt to measure cognitive skills in a nonverbal approach. The new manual includes demographic information, which was needed to establish additional reliability and validity data for this instrument. The STD has been widely used as a pre and posttest measure. Further, it is being used not only in the United States, but abroad. It is an excellent tool for assessing children's cognitive abilities and emotional capacities. This assessment has been translated, standardized, and published in Brazil and in Russia.

DRAW A STORY TEST (2002)

The DAS was created as a screen for depression for children, adolescents, and adults (Silver, 2002). This is an interesting assessment, which potentially yields information about the artist's affective state. Interscorer reliability is high for art therapists. Some training may be required for other professionals outside of the field of art therapy to reliably score the DAS.

The validity evidence suggests that it may be a screen for depression for children. Additional research is needed to state the DAS accurately screens for depression in adolescents or adults. There is no evidence at this point that the DAS can screen for depression with adults. Separating adults from adolescents, as Silver (2002) suggested, may be a key in providing more validity evidence for these populations.

It would be appealing to see more research related to the occurrence of ambivalent and ambiguous themes in the DAS and depression. Although some researchers have used the DAS (Cohene & Cohene, 1989) with hearing impaired children, additional research is needed with this population as well.

DRAW A PERSON: SCREENING PROCEDURE FOR EMOTIONAL DISTURBANCE (1991)

The DAP: SPED (Naglieri et al., 1991) was developed to serve as an aid in the identification of children or adolescents who may be behaviorally or emotionally disordered. The manual was clear and concise. Administration and scoring guidelines were clearly outlined. Case examples were well-structured and demonstrated the scoring system adequately. The test designers provided an excellent standardization sample that outlined demographic characteristics clearly and completely. Instructions for administration, scoring, and interpretation were very detailed.

Construct validity evidence was weak. This was a general complaint about most human figure drawing tests (Motta et al., 1993). Discriminant validity evidence was moderate to strong. The DAP: SPED appeared to discriminate between normal populations and special populations. Reliability evidence appeared strong. No significant differences were found after a one-week interval, indicating the stability of the instrument. Although the manual stated that the drawings could be used as measures of intellectual functioning, there was no evidence provided to confirm this assertion. Therefore, the DAP: SPEED should not be used as a measure of intelligence. I highly recommend the DAP: SPEED, especially in cases where a child or adolescent is suspected to suffer from emotional disturbance.

MAGAZINE PHOTO COLLAGE (1993)

The MPC (Landgarten, 1993) was designed to reveal a client's conflicts, defense mechanisms, and styles of functioning. This approach evaluated collage images as opposed to drawing style. Landgarten (1993) designed a four-task assessment protocol that was simple to administer and fit into the treatment process easily. Interpretation was based on the client's free associations and the therapist's observation of the manner in which the collage was completed. Landgarten (1993) presented clear guidelines for the administration of the MPC, materials needed, and case examples. Also, the MPC appeared to counter some of the problems inherent in cross-cultural counseling by taking into consideration images familiar to clients with diverse backgrounds.

The assessment used only images of people and inanimate objects. This limited the scope of the assessment in that animal and nature images were not considered. The fact that the MPC was to be completed in one session may be limiting. Another shortcoming was that the tasks were viewed separately. With an assessment of this nature, common themes among the tasks should be noted. Interpretation of the tasks may be difficult. The exact nature of how the collage measured transference and countertransference issues was unclear. The same holds true for the interpretation of the client's attitude from one particular image. Additional information was needed too, on the interpretation of the collage tasks.

The MPC lacked validity and reliability evidence. Since Landgarten (1993) claimed that the MPC was a multicultural assessment, research should be completed to support this point. Overall, the MPC appeared to be an empowering approach when working with clients. It offered the client a choice in image selection and interpretation of the collage. Additionally, it reduced the possibility of cultural bias by including images consistent with a client's cultural background. The MPC may increase a client's awareness of self by yielding information about inner conflicts and relationships with others. It may be a particularly useful tool for therapists engaged in cross-cultural counseling.

BELIEF ART THERAPY ASSESSMENT (2002)

Horovitz (2002) created the BATA to provide a profile of a client's spiritual development. The BATA offered a free choice of art media. Given that some clients may be anxious about exploring spiritual issues, this was a valuable improvement over other art therapy assessments that were limited to using only pencil drawings. Also, the BATA can be used with agnostics or atheists. Horovitz (2002) furnished a list of questions and suggestions when working with these individuals. The manual was very descriptive and included several case examples that demonstrated the use of the BATA.

Since examiner qualifications were not discussed, guidelines for interpretation could have been more detailed. Individuals with little clinical experience or training in art therapy may find the BATA difficult to interpret. Horovitz (2002) described Fowler's (1981) theory of spiritual development in detail; yet, she did not address its application in several of the case examples.

To date, the BATA is the only assessment in art therapy that explores a client's spiritual development. Since spirituality is an important facet of many people's lives, this assessment is long overdue. As opposed to most art therapy assessments, the client was offered a wide variety of media. Although the BATA may not be appropriate for all clients, particularly disturbed clients or school children, it did offer an option to those individuals who were ready to explore their spiritual nature.

ART THERAPY DREAM ASSESSMENT (1999)

The ATDA is simple and easy to administer. Given that the assessment does not have scoring criteria or guidelines for interpretation, clinical experience with dream interpretation and art will be necessary to interpret the ATDA. The assessment is new; therefore, it needs to be standardized and research has to be conducted to establish reliability and validity data.

The process of dream interpretation is imaginative in itself, and through the ATDA, it becomes poetic and artistic. Psychologists have long realized the importance of dreams to physical, emotional, and mental well-being, leading to the development of dream therapy and a growing application of dream art. The ATDA is one of the first assessments to combine dream analysis and art therapy.

FACE STIMULUS ASSESSMENT (2001)

This is a new art therapy assessment. Normative research and information on reliability and validity have to be established. Further, the guidelines for interpretation need to be formalized so people other than experienced art therapists will be able to use the assessment.

Betts (2003) suggested that a rating scale be developed for the FSA. "In order to develop a valid and reliable rating method for the FSA, researchers would need to establish a method to rate those elements in the drawings that graphically demonstrate the identified concept, ability, or skill, such as the role of color, figural and size differentiation, drawing systems, compositional strategies, the incidence of bizarre or unconventional elements, and the use of pictorial space" (Betts, 2003, p. 80).

Given that the assessment originated out of work with children who were developmentally delayed, additional research is needed with this population. Correlations with emotional disturbance and or developmental delays or communication problems should be established. Since FSA seems to reveal information about the artists' self concept, it can be paired with standardized self-esteem measures.

FORMAL ELEMENTS ART THERAPY SCALE (1990)

The PPAT and FEATS (Gantt & Tabone, 1998) attempted to link psychiatric symptoms to graphic indicators. Unfortunately, the sample sizes in the manual and for Gantt's follow-up research using FEATS were small. Also, it is not certain if psychiatric conditions were present in the control groups.

The participants in the manual also represented a rather homogenous group. It would be interesting to see if there are cultural differences with the PPAT. It is not known if the PPAT/FEATS can be used effectively with children; however, Gantt (2004) is currently working on developing a normative sample of children's work on the PPAT using FEATS.

The FEATS is an excellent quantitative assessment. The rating criteria are clearly outlined with example drawings for the scales. FEATS shows a great deal of promise as a research tool. Clearly, it does distinguish between groups with psychiatric diagnoses. Additional validity studies using the PPAT and FEATS are needed, particularly to determine if there are cultural differences.

LEVICK EMOTIONAL AND COGNITIVE ART THERAPY ASSESSMENT (2001)

Both manuals were detailed and easy to read. Specific guidelines were established for administration procedures, scoring, and interpretation. Particularly valuable were the appendixes in the test administration and scoring manual. Broken down by age, Levick (2001-b) described cognitive, artistic, psychosexual, and defensive development of children. Additionally, she listed the major defenses, defined them, and provided a list of graphic indicators. Scoring guidelines were clearly outlined and conversion tables were easy to use. Levick (2001-b) also provided a generic sample report form.

The largest weakness was the lack of a norm population. Levick (2004) noted that these norms are currently being developed and should be available in September, 2004. There was some reliability evidence; yet more research is needed on this assessment. Rater reliability, internal consistency, content validity, criterion-related validity, and construct validity have yet to be established for this assessment.

There is a great deal of research potential using this tool. For instance, how does the LECATA correlate with assessments such as the DAP, KFD, and DDS? These assessments can be correlated specifically with different drawing tasks: DDS–task one; DAP–task two, and DDS–task five. Does the LECATA adequately discriminate between "normal" children and those children diagnosed with cognitive and or emotional deficits? Can therapists generate the same scores for an artist's work based on the scoring criteria in the manual or is further training necessary? All these questions must be addressed to establish credibility that this assessment is a reliable and valid instrument for assessment cognitive and emotional development in children.

Of all the assessments that I have reviewed to date, the LECATA is the most comprehensive in terms of explaining the theoretical constructs upon which the assessment was based. Artistic, cognitive, and emotional criteria were clearly explained and examples provided. Articles on art therapy and a list of art therapy resources was also included in the procedural manual.

CONCLUSION

The assessments reviewed within this text represent only a few of the art therapy assessments available today. Given that practitioners differ in their assessment needs, it was my intention to provide them with a broad range of possible assessments. Family dynamics, multicultural issues, self-perception, spirituality, and relationship issues were just a few of the areas covered within this text. Although many of the assessments lacked reliability and validity evidence, some demonstrated clinical usefulness. The next chapter will present a method for utilizing and writing the results of art therapy assessments.

REFERENCES

Andrews, J., & Janzen, H. (1988). A global approach for the interpretation of the Kinetic School Drawing (KSD): A quick scoring sheet, reference guide, and rating scale. *Psychology in the Schools, 25,* 217–237.

Betts, D.J. (2003). Developing projective drawing test: Experiences with the Face Stimulus Assessment (FSA). *Art Therapy: Journal of the American Art Therapy Association, 20*(2), 77–82.

Brooke, S.L. (1996). *Tools of the Trade: A therapist's guide to art therapy assessments.* Springfield, IL: Charles C Thomas Publishers.

Brooke, S.L. (1997). *Art therapy with sexual abuse survivors.* Springfield, IL: Charles C Thomas Publishers.

Buck, J.N. (1987). *The House-Tree-Person Technique: Revised manual.* Los Angeles, CA: Western Psychological Services.

Burns, R.C. (1990). *A guide to family-centered circle drawings.* Brunner/Mazel Publishers: New York.

Burns, R.C. (1987). *Kinetic House-Tree-Person-Drawings: An interpretive manual.* New York, NY: Brunner/Mazel Publishers.

Burns, R.C., & Kaufman, S.H. (1972). *Actions, styles, and symbols in Kinetic Family Drawings (K-F-D): An interpretive manual.* New York: Brunner/Mazel.

Cabacungan, L.F. (1985). The child's representation of his family in Kinetic Family Drawings (KFD): A cross-cultural comparison. *Psychologia, 28,* 228–236.

Cohen, B.M. (Ed.). (1985). *The Diagnostic Drawing Series Handbook.* Alexandria, VA: Barry Cohen.

Cohene, S. & Cohene, L.S. (1989). Art therapy and writing with deaf children. *Journal of Independent Social Work, 42*(2), 21–46.

Crehan, K.D. (1989). Review of the Silver Drawing Test of Cognitive Skills and

Adjustment. *Mental Measurements 1989 book.* (10 333). Lincoln, NE: Burrs Institute of Mental Measurements.

Cummings, J.A. (1980). An evaluation of an objective scoring system for the KFDs. *Dissertation Abstracts, 41*(6-A), 2313.

Fowler, J.W. (1981). *Stages of faith: The psychology of human development and the quest for meaning.* San Fransciso, CA: Harper.

Gantt, L. (2004, January 22). Personal communication.

Gantt, L., & Tabone, C. (1998). *Formal elements art therapy scale: The rating manual.* Morgantown, WV: Gargoyle Press.

Horovitz, E.G. (2002). *Spiritual art therapy: An alternate path,* second edition. Springfield, IL: Charles C Thomas, Publisher.

Knoff, H.M., & Prout, H.T. (1985). *Kinetic Drawing System for Family and School: A Handbook.* Los Angeles, CA: Western Psychological Services.

Koppitz, E.M. (1968). *Psychological Evaluation of Children's Human Figure Drawings.* New York: Grune & Stratton.

Landgarten, H. B. (1993). *Magazine Photo Collage.* New York, NY: Brunner/ Mazel Publishers.

Levick, M.F. (2001-a). *The Levick Emotional and Cognitive Art Therapy Assessment (LECATA): Procedures.* Florida: Myra F. Levick.

Levick, M.F. (2001-b). *The Levick Emotional and Cognitive Art Therapy Assessment (LECATA): Test administration and scoring manual.* Florida: Myra F. Levick.

Levick, M.F. (2004). Personal communication, February 7, 2004.

Lingren, R.H. (1971). An attempted replication of emotional indicators in human figure drawings by shy and aggressive children. *Psychological Reports, 29,* 35–38.

Marzolf, S.S., & Kirchner, J.H. (1972). House-Tree-Person drawings and personality traits. *Journal of Personality Assessment, 36*(2), 148–165.

Maslow, A.H. (1954). *Motivation and personality.* New York: Harper and Row.

McPhee, J., & Wegner, K. (1976). Kinetic-Family-Drawing styles and emotionally disturbed childhood behavior. *Journal of Personality Assessment, 40,* 487–491.

Mostkoff, D.L., & Lazarus, P.J. (1983). The Kinetic Family Drawing: The reliability of an objective scoring system. *Psychology in the Schools, 20,* 16–20.

Motta, R.W., Little, S.G., & Tobin, M.I. (1993). The use and abuse of human figure drawings. *School Psychology Quarterly, 8*(3), 162–169.

Naglieri, J.A., McNeish, T.J., & Bardos, A.N. (1991). *Draw a person: Screening procedure for emotional disturbance.* Austin, TX: Pro-Ed.

Neale, E.L., & Rosal, M.L. (1993). What can art therapists learn from the research on projective drawing techniques for children? A review of the literature. *The Arts in Psychotherapy, 20,* 37–49.

Norford, B.C., & Barakat, L.P. (1990). The relationship of human figure drawings to aggressive behavior in preschool children. *Psychology in the Schools, 27,* 318–325.

Silver, R. (1990). *Silver Drawing Test of Cognitive Skills and Adjustment.* Sarasota, FL: Ablin Press.

Silver, R. (2002). *Three Art Assessments: The Silver Drawing Test of Cognition and Emotion; Draw a Story: Screening for Depression; and Stimulus Drawing and Techniques.* New York: Brunner-Routledge.

Chapter 19

AN APPROACH TO USING
ART THERAPY ASSESSMENTS

A Case Study

S ince art-based assessments have strengths as well as weaknesses, the most logical approach to evaluating clients is to combine several assessments. This method yields more information on client issues. Additionally, common themes may be noted by the therapist that would otherwise remain illusive if only one assessment is used. The following represents one technique for evaluating clients. This format was developed by Ellen Horovitz (1994; personal communication) to help her graduate students present a clinical evaluation of clients. The case example will demonstrate how these instruments may be combined to create a profile of a client. Sommer volunteered to participate and gave her permission to use the evaluation and art work.

ART THERAPY DIAGNOSTIC ASSESSMENT

NAME: Sommer
DOB: 6/13/1980
CA: 23 years
REFERRAL: volunteer
TESTS ADMINISTERED: Kinetic House-Tree-Person Test (KHTP)
                             Kinetic Family Drawing (KFD)
                             Diagnostic Drawing Series (DDS)
                             Person Picking an Apple from a Tree (PPAT)
                             Belief Art Therapy Assessment (BATA)
                             Art Therapy Dream Assessment (ATDA)
                             Symbol Centered Circle Drawings (SCCD)

ADMINISTRANT: Stephanie L. Brooke, MS, NCC
                                   Art Therapist

OBSERVATIONS, BEHAVIORAL IMPRESSIONS

Sommer, a thin, tall, white female with red hair and blue eyes, volunteered to participate in the diagnostic assessment. Sommer is working on her degree in psychology and has another year before she graduates. Sommer has had experience with art and was engaged in the process, with the exception for the KFD. She did not show a marked directional preference The quality of her strokes was soft; yet, determined. Sommer did not ask for suggestions or help during the session. Form was more important for Sommer than color. Her work was full, original, and integrated. She worked best with pastels.

TEST RESULTS

Kinetic House-Tree-Person Test

Sommer drew her house first which suggests a need to belong to society, to have a home for nurturing, and to belong to the earth. The house was one she would like

Figure 1. Kinetic House-Tree-Person Test.

to have one day. The house had many windows, and a sun roof, which may represent openness and desire for environmental contact. There were many plants in the windows suggesting a desire to nurture.

Next, Sommer drew the tree right next to the house and in fact, touching the roof of the house. Although the tree is not leaning toward the house, it may indicate movement toward family attachments. The tree was the largest object on the page, which represents a strong life force. The foliage was circular suggesting a possible lack of direction in Sommer's energy system. Additionally, the branches were fragmented, which may characterize a person who has ideas but does not complete them.

The last item drawn was the person, and Sommer seemed a bit stuck on this at first. She drew the person, herself, sitting by the brook making a painting. She said that she used to do this quite a bit when she was younger. The expression on the face is sad. Further, there is heavy shading on the hair and hat, indicating anxiety. Hats usually suggest a need for containment with respect to cognitions.

There is a pet cemetery behind the tree, and in between the house and the tree. She said that she has a pet cemetery at her parents' house. It is interesting to note that there are less windows on this side of the house. Additionally, windows that are there have curtains which limit the view.

Kinetic Family Drawing

Sommer was highly resistant to completing this drawing. She was defended and insisted that she could not draw people. She invested little effort and detail, completing the drawing in less than five minutes.

The drawing shows a great deal of compartmentalization. Each member of the family is separated from each other by lines. There is no clear point of access. She drew her brother laying in his bed, reading. The bed almost resembles a tomb. Sommer drew herself, with her back to all other figures, alone in her room studying. Again, the hair is shaded heavily suggesting anxiety. Sommer drew her mother in the parent's bedroom, curled up in a ball, in fear, and crying. The step-father is outside the door banging on it and looks very angry. Everyone in the family was isolated. Compared to her other drawings, this one is impoverished.

Sommer had been through counseling for sexual abuse, at the hands of her stepfather, which is why it was difficult for her to complete the drawing. She was taking medication for anxiety and depression during her course of therapy and continues today. She does not feel close to any of her family members, as indicated graphically in her drawing, and in fact, and has a very distant relationship with them presently. Sommer remembers her stepfather as an angry person, fighting with her mother, breaking down the door to the bedroom when they were fighting. Sommer and her brother spent a great deal of time in their rooms to escape from the parental fighting. She said she was not aware of any physical abuse in the house but the fear was always there.

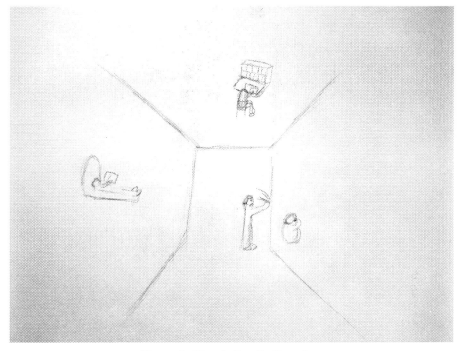

Figure 2. Kinetic Family Drawing.

Diagnostic Drawing Series

The first picture was the free drawing and it was very colorful. On the lower left hand side of the page, there is a floating pink flower.

Sommer was highly invested with this drawing. When asked about it, she said that it was similar to a drawing she made a few years ago after her suicide attempt. She said it represented hope and life. It gave her a sense of peace.

The next drawing was the tree drawing. Once again, Sommer was highly invested in her work and enjoyed the drawing task.

She stated that Autumn is her favorite season. She loves the colors in the tree. "It is like God takes a paint brush across the landscape." Sommer did show some perseveration in the creation of the leaves for this tree. The base of three is strong with a solid root foundation.

The last drawing was the picture of how you are feeling. At first, Sommer seemed a bit stuck on this but then drew an image of a mermaid.

It is a floating figure DONE mostly in one color. When asked about the painting, Sommer replied that mermaids represent beauty and freedom. Sommer said that she has been feeling free of many of the issues that have been weighing on her.

Sommer did have a dual diagnosis two years ago, depression/anxiety and alcohol dependence. Her drawings did not show graphic indicators of depression but she has been on medication for depression and anxiety for the past two years.

Figure 3. Diagnostic Drawing Series #1.

Figure 4. Diagnostic Drawing Series #2.

Figure 5. Diagnostic Drawing Series #3.

Person Picking an Apple from a Tree

Sommer did this drawing quickly but was highly invested. She drew herself riding on horseback picking an apple from the tree.

The person has a more pleasant affect and reaches easily to pick the apple from the tree. Again, she drew herself with a hat. It should be noted that some of the apples have fallen from the tree.

For the first scale, prominence of color. This therapist rated the drawing 3 indicating two or more forms or objects were colored in. The color fit scale was rated 5, showing that all colors were appropriate to the specific objects in the drawing. There was a moderate amount of energy in the drawing earning a rating of 3. Sommer used approximately 75% of the space, earning a score of 4 on the space scale. The composition was well-integrated earning a score of 5 on the integration scale. Further, there were no bizarre or illogical elements in the drawing, earning a rating of 5 on the logic scale. The PPAT was drawn realistically with shading on the tree, earning a score of 5 on the realism scale. For the problem-solving scale, the PPAT earned a score of 5, indicating that the person is in the process of picking the apple using a reasonable support, the horse. On the developmental level, the PPAT earned a score of 5 indicating that it was an adult drawing and showed some artistic sophistication or training. For details of objects and environment, the PPAT earned a score of 2

Figure 6. Person Picking Apple from Tree.

with a horizontal line indicating grass, but nothing else in the environment. For line quality, the PPAT earned a score of 4, indicating that the lines used were under control. For the person scale, the drawing earned a score of 5, showing that the person was drawn with articulated body parts. There was no rotation of objects, indicating a score of 5. There was no perseveration, earning a score for the last scale of the FEATS.

The picture is oriented horizontally. Only a few colors were used in the drawing: red, light green, dark green, orange, and brown. For the person, orange, red, and dark green were used. As for the energy of the person, she is sitting on the horse, reaching for the apple. The person is in profile and appears to be an adolescent or adult. The person is wearing a hat and one uniform outfit for the clothing. The tree has 10 or more apples with three that fell to the ground. All the apples are red. There is very little detail in the environment–the figures are grounded on a grass line.

Belief Art Therapy Assessment

Sommer chose oil pastes and paint to complete the BATA. When asked to depict what God means to her, Sommer drew a series of images which she associates with religion: a heart, ankh, and the Yin/Yang symbol. She said the heart represents the key to life and spirituality–love. Another image was the ankh, for her, it represented the continuous circle of life and how we are each a part of that circle, into infinity. The last image was the

Figure 7. Belief Art Therapy Assessment of God.

Figure 8. Belief Art Therapy Assessment of Antithesis of God.

Yin/Yang symbol, which she described as the Asian symbol for masculinity and femininity. Sommer felt that it also represents the light and dark parts of herself.

After sitting for about five minutes, Sommer took a different approach to completing the antithesis of God. She used black construction paper and tissue paper to create a stained glass window.

She said the opposite of God is like looking through a fragmented window, when light is promised but never comes. It is deceiving. She invested a great deal of time creating this portion but seemed resistant to talking about the finished product.

Art Therapy Dream Assessment

Sommer was particularly troubled by a recent dream. She said she woke up crying and very frightened. She chose pencil to complete the ATDA. At first, Sommer said that she could not remember the dream so Gestalt techniques were used to help her come up with the dream text.

Figure 9. Art Therapy Dream Assessment.

Script 1: *The animal soldier is yelling at me. It is a German soldier. I am very frightened because he is yelling and has a gun. He is saying, "You are out of order! We must have peace and quiet around here and you are out of order!"*

Script 2: *"You are out of order! We must have peace and quiet around here and you are out of order!"*

Script 3: *You are out of order!*

In the past week, Sommer was battling a severe depression over a relationship. She knew that it was not right for her but did not know what to do about it. The turmoil of this was creating havoc in her life, triggering suicidal ideations, and essentially knocking her out of emotional kilter so that she was "out of order." She felt a great deal of relief working through this dream and did come to some closure about her relationship issues which she had been keeping to herself and trying to contain.

Symbol Centered Circle Drawings

When Sommer came to art therapy session, she wanted a directive as to what to create. This therapist suggested a drawing of what her life was like now, the people that were around her, and how she saw herself. She was resistant to drawing people so this therapist suggested using collage images. Instead, Sommer chose colored pencils and pastels to create the following symbol drawing:

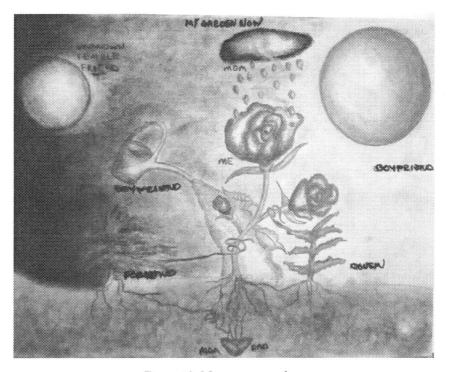

Figure 10. My current garden.

Of all the drawings that she completed in therapy, Sommer was highly invested in this one, showing a great deal of detail, depth, color, and the utilization of space. She labeled each part of the picture as representing those significant people in her life. Sommer stated that she felt that she was somewhere in between the light and the dark, a theme that emerged in her BATA.

The first symbol that was centered was the image of her mother as the thunder cloud.

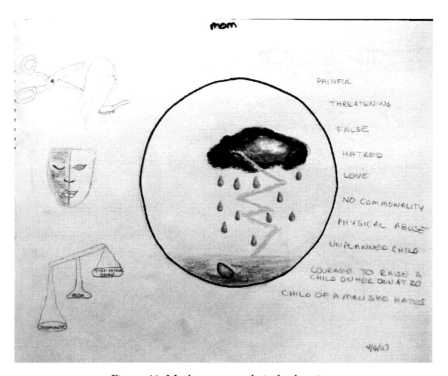

Figure 11. Mother-centered circle drawing.

On the left hand side of the page, she drew symbols and used words on the right. She said she remembers her mother verbally striking without warning. From the time she was little, Sommer remembers her mother being very angry, like a dark cloud over her head all the time. Yet, she did remember times when her mother was nurturing, as symbolized by the rain. Her mother was always harsh when combing her hair, a regular battle in the mornings that she dreaded. When they fought, Sommer's mother would always threaten to cut her long hair. The mask represented the false face her mother put on in front of her friends and family: She would dote over Sommer in front of them and then physically abuse her when they were gone. As for the scale, Sommer felt that her mother put everyone else, her brother, her stepfather, before her. Sommer said that she felt that her mother always hated her

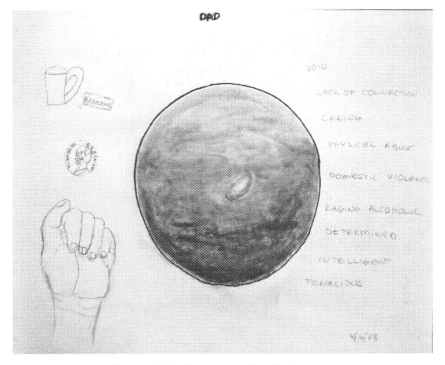

Figure 12. Father-centered circle drawing.

because she looked like her father, a man the mother detested.

The next symbol was in half seed representing her father.

Sommer did not remember her father as her parents were divorced when she was barely two years old. What she does know of him is through her mother's stories. Sommer said that her father was physically abusive to her mother and was an alcoholic. She drew a fist to represent anger, an image that came up in her stepfather figure in the KFD.

Two symbols of the boyfriend appeared in the drawing. One was of the sun and the other a watering pot. The sun was the largest image on the page.

This drawing was done when her relationship with her boyfriend was new. She viewed him as holding her heart, intelligent, fun, and free. The yin/yang symbol appears again as it did in her spirituality drawing. She felt that he brought peace to her life at a time when she was struggling with a drinking problem.

As the sun provided her with nourishment so did the watering pot. She stated again that he brought balance to her life as well as love. They were friends for four years before dating. She drew the willow tree to represent flexibility. The willow tree is taking nourishment from the brook, which she associated with herself.

The next symbol centered drawing is of her cousin—a weed in the garden.

Her cousin was one of her enablers to drink, always getting wine for her when she said she probably should not have had it. He would get drunk right along with her.

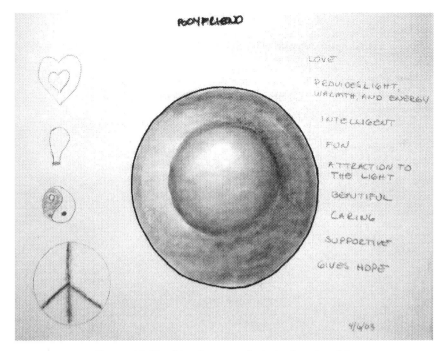

Figure 13. Boyfriend-centered circle drawing #1.

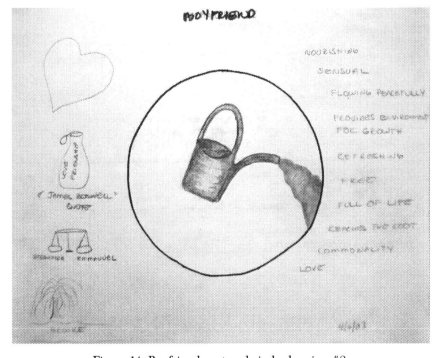

Figure 14. Boyfriend-centered circle drawing #2.

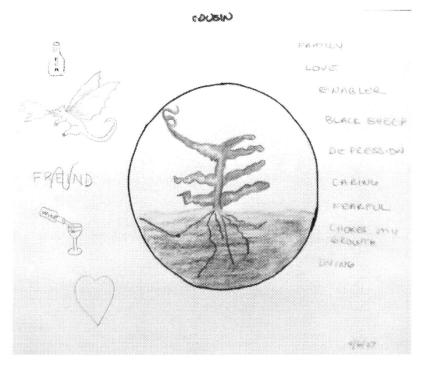

Figure 15. Cousin-centered circle drawing.

Although she described him as her best friend and a person with a big heart, she felt that he did not have her best interests at heart sometimes and thus would choke her.

The weed symbol was also used for a close male friend of hers–another enabler according to Sommer. This friend would be her travel companion on European trips but she felt that he sometimes attached himself to closely too her and asked too many questions. Although she said he cared, he always encouraged her to drink.

The moon image was of an unknown female friend.

Although Sommer longs for a female friend, she feels that this eludes her. Sometimes, she feels that there is a lack of trust with women and she admits to putting a wall up. She said that her past friendships with women wax and wane, like the cycle of the moon. "It is like jumping from a plane for the first time and someone moved the safety net."

The last symbol centered circle drawing is of her, represented as a rose vine.

The rose has no thorns which may suggest vulnerability. She thought of the music video, "Brave" by her favorite band Marillion as characterizing herself. In the video, the woman, a sexual abuse survivor, battles her demons, tries to be brave, but then ends up taking her life. There was a great deal of pain in this drawing with the symbol of the wounded heart: "I have been wounded by ALL significant figures in my life." For her, the butterfly represents freedom and the rose, growth. She said her life has been the long search for balance between being a victim and being a survivor.

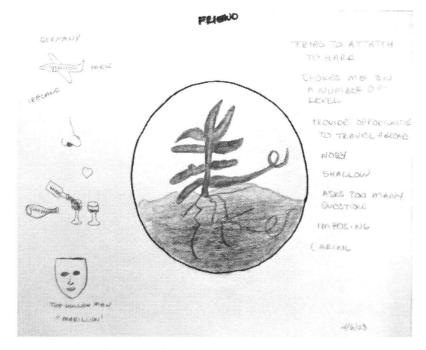

Figure 16. Friend-centered circle drawing.

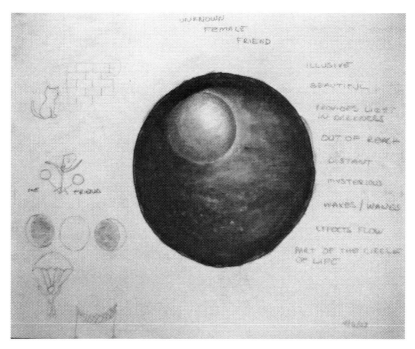

Figure 17. Unknown female friend-centered circle drawing.

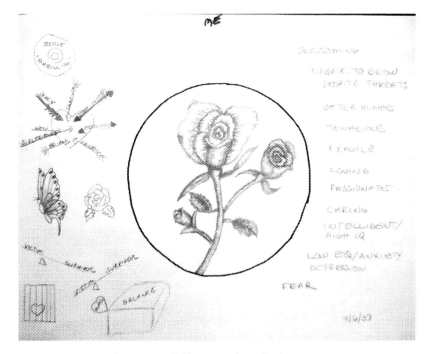

Figure 18. Self-centered circle drawing.

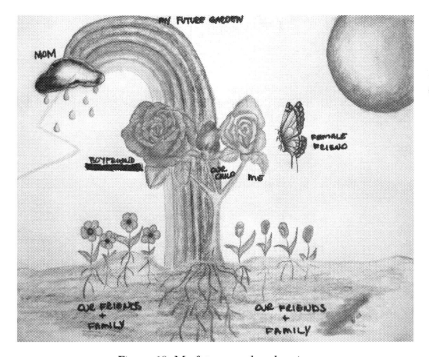

Figure 19. My future garden drawing.

Sommer drew a heart which looks like it is falling off a box. To this she replied, "My heart is made of glass, searching for stability, constantly in jeopardy of shattering, above all, a broken heart will trigger me to drink."

The last drawing is of how she would like her life to be in the future. The darkness is gone. The angry cloud, mother, is passing leaving behind a colorful rainbow. She and her boyfriend are the roses, with a bud between them, representing a desire to have a family. The female friend is now a butterfly coming close to the rose which represented her. There are no more weeds in the garden, only flowers which represent her family and friends. She titled this, "My future garden."

SUMMARY

Sommer's work appears to be in the Pseudo-Naturalistic Stage of artistic development (12–14 years) according to Lowenfeld and Brittain (1987). Although Sommer worked well with the materials, she was resistant to some of the drawing tasks, particularly the KFD. Talking about family issues is still very difficult for her.

The predominant themes were a need for nurturing and a desire for familial contact as depicted in her KHTP and free drawing from which she created the symbol centered circles. Sommer was able to successfully conceptualize her ideas and was highly invested in the art process. She did not display any anxiety or reluctance to the art media, just some of the art tasks. She had difficulty expressing affect related to her family of origin. Overall, she demonstrated reflection and attended well.

RECOMMENDATIONS

Sommer was very eager about the art process initially and was engaged and invested in most of the drawings. She did much better with free drawings suggesting a need for autonomy and independence and was stubborn with tasks she did not want to complete. Form was more important than color. Overall, Sommer worked in the pseudo-naturalistic stage of development (12–14 years) according to Lowenfeld and Brittain (1987). This therapist highly recommends that Sommer continues with individual art therapy. Her past suicide attempt, difficulty with relationships, and struggle to battle the drinking problem are room for concern and indicate the need for continued support and therapy. It is felt that the art materials and support of the therapist might provide an avenue for expressing her feelings, particularly in relation to family of origin work. Working in clay may help her channel possible aggressive energy associated with her family. In addition, art therapy may help her improve her self-esteem.

Stephanie L. Brooke, MS, NCC
Art Therapist

APPENDIX I
BELIEF ART THERAPY ASSESSMENT INTERVIEW

Stephanie (T):   What is your religious affiliation?

Sommer (C):   I don't know. I was baptized Protestant as a baby. My mother is Catholic and my stepfather was Protestant. I have been going to a Catholic church lately.

T: Have there ever been any changes in your religious affiliation?

C: No, but I did decide to go to a Catholic church. I am not sure about converting though.

T: When did these changes take place and what were the circumstances that caused this change?

C: I tried to commit suicide a few years ago and went to a Catholic hospital. A nurse there suggested that I try this church because they were more open than most Catholic churches. People from all walks of life go there, even Protestants can go there.

T: What is the level of your present involvement with your church, temple, or faith community?

C: I have always considered myself a spiritual person but have been resistant to the whole organized religion thing. This church that I am going to now seems different.

T: Yet you say you are spiritual. How would you characterize your spiritual life?

C: I guess I am a hodge podge of different spiritual concepts from Christianity, Taoism, Wicca, etc.

T: What is your relationship with your pastor or minister?

C: I know him but that is it.

T: Do you have any religious/cultural practices that you find particularly meaningful?

C: I pray every day, usually in the morning and in the evening. I celebrate the traditional Christian holidays.

T: What kind of relationship do you have with God?

C: I think it is a good one between church and the support groups I go to. I try to practice my spiritual principles daily.

T: What gives you special strength and meaning in your life?

C: Love–love for other people, love of self, and love of nature.

T: Is God involved in your problems? Do you blame God for your problems?

C: No I do not blame God. I have a poem, *Footprints,* that my grandmother gave me. Whenever I feel that God has abandoned me, I read that poem. I have gone through some pretty horrible experiences in my life but it has made me a stronger person.

T: Have you ever had a feeling of forgiveness from God?

C: Sure. We all make mistakes and I am no exception. As long as you honestly ask for forgiveness and try to make a positive change, I feel God forgives.

T: What does the ankh mean to you?

C: Everlasting life. It is symbolic of how we are all connected to one another—we are all part of God's plan and circle.

T: And the Yin/Yang?

C: We all have a dark and a light side, they are part of one another. You cannot have light without darkness. They flow from and into one another.

T: What about your antithesis to God?

C: I don't know. It is a stained glass window without any light. There is the promise of light but none comes. It is fragmented.

REFERENCES

Horovitz, E. (1994). *Personal Communication.*

Lowenfeld, V., and Brittain, W.L. (1987). *Creative and Mental Growth.* 8th ed. New York: Macmillan.

Chapter 20

INTERNET RESOURCES

This chapter will provide some links to helpful information on art therapy including art therapy organizations, news articles on art therapy, frequently asked questions, and much more. Further, some links are provided here for the art therapy assessments reviewed in this book.

Research for this site was conducted primarily through Google.com and Netscape. Also, I created a AOL news alert for any articles on the topic of art therapy. It should be noted that this is not a comprehensive list but should provide enough resources to get you started on your search!

Stephanie L. Brooke, MS, NCC

http://StephanieLBrooke.com

Title: *Albuquerque Tribune* Online

Website: http://www.abqtrib.com/archives/neighbors04/012204_neigh
                 bors_mailbox.shtml

Abstract:

An article by Albuquerque Tribune Online talks of Santa Fe Mountain Center, Santa Fe, for an empowerment project. Southwestern College, Santa Fe, for an art therapy program to help girls with eating disorders.

Title: American Art Therapy Association (AATA)

Website: http://www.arttherapy.org/

Abstract:

This site contains information on AATA, a national organization founded in 1969. Information about the organization and membership requirements are discussed. The News and Events lists contains links to job opportunities, legal issues, conferences, and continuing education. Registration guidelines and approved art therapy programs are also presented.

Title: Art, music, and culture: Iraqis taking care of their own

Website: http://electroniciraq.net/news/1321.shtml

Abstract:

This article from Electronic Iraq (January 9, 2004) discusses Childhood's Voice Art Therapy School. This school is associated with the Season's Art School, which provides services to children suffering from PTSD, poverty, and other traumas and disabilities.

Title: Art therapy

Website: http://www.cancer.org/docroot/ETO/content/ETO_5_3X_Art
                _Therapy.asp?sitearea=ETO

Abstract:

Sponsored by the American Cancer Society (2003), this site talks about the benefits of art therapy. It considers the historical evolution of art therapy, evidence to support benefits, and possible complications of using art therapy.

Title: Art therapy

Website: http://www.healthatoz.com/healthatoz/Atoz/ency/art_therapy
                .html

Abstract:

Ford-Martin (2002) published this online essay about art therapy that is a good overview of the field. She provides a detailed description of the origins of this field including information on early assessments such as the DAP and more. The work of the early founders of the field is also discussed. A list of books in the field is also included.

Title: Art therapy

Website: http://www.wholehealthmd.com/refshelf/substances_view/
             1,1525,671,00.html

Abstract:

This site is sponsored by whole health md.com (2004) and provides a description of art therapy, how it works, what people can expect from the therapeutic process, health benefits, and how to choose a practitioner.

Title: Art therapy and the brain

Website: http://www.schoolintrosite.brainyart.com/

Abstract:

Del Giacco's Art Therapy Institute sponsors this site. The institute offers a certificate course online on Neuro art therapy and the Therapeutic Drawing Series (CEU available). This site also provides a free learning module on the brain and brain injury.

Title: Art therapy at work

Website: http://home.flash.net/~redthumb/favorite.htm

Abstract:

This site discusses the long-term benefits of art therapy for children and their families. Benefits to people with term needs as well as people in crisis can work through their problems in a secure holding environment created by the art therapist.

Title: Art Therapy Credential Board (ATCB)

Website: http://www.atcb.org/applicants.htm

Abstract:

This site contains information on the registration process for art therapy. Four options are presented. Code of professional practice is discussed. Frequently asked questions, newsletters, exam, and re-certification links are provided. Applications for registration are available.

Title: Art therapy FAQ

Website: http://www.ctarttherapy.org/information/

Abstract:

This site provides some answers to commonly asked questions about art therapy such as the definition, expectations of a session, information about graduate programs, art therapy credentials, and information on the job market.

Title: Art therapy helps Iraqi children recover from war

Website: http://www.stuff.co.nz/stuff/0,2106,2783074a12,00.html

Abstract:

Sunday Times News Article (January 14, 2004) discusses the Seasons Art School. This school is designed to give back Iraqi students their childhood as opposed to a teaching/learning environment. The school serves 180 students from five to 18 years of age. Students come to the school a few hours a day and participate in creative arts therapy.

Title: Art therapy graduate school programs

Website: http://www.gradschools.com/listings/menus/art_therapy_
              menu.html

Abstract:

Gradschools.com provides a comprehensive list of graduate schools in art therapy, creative arts therapy, and music therapy. A list of programs outside the U.S., distance/online learning programs, and certificate programs. Further, links to dissertation thesis advisors is also provided.

Title: Art therapy on the web

Website: http://www.sofer.com/art-therapy/

Abstract:

This site was developed by Danny Sofer, originally designed to compliment a talk given in July 1996 to the London Regional Group meeting of the British Association of Art Therapists. Art therapy links , art therapy forum, and a short paper on art therapy are provided. Information about jobs, training, research, and conferences are also provided.

Title: Art therapy resources at Questia

Website: http://www.questia.com/Index.jsp?CRID=art_therapy& OFFID=se1

Abstract:

This online library contains links to art therapy books, journals, and new articles. A demonstration link is provided. If you like the site, you can subscribe to it for $9.99 to $19.99/month.

Title: Art therapy student networking forum

Website: http://forums.delphiforums.com/ATstudents

Abstract:

Established in 1999, the form was created for art therapists and students and provides an online network community. Links to other art therapy forums are provided.

Title: Art therapy student website

Website: http://www.art-therapy-canvas.org/

Abstract:

This site is a communication port for art therapists and students sponsored by the Canvas. It provides resources for advanced art therapists and students alike. It includes state pages, legislative information, research, and networking resources.

Title: Art therapy: Visualizing Emotions

Website: http://www.bluejeanonline.com/features/features_archives/
                features0301g.html

Abstract:

Kotwas (2002), senior editor of Blue Jean Magazine, interviewed Colleen Kunz, art therapist at a battered women's shelter in Rochester, New York, to get a overall view of the nature of art therapy. Career possibilities for art therapists are also briefly discussed.

Title: Artful Hands

Website: http://www.zwire.com/site/news.cfm?newsid=10924131&BRD
                =1649&PAG=461&dept_id=11971&rfi=6

Abstract:

This article on the RockyHillPost.com discusses the growth of an art therapy program at the Veterans Home and Hospital in Rocky Hill. Starting out as an art class, the program grew rapidly. Fifty veterans showed their work at the third annual art show.

Title: Arts in Therapy Network

Website: http://www.artsintherapy.com/

Abstract:

AIT is an international, nonprofit organization, which provides an online community for people interested in creative healing therapies. Membership for this site is free. It provides information on different types of therapies including the following: art, music, dance, drama, psychodrama, poetry, bibliotherapy phototherapay, and expressive arts therapy. News articles are also presented. Links to state art therapy associations are provided.

Title: The Arts We Need

Website: www.theartsweneed.org

Abstract:

The Arts We Need (TAWN) is a nonprofit organization that provides creative arts therapies to people with special needs.

Title: Benefits of art therapy

Website: http://www.mainchance.org/upward/read/september2002/therapy.html

Abstract:

In this article by Brenner (2002), the benefits of art therapy are delineated. Brenner is a creative arts therapy working for the VA New York Harbor Healthcare system. The site contains some drawings by clients.

Title: Cancer fools women

Website: http://www.sundaytimes.news.com.au/common/story_page/0,7034,8482939%255E2761,00.html

Abstract:

This article in the *Sunday Times,* January 24, 2004, talks about a cancer patient's participation in the Edith Cowan University study on the benefits of art therapy.

Title: Creative-healing therapies for mentally challenged

Website: http://timesofindia.indiatimes.com/articleshow/468786.cms

Abstract:

This article in the *Times of India* (2/2/04) talks about the use of creative therapy with the mentally challenged in a residential care facility. The center specializes in work with the following disabilities: epilepsy, autism, and other neurological disorders.

Title: Cult Survivors Handbook

Website: http://surrealist.org/norimuster/handbook6.html

Abstract:

Written by Muster (2000), this site discusses creative art therapy in combination with Gestalt techniques.

Title: Drawings

Website: http://www.ipt-forensics.com/library/images5.htm

Abstract:

Sponsored by the Institute of Psychological therapies, this site provides a nice overview of art therapy assessments used with children. Graphic indicators of sexual abuse are briefly discussed. Empirical strengths and weaknesses are also delineated.

Title: Drawings as a method of program evaluation and communication with school-aged children

Website: http://www.joe.org/joe/1996december/a2.html

Abstract:

This is an online journal article, *Journal of Extension,* written by Evans and Reilly (1996). The author looks at the use of projective drawing techniques in the evaluation of prevention programs working with school aged children. Problems using these activities and implications for practitioners are discussed.

Title: Ernest Seigler

Website: http://www.cleveland.com/news/plaindealer/index.ssf?/base/news/1074853831256800.xml

Abstract:

This article on Cleveland.com talks about entrepreneur Earnest Siegler who died 1/22/04. He and his wife Norma were one of the first contributors to the Gathering Place, a cancer support and research center. The Norma C. Seigler Garden is scheduled to open in 2005 and will feature 12 areas dedicated to meditation and art therapy.

Title: Face Stimulus Assessment (FSA)

Website: http://www.art-therapy.us/FSA.htm

Abstract:

This site provides information on the FSA including recommended materials and background of the assessment. Pricing information on clinician and researcher's packet are provided. Also, references about the FSA are listed.

Title: Funding Opportunities for Research

Website: http://www.arttherapy.org/resources/research/assessments.htm

Abstract:

The American Art Therapy Association sponsors this site. It lists information about the BATA, CATA, DDS, FSA, LECATA, MARI, PPAT, SDT, UPAP. Description, costs, and contact information for the assessments are provided. Other helpful links are provided.

Title: International Expressive Arts Therapy Association (IEATA)

Website: http://www.ieata.org/

Abstract:

IEATA is a nonprofit organization that supports the expressive arts in therapy, education, and artists.

Title: Julia Productions Inc.

Website: http://www.arttxfilms.com/

Abstract:

This site features art therapy instructional films. Samples are available for download. Additionally, the work of E.G. Horovitz, Director of Nazareth College Art Therapy Program and BATA Assessment author is also featured.

Title: Katoomba woman draws comfort for UN bomb victims

Website: http://bluemountains.yourguide.com.au/detail.asp?class=news &subclass=local&category=general%20news&story_id= 280521&y=2004&m=1

Abstract:

This article (January 21, 2004) in the *Blue Mountain Gazette* Sue Sweeny's trip to Iraq. A graduate in art therapy, Sue accepted a contract from the United Nations to provide counseling support and art therapy for the survivors of the United Nations Headquarters attack in Baghdad.

Title: Making mandalas

Website: http://www.nyjournalnews.com/newsroom/012704/e01w27 mandalas.html

Abstract:

This article in *The News Journal*.com (January 27, 2004) discusses the foundation of this ancient form of Hindu art. The article discusses the relationship of mandala drawing and art therapy. Comments from art therapist about mandala drawings are included.

Title: The Mandala Project

Website: http://www.mandalaproject.org/

Abstract:

This site discusses mandala drawings, provides resources, and educational links. The Mandala Project is a nonprofit organization that provides workshops on mandalas and with custom tailoring workshops for interested parties. Links to mandala exhibits are also provided.

Title: National Coalition of Art Therapies Associations
             (NCATA)

Website: http://www.ncata.com/

Abstract:

NCATA is an alliance of professional associations dedicated to the advancement of the arts as therapeutic modalities. It covers art therapy, music therapy, psychodrama, poetry therapy, drama therapy, and dance–movement therapy.

Title: Nazareth College Graduate Art Therapy Program

Website: http://www.naz.edu/dept/art_therapy/

Abstract:

The site provides information on Nazareth College's art therapy program, which is approved by American Art Therapy Association. A program description, admission requirements, program requires, faculty, and course work are provided. The site also features the artwork of the students and faculty. A list of upcoming workshops is also provided.

Title: ProEd Online

Website: http://www.proedinc.com/index.html

Abstract:

This site is sponsored by the leading publishers of nationally standardized assessments, including the DAP: IQ and DAP: SPED. Additionally, ProEd resources, texts, and journals in the following areas: speech, language and hearing; psychology and counseling; special education; gifted childhood intervention; occupational and physical therapy. The organization also sponsors online continuing education courses.

Title: Projective use of drawings

Website: http://www.arttherapyincanada.ca/pages/bookproj.html

Abstract:

Sponsored by Canadian art therapist, Hansen-Adamidis, this site provides a list of art therapy journal articles related to the projective use of drawings. Links to articles on the following are provided: art therapy and cancer; art therapy and HIV; art therapy for trauma and bereavement issues; art therapy with children, groups, and families, and new books in the field of art therapy.

Title: Psychology art therapy

Website: http://www.powells.com/subsection/PsychologyArtTherapy.5
              .html

Abstract:

Powell.com offers over 131 books on art therapy. A short description of each book is provided and includes authors such as Wadeson, Malchiodi, McNiff, Kramer, Silver, and more.

Title: Rawley Silver, Ed.D, ATR

Website: http://www.rawleysilver.com/index.html

Abstract:

Rawley Silver, author of the Silver Drawing Test, sponsors this site. The site includes her list of publications, articles in PDF format. Also, Silver's research endeavors, teaching experiences, and work experience are outlined.

Title: School Security

Website: http://www.gothamgazette.com/article/issueoftheweek/
              20040117/200/843

Abstract:

This article by *Gothem Gazette* (January 17, 2004) outlines the problem of crime and violence in schools. It provides an academic program as well as counseling and less traditional approaches, such as music and art therapy—all aimed at preparing students with behavior problems to return to school.

Title: Survivors Art Foundation

Website: http://www.survivorsartfoundation.org/

Abstract:

SAF is a nonprofit organizations that focuses on survivor trauma issues and the use of expressive art therapies as healing and treatment approaches. The artwork of trauma survivors is presented in a virtual gallery show. An extensive resource list of organizations dealing with arts and trauma is provided. Additionally, people can send SAF e-cards featuring the artwork of trauma survivors.

Title: Test Reviews Online

Website: http://buros.unl.edu/buros/jsp/lists.jsp?letter=D

Abstract:

Burros Institute sponsors this site. It includes an extensive list of assessments, which are critically reviewed, including the Draw a Person Test, Draw a Story, and the Silver Drawing Test. Reviews are available for $15 per test title.

AUTHOR INDEX

A

Abell, S.C., 77, 80
Agell, G., 173, 178
Allessandrini, C.D., 107, 109, 110
Alley, T.R., 163, 165
Ambramovitch, R., 97
Amos, S., 175, 176
Anastasi, A., 5, 6, 10, 97, 133, 175, 176
Anderson, V., 104, 110
Andrews, J., 52, 53, 54, 55, 190, 198
Anthony, E., 3, 10
Ardon, A.M., 63, 65, 66
Armstrong, D.C., 53, 55

B

Bakarat, L.P., 22, 27, 199
Bardos, A.N. 124–134, 133
Barrett, A.M., 78, 80
Bergland, C., 175, 176
Betensky, M., 96, 97
Betts, D.J., 9, 10, 157, 158, 160–166, 196, 198
Billingsley, G., 63, 66
Black, F.W., 21, 26
Bloom, A., 36, 45
Bolander, K., 59, 66
Bouchard, R.R., 4, 10
Brandt, M., 120, 122
Breslin, K.T., 151
Brewer, F., 36, 43
Brueing, C.C., 131, 134
Briccetti, K.A., 131, 134
Brittain, W., 148, 150, 217
Bronson, G.W., 163, 165
Brooke, S.L., 6, 24, 26, 37, 43, 109, 110, 115, 117, 122, 146, 165, 168, 169, 171, 176, 189, 192, 193, 198, 216, 221
Browne, K.D., 37, 38, 45, 46
Buck, J.N., 59, 66, 68–80, 85, 87, 89, 191, 198
Buckner, S., 157, 158
Burgess, A.W., 37, 43
Burns, R.C., 29–46, 47, 51, 55, 57, 59, 66, 82–89, 90–97, 148, 151, 189, 191, 192, 198
Burns, W.J., 163, 165
Burt, H., 66
Butler, R.J., 129, 134

C

Cabacungan, L.F., 39, 43, 189, 198
Carpenter, W., 175, 178
Casulla, M.M., 21
Catell, R.B., 74, 80
Cates, J.A., 22, 23, 26
Chandler, L., 22, 26
Chapman, J., 6, 10
Chapman, L., 6, 10
Chase, C.I., 110
Chiaia, M.E., 158
Clemer, D.S., 49, 50, 52, 55
Cohen, B., v–x, 5, 8, 9, 10, 56–67, 163, 165, 190, 198
Cohen, F.W., 37, 44
Cohene, S., 122, 198
Cohene, L.S., 122, 193
Coles, R., 149, 151
Cooper, S.H., 183, 186
Coopersmith, S., 165
Corsini, R.J., 146, 151
Couch, J.B., 61, 66

233

SUBJECT INDEX

A

Abuse
  Physical, 36–39, 75, 78, 113
  Sexual, 23, 24, 36–39, 43, 77, 78, 117, 131, 169, 188, 189, 192, 202
Achievement, 20, 31, 48, 50, 51, 52, 188, 190
Action, 30, 31, 32, 39, 40, 50
Aggression, 19, 20–21, 22, 26, 35, 75, 76, 114, 188
Alexithymia, 77
Alzheimer's, 61, 62
Approachers, 87
American Art Therapy Association, vi, vii, ix, 114, 221, 228, 230
American Psychological Association, ix, 80, 99
Anxiety, 23, 40, 42, 50, 51, 75, 76, 79, 120, 138, 149, 164, 184, 185, 195, 202
Art therapy assessment, 4–10
Art Therapy Dream Assessment (ATDA), 9, 153–159, 196, 208–209
Attachment, 82, 83–84, 86, 87, 192
Avoiders, 50, 51, 83–84, 87

B

Belief Art Therapy Assessment (BATA), 145–152, 195, 206–208

C

Children's Diagnostic Drawing Series (CDDS), 62–63, 65
Color assessments, 56–67, 68–80, 135–144, 145–159, 167–178, 179–187

Cognitive Art Therapy Assessment (CATA), 150
Compartmentalization, 31, 34, 37, 40, 202
Cookbook approach, 8, 95, 141, 171
Cultural differences, 21, 24, 39–40, 43, 51–53, 74, 77–78, 107–108, 128, 135–144, 163–164, 174, 176, 189, 197

D

Deaf (*see* hearing impaired)
Dementia, 23, 62
Depression, 42, 53, 60, 61, 63, 65, 77, 87, 112–123, 138, 168, 169, 172, 173, 174, 184, 190, 193
Developmental indicators, 14–18, 23, 188
Diagnostic Drawing Series (DDS), v, x, 9, 56–67, 186, 190, 191, 197, 203–205
Diagnostic Systems Manual (DSM), 56, 57, 61, 62, 114, 168, 171
Disassociative Disorders, 62, 63, 64, 65
Draw A Person Test (DAP), 77, 78, 82, 124–134, 182, 186, 194, 197, 221, 230
Draw A Story Test (DAS), 9, 110, 112–123, 193
Drawing Analysis Form (DAF), 59, 62
Dreams, 59, 76, 153–159, 196
Dysthymia, 60, 65

E

Eating disorders, 62, 93, 136, 148
Emotional disturbance, 43, 50, 52, 54, 75, 103, 112–114, 116, 118, 119, 120, 124–134, 146, 148, 165, 194
Emotional indicators, 14, 15, 17, 20, 21, 22, 23, 24, 38, 39, 180, 188

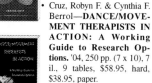

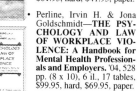